Death in the Classroom

Other Books by the Author
Joseph Conrad: Writing as Rescue
The Talking Cure: Literary Representations of Psychoanalysis
Narcissism and the Novel
Diaries to an English Professor: Pain and Growth in the Classroom
Surviving Literary Suicide
Risky Writing: Self-Disclosure and Self-Transformation in the Classroom
Empathic Teaching: Education for Life
Dying to Teach: A Memoir of Love, Loss, and Learning
Cutting and the Pedagogy of Self-Disclosure (with Patricia Hatch Wallace)

Death in the Classroom
Writing about Love and Loss

Jeffrey Berman

State University of New York Press

Published by
State University of New York Press, Albany

For information, contact State University of New York Press, Albany, NY
www.sunypress.edu

Production by Dana Foote
Marketing by Fran Keneston

Library of Congress Cataloging-in-Publication Data
Berman, Jeffrey, 1945–
    Death in the classroom : writing about love and loss / Jeffrey Berman.
        p. cm.
    Includes bibliographical references and index.
    ISBN 978-0-7914-7631-4 (hardcover : alk. paper)—ISBN 978-0-7914-7632-1
(pbk : alk. paper)
    1. Death—Psychological aspects—Study and teaching. 2. Death in literature—
Study and teaching. 3. English language—Rhetoric—Study and teaching—
Psychological aspects. I. Title.
BF789.D4B466   2009
808′.042′0711—dc22

                                                                    2007052668

10 9 8 7 6 5 4 3 2 1

For our grandchildren: Max, Nate, Talia, and Skyler   ∼

Death destroys a man: the idea of Death saves him.
—E. M. Forster, *Howards End*

Contents

Acknowledgments

As usual, my students are my teachers, and their writings have deepened my understanding of love and loss. I am grateful to the students who took Love and Loss in Literature and Life with me in the spring of 2006: Jonathan Abel, Sally Adams, Katheline Alcantara, Stephen Arena, Joseph Bauer, Juliana Bayne, Stefanie Bizan, Camerin Blomquist, Corey Brown, Amanda Calvagno, Krista Cameron, Marie Cantalino, Sarah Coon, Lisa Cooperstein, Vanessa D'Arcy, Jessica Deatcher, Matthew Dreitlein, Tran Duong, William Eckert, Yosbelky Espinal, Tracy Estriplet, Steven Figueroa, Kyle Filiault, Amelia Gagliano, Allison Gates, Sarah Graham, Kristen Hagan, Christopher Hartnett, Monica Jones, Jennifer Kim, Bethann Leigh, Natalie Lesser, Jessica Mathias, Meredith Matty, Casey McLeod, Caroline Mecca, Elizabeth Mullarkey, Jay Peck, Stephanie Pincar, Lindsay Ragozzino, Christine Reis, Lianna Robins, Jennifer Robinson, Matthew Rogulski, Erin Ross, Christina Russo, Veronica Scarlett, Scott Schulman, Ashley Tyrell, Nicaury Vargas, and Ruth Williams. Special thanks to Jaclyn Ippolita, Marcy Isabella, Clifton Johnson, Laura Mulvey, Sara E. Murphy, Gabrielle Sierra, and Megan Tarquinio, who made important contributions to the book. Throughout the semester I regarded myself not only as the teacher but also as a student, intent on learning how my classmates reacted to death education. We were all in different ways students of sorrow, and we tried to teach each other what we were learning about love and loss. As my student Breanna wrote to me in an email after the course ended, "We were all fellow mourners over someone or something." Without being sentimental, I believe that many of us felt pedagogical love for each other, love that is neither transgressive nor exploitive.

I'm grateful to Richard Bower, a tenured professor at Cayuga County Community College who is now pursuing a doctoral degree in our program. Richard wrote a diary entry for each class he attended, helped me grade papers, interviewed several students, and wrote an essay that appears in appendix A. In helping me with the course, he was less a teaching assistant than a colleague.

I'm grateful to the entire staff of the State University of New York Press, especially to James Peltz, interim director, Jane Bunker, editor in chief, and the two anonymous readers whose suggestions for revision strengthened the book. This is my sixth book copyedited by Anne R. Gibbons, who not only improved my prose but also made the book more reader-friendly. Here is an example of

Anne's passion for revision. I wrote about Barbara: "Ironically a lifetime of excellent health worked against her, and she died a lingering death, her body wasting away to a shadow of her former self." Anne commented, "You may want to reword, but I suggest you avoid the 'shadow of her former self' cliché," and she then revised the ending of the sentence: "and she died a lingering death, her body wasting away while her warrior spirit refused to surrender." Good writing is so important to Anne that she had to restrain herself from revising several of the published scholarly passages that I quoted throughout the book. Thanks also to Dana Foote, the State University of New York Press production editor who also supervised the publication of *Dying to Teach*.

Finally, my greatest debt is, as usual, to Barbara, who has been my muse in life and in death. She continues to inspire her family and friends, and now many of my students.

Introduction

Dear Jeff,

During my last semester of college, I enrolled in Love and Loss as an elective for my major. I was unaware of the huge impact that the course would have on me. There were times when I felt like an outsider in the class; unlike my professor and many of my classmates, I was fortunate enough to have never lost a loved one. Even though I had not shared the same feelings of loss as others in my class, the course required us to open up to one another. Every day that I entered the classroom for Love and Loss, I knew that we would be confronting a difficult aspect of life. I knew that contemplating death would prepare me for loss in the future; however, I never imagined that I would be tested so soon after the course ended.

Barely two weeks after the conclusion of the course, I received a phone call from my father with the news that my grandfather had died. His death came as a surprise and greatly affected me. I cried when I heard the news. Though this is a likely reaction to loss, I was surprised by my emotions. I had reflected on my grandparents dying throughout the course, and I did not think I would be terribly emotional when they died. This is not to say that I do not love them; I simply thought that I came to terms with the inevitability of death. I was wrong. I even lost my composure when I told the professor of my summer course that I would be absent for the remainder of the week.

During my ride from Albany to Queens, I was flooded with memories of my grandfather. I imagined what I would say in his eulogy. If I had not taken Love and Loss, I would not have considered writing a eulogy. Prior to the course, I did not even know the difference between an obituary and a eulogy, nor did I know how to write either. I spent most of that night in front of my computer, going back and forth between crying and typing his eulogy. I was not sure whether or not I would actually read the eulogy at the funeral; however, the act of writing it made me feel connected to my grandfather, as I was commemorating his life. I ultimately did not read the eulogy at the funeral because I could not stop crying.

1

At the funeral, and for the days and weeks that followed, I experienced tremendous guilt. Even though my grandfather was healthy, I felt that I should have called him more. I realized how selfish I was. Through the loss of my grandfather, I recognize the importance of reaching out to my family and friends. It is not difficult to make a phone call to tell someone that you love them; it is a simple act that can mean so much to someone. I try to remind myself that every day.

Loss is not something that is easy to accept. I also do not believe that it is something that you get used to. Very soon after I lost my grandfather, my dog died. It seemed as though death waited, and waited, and then stormed into my life full force. Even though it was hard to cope with my losses, Love and Loss allowed me to consider and prepare for loss.

Thanks again for everything, and good luck with your book.

Madison

Madison's letter, emailed to me in September 2006, four months after the end of Love and Loss, reveals so many of the expected and unexpected consequences of a loved one's death. Just as every death is different, so is every person's reaction to death different. Despite these differences, death usually comes as a shock to most of us, even when anticipated, and few can prepare adequately for the pain and sorrow arising from loss. Many people find themselves losing their composure, as Madison did, not only at the funeral but also when thinking or talking about the deceased. This too is common. But what may not be anticipated is the "tremendous guilt" following a person's death, guilt that may arise from the fear that one has not been a good enough relative or friend to the deceased. This guilt may be in addition to the "survivor guilt" or "existential guilt" that so many people feel. Guilt may be implied in the many questions we ask ourselves following a death. Why did he or she die instead of me? Could I have done something to prevent this death? How do I say farewell to other dying loved ones in the future?

Madison's email reminds us that although we can never entirely "get used" to death, we can "consider and prepare for loss." There is nothing new about such a belief. Socrates believed that studying philosophy is a preparation for death, and each day stories like Tolstoy's *The Death of Ivan Ilych* are discussed in schools and colleges. Teachers who are interested in narrowing the distance between literature and life may invoke Elisabeth Kübler-Ross's influential "stage theory of dying," in which we see Ivan Ilych moving in a sequential way from initial shock and denial to anger, bargaining, depression, and final acceptance. The words that are inscribed on his watch-chain— *respice finem* (reflect on your end)—reflect the theme of the story. "If all of us would make an all-out effort to contemplate our own death," Kübler-

Ross writes in *On Death and Dying,* "to deal with our anxieties surrounding the concept of death, and to help others familiarize themselves with these thoughts, perhaps there could be less destructiveness around us" (13). Yet despite her injunction, Tolstoy's story remains distant from most readers. Thus we may feel, as Madison did throughout the course, "like an outsider." Like Ivan Ilych, we know that we will die one day, but this intellectual knowledge is rarely translated into deeper emotional knowledge. Death awakens such intense emotional resistance within us that we distance ourselves from dying characters. "It's only a story," we say to ourselves with relief as we return to the business of living.

Death Education

In *A Treasury of Comfort,* a collection of writings about death, mourning, and solace, Sidney Greenberg notes: "Realistically speaking, we are all potential mourners. The time to develop a mature philosophy toward death is before, not after, it strikes, just as one should learn to swim before one gets shipwrecked, not after. The analogy suffers in only one respect. Most of us will never be shipwrecked but the need for a sustaining outlook upon death and a reasonable knowledge of how to handle our grief is one which we shall almost all certainly experience" (ix–x). Virginia Morris offers an equally striking metaphor that explains the need to prepare for the inevitable. "Hanging on the edge of a precipice, engulfed by terror, is not the time or place to learn about emergency rock-climbing procedures; you have to learn them before you start the expedition. Likewise, we have to start learning about death now, while we are still healthy. We have to start before illness is upon us, before we are in the swamp and our primal instincts take over, before we are blinded by denial and fighting valiantly for hope. We have to start today, whether we are twenty-eight or seventy-four, coming to terms with our mortality, understanding the medical choices that can arise, and developing an entirely new way of thinking about life and death" (3). And Jonathan Silin, an early childhood educator, writes that "when we attempt to exclude death, we also exclude the life-affirming understanding of human temporality" (40).

Death education is generally reserved for health professionals, but college teachers can initiate awareness by encouraging students to write about their own experiences with loss. Since the middle 1970s, when I began asking undergraduates to turn in a weekly "Freudian Diary" in my literature and psychoanalysis classes, scores of men and women have written about various forms of loss, including death, and their diaries and essays appear in several of my books: *Diaries to an English Professor* (1994), *Surviving Literary Suicide* (1999), *Risky Writing* (2001), *Empathic Teaching* (2004), and *Cutting and the*

Pedagogy of Self-Disclosure (2007). These books focus primarily on my students' experiences, not my own.

My life changed irrevocably on August 12, 2002, one day after my thirty-fourth wedding anniversary, when my beloved wife, Barbara, was diagnosed with terminal pancreatic cancer—a redundancy since pancreatic cancer is one of the most dreaded diseases, with a 99 percent mortality rate. The average survival time of pancreatic cancer patients following diagnosis is three to seven months. Thanks to an experimental pancreatic cancer vaccine, she lived longer than her oncologist predicted. She died on April 5, 2004, after a valiant twenty-month struggle. Our attitude toward death changed radically; immediately after her diagnosis, death was the feared and hated adversary from which we did everything to escape, but as her suffering increased and she was no longer able to walk or talk, eat or drink, death became an ally that could not come quickly enough. Ironically, a lifetime of excellent health worked against her, and she died a lingering death, her body wasting away while her warrior spirit refused to surrender.

With Barbara's permission, I read to my Expository Writing students in March 2004 my eulogy for her, and I began writing a book about her immediately after her death. I never stopped thinking about her, day and night, for the eighteen months it took me to complete *Dying to Teach*. Writing and teaching were the major ways in which I grieved her death, the only solemn daily death rituals that I observed. Her death will always be the major loss in my life, the absence of the center of my life. I have long known about the healing power of the "talking cure" and the "writing cure." I never missed a day of teaching while caring for Barbara in our home, and I suddenly discovered the potent benefits of the "teaching cure." It is no exaggeration to say that teaching preserved my sanity during this excruciating time. Twenty-one months after Barbara's death, I taught a new course at the University at Albany called Love and Loss in Literature and Life that focused on the stories, poems, and memoirs that may be classified as the literature of bereavement. I began this book as soon as I completed that course.

There are other less personal reasons that compelled me to teach Love and Loss and to write *Death in the Classroom*. Until around the middle of the twentieth century, most Americans died in the comfort of their homes, surrounded by their loved ones. Now 80 percent of Americans die in hospitals, nursing homes, or other impersonal institutions. One consequence of separating the dying from the living is that death has become an unspeakable subject. I don't mean that teachers fail to speak about death in literature courses. Literature abounds in death scenes, and there are few stories, poems, plays, or memoirs in which the grim reaper does not make an appearance. But teachers rarely if ever speak about real as opposed to fictional or philosophical death. By "real" death I mean our relatives' and friends' deaths—and our own. There seems to be an unwritten rule that real death is not an appropriate subject for discussion in a literature classroom, and it seems especially inappropriate to speak "personally" about death.

There are a spate of books about death in academia—books with titles such as *Death in the Quadrangle*, *Death on the Campus*, *Death of a Department Chair*, *Murder at the MLA*, *Murder in the English Department*, and *Death in a Delphi Seminar*. According to an article in the *Chronicle of Higher Education*, "For more than half a century, writers have used the murder mystery as a vehicle for explorations—sometimes playful, sometimes deeply serious—of the sins and foibles of academe" (22 September 2006). By contrast, *Death in the Classroom* is about real death, *personal* death: Barbara's death, my students' grandparents' (or parents' or siblings') deaths, and our own impending deaths, which for the moment we can only imagine and try to postpone. I have chosen a title that represents accurately the content of this project, but let me observe at the beginning, lest readers be unduly intimidated by the subject, that it has not been depressing or morbid to write this book. Nor do I think it will be depressing or morbid for my readers. I looked forward to writing every morning, just as I looked forward to teaching every Love and Loss class, and though the course was often emotionally charged, there were many more smiles than tears for the majority of students and for myself. To give one example, many students imagined their "last words" to be flippant, light-hearted, or ironic, affirming the importance of humor when confronting death. It is perfectly appropriate, indeed, often necessary, to use humor to confront the end of life, and one thinks of Woody Allen's sardonic observation: "I'm not afraid of death. I just don't want to be there when it happens." There were many times during class when our discussions erupted into unexpected laughter, and I have tried to include these moments in this book. Whenever possible I invoke the long and honorable tradition of "Jewish wry" to fortify body and spirit in the presence of death. One can have pleasure while fulfilling a sacred duty.

Writing about death is often writing about disaster, and Maurice Blanchot's remarks come to mind here: "The disaster, unexperienced. It is what escapes the very possibility of experience—it is the limit of writing. This must be repeated: the disaster de-scribes." Yet this does not mean, Blanchot continues, that the "disaster, as the force of writing, is excluded from it, is beyond the pale of writing or extratextual" (7). Death forever escapes any attempt to understand it. As Garrett Stewart points out, death is the single event in life that novelists can only imagine rather than know. "Despite its brutal factuality at the close of life, dying is by nature the one inevitably fictional matter in prose fiction. Death for the self exists only as nonexistence, is not a topic so much as a voiding event, has no vocabulary native to it, would leave us mute before its impenetrable fact" (4). We can never know death, but writing about it can help us to understand, to a limited extent, how the dying feel about death and, to a larger extent, how relatives and friends feel about a loved one's death.

The Denial of Death

Denial may be the main obstacle to death education. "The twentieth century crystalized a new attitude toward dying and death," declares sociologist David Wendell Moller. "In this modern era, dying and death were no longer considered to be important experiences that would absorb the attention and energies of humanity. To the contrary, death and dying became something to be shunned, avoided, denied, and, if possible, conquered. Contrary to earlier times, dying and death in the twentieth century have become devoid of meaning, ritual support, and cultural approval. What has been termed the 'age of denial' has arrived" (15). Moller cites Kübler-Ross as an example of a "conqueror" of death. He praises the seriousness of *On Death and Dying*, which has never been out of print since its publication in 1969, and her advocacy of the rights and needs of the terminally ill, but he also criticizes as over-simplifications her stage theory of dying and her belief in a "good death." He characterizes Kübler-Ross and her disciples as "travel agents for the dying, offering therapeutic intervention to a singular destination: tranquil, peaceful death" (51).

One should not underestimate the resistance to death education. Indeed, Barbara's doctors and nurses seldom used the words "dying" or "death"; instead, they talked about a patient's "passing." For the same reason, cancer is often referred to as "CA." Just as dying and death have many euphemisms, so does cancer, a word too dreadful for many people to utter. Barbara's oncologist Fred Shapiro is unusually plain speaking and direct, but more often than not he used the word "disease" rather than "cancer," and when her health deteriorated rapidly in the last few months, he referred to the "natural course of the disease," which doesn't sound as horrifying as "the cancer is spreading." Moller begins *Confronting Death* with a telling anecdote. "When I called the American Cancer Society to request permission to include some of their materials in this book, their representative responded, '*Absolutely not. In no way do we want to be associated with a book on death. We want to emphasize the positive aspects of cancer only*'" (vii; emphasis in original).

Dominick LaCapra distinguishes between *writing about trauma*, which he calls an "aspect of historiography related to the project of reconstructing the past as objectively as possible," and *writing trauma*, a process of "acting out, working over, and to some extent working through" a traumatic experience (*Writing History, Writing Trauma* 186). The latter is more personal and dangerous than the former. A similar distinction may be made between "writing about death" and "writing death." The former does not involve the same personal experience or confrontation with death that is implicit in the latter. Most of the student writings in this book fall into the category of "writing about death," but a few involve "writing death." Peter Goggin and Maureen Daly Goggin make a further distinction between *metadiscourse on writing (about) trauma* and *writing during trauma*, the former involving "critical or scholarly practices of studying and writing about either of the two discourses LaCapra identifies," the latter involving "any kind of writing undertaken during a traumatic period whether or not it is directly linked or generated by the trauma" (34). Some of the student writings in this book may be viewed as "metadiscourse on writing (about) death," but other writings about recent endings are "writing during death."

Writing a personal essay on death—writing death—is risky because it generally involves pain and, as we see in Madison's email, guilt. Writing about certain forms of death, such as suicide, may also involve shame. "In autobiography," Nancy K. Miller states, "the acts—performed and witnessed—that might seem to beg not to be revealed are the very ones that produce writing. Thus the private, silent images of the scene in the basement are transformed into a shareable narrative when finally, with the logic of deferral always at the heart of trauma, they are put into words for others; secret knowledge becomes public shame" (210). To write about a relative's or friend's death is to bear witness through testimony, which poses special difficulties. "Testimony," as Dori Laub suggests, "is inherently a process of facing loss—of going through the pain of the act of witnessing, and of the ending of the act of witnessing—which entails yet another repetition of experience of separation and loss" (91). Students sometimes experience what LaCapra calls "empathic unsettlement," in which "secondary witnesses" feel partial identification with victims of atrocity ("Trauma, Absence, Loss," 722).

Geoffrey Hartman remarks in *Scars of the Spirit* that "autobiography, whether it deals with private acts and feelings or a life of public service, cannot escape suspicion. . . . Stories about oneself, whether performed within the 'public square' of encomium, funeral oration, and sanctioned self-praise, or outside of it, never quite detach from narrative fiction" (17). Hartman implies that although the writer may strive for "transparency—a standard of honesty that would allow us to discern truth freed of manipulation and deception" (12), "no one is so naive as to think all masks can be removed, all memories unified, all shadows dissolved. Shadows may be deliberately added, in fact, and often to reveal rather than conceal" (9). I agree with Hartman, and in my literature classes I explore with my students the masks of "fictional" and "real" characters. I do not call into question, however, the authenticity of my stu-

dents' personal writings, not because I believe the writings are perfectly transparent, an impossibility, but because I believe that students would become
defensive and resistant if a teacher challenged the truthfulness of their diaries
and essays.

Students who hear personal essays develop a bond with each other, and
they learn that others can empathize with their fears and disappointments. It is
not that all our secrets are the same; rather, we all have secrets which, if shared
in an empathic classroom, result in greater understanding of each other and, in
many cases, a lessening of pain and shame. The connection that students feel
with each other resembles the "community" about which Nancy K. Miller and
Jason Tougaw speak in *Extremities:* "The culture of first-person writing needs to
be understood in relation to a desire for common grounds—if not an identity-
bound shared experience, then one that is shareable through identification,
though this too will vary in degrees of proximity. The memoir and all forms of
personal testimony not only expand the boundaries of identity construction
and the contours of the self but also lay claim to potential territories of
community" (2–3).

Unlike speaking, which is generally spontaneous and uninterrupted,
writing is deliberate and lends itself to reflection and revision. Writers can
pause if they find their words or thoughts emotionally wrenching and return to
their writing when they feel more in control. In *Men Don't Cry . . . Women
Do*, Terry Martin and Kenneth Doka say of bibliotherapy: "It allows dosing[;]
that is, if the griever finds something too painful or difficult, he or she can set it
aside for a while. And certainly it offers control. Grievers can choose the time
and place they use it" (148–49). This formula applies equally well to writing
about death. Martin and Doka also use the term "normalization" (148) to
describe the moment when grievers recognize that others experience their
own complicated feelings. Normalization validates grievers with the knowledge that their anger, sadness, confusion, and guilt are typical of others in the
same situation. The knowledge they are not alone is reassuring.

Death education creates the opportunity for what Richard Tedeschi and
his associates call "posttraumatic growth," the positive changes that may arise
from a crisis. These changes may be the recognition that we can survive the
deaths of beloved relatives and friends—we go on living even when we think
our hearts are broken. In Anna Quindlen's novel *One True Thing*, Ellen
Gulden experiences posttraumatic growth as a result of caring for her mother.
She develops an understanding of and love for Kate, with whom she has had a
conflicted relationship; she learns who her real friends are; and she enters a
profession that allows her to work with adolescents suffering from depression
and despair. As close as our family was before Barbara's illness, we became
closer afterward, and we discovered that love and devotion can survive the
worst suffering.

The Personal and the Pedagogical

I knew when I was teaching Love and Loss that I wanted to write a book about the course, and so I kept a diary throughout the semester, recording my impressions of each class. These diary entries form the core of *Death in the Classroom* and mark the striking tonal shifts in many classes. One moment we felt glad when contemplating love; the next moment we felt sad when confronting loss. I wrote each entry either immediately following each class or, if fatigue prevented me from writing, the next morning. I note in each entry the eventful moments of the class, including my observations about the poems and stories I was teaching, my musings on love and death, the books I was reading for the course, and my students' responses both in and out of the classroom. (They often emailed me before or after class to tell me how they felt about the course.) I began writing the book after the course ended, revising my prose (I can't write a simple declarative sentence on the first try), filling in some of the details of each class, omitting other details that no longer seemed important, adding some of my students' emails and notes to me, quoting academic books that relate to a particular class, and sharpening the thematic focus of each chapter. After completing a draft of the book, I occasionally came across new information published in a newspaper, magazine, or scholarly journal that was relevant to my own work; I include this information in brackets.

There is probably nothing in life more terrifying (except perhaps for certain dreaded illnesses or injuries) than death, and this was the first time my students had taken an entire course on the subject. It was also the first time that a teacher encouraged them to write about their *feelings* as well as their thoughts about this dark subject. Wherever possible, I try to connect in my diary the personal and the pedagogical: how my feelings and thoughts about death affected my spoken and unspoken comments in class, and how my teaching influenced my life. I also record in the diary entries the surprises that occurred in class.

And indeed, there were many surprises. I could not predict when I was planning the course that both the teacher and his students would become more intrigued by the writing assignments than by the class readings. The seven essays each student wrote turned out to be more intense than many of the class readings—largely because the writings were so *personal*. Before returning each set of essays, I decided to read three or four aloud, anonymously and always with the authors' permission; these essays were insightful, heartfelt, and moving. I soon realized that I was interested not only in how my students wrote about death, such as in an obituary or a eulogy, the first two writing assignments, but also in how they felt about each essay. After reading aloud a few essays and then returning all of them, I asked students to write a brief (and anonymous) evaluation of each writing assignment. I would then summarize their responses in the next class. We probably spent as much time on the students' writings as on the class readings. Seeing how my students reacted, week after week, to the course was helpful. I have included some of these anonymous responses.

Another surprise was the many students who have suffered major losses in their lives: not only grandparents and aunts and uncles but also in several cases parents, siblings, and close friends. Loss figures prominently in these student's writings, and in the following pages I focus on several of these young men and women. Their writings tell us a great deal about how death has shaped their lives. Many of them discovered that writing itself is one of the best ways to cope with death and memorialize loss. Others enrolled in the course because they knew that sooner or later it would be relevant to their lives.

Still another surprise, though perhaps it should not have been, is how many students have strong religious beliefs. The only reason I was surprised is because of my own lack of religious belief. Anyone who tries to understand college students' attitudes toward death must also try to understand the role of religion in their lives. And so one of the essay topics asked students to explore how their religious beliefs or disbeliefs influence their view of death.

There were many other surprises throughout the semester. The students were constantly surprised by the power of the essays I read aloud, and many of them were impressed with their classmates' writing skills. They were surprised that so many of their classmates had survived devastating losses; one student lost both parents in early childhood, and it was a challenge for him to avoid becoming "very callous." They were surprised by how teary-eyed they became not only when they wrote their essays but also when they heard me read aloud their own and classmates' writings. (One student reported in an anonymous response that he or she did not cry when writing an essay but did cry upon hearing me read the essay aloud.) They were surprised when they suddenly remembered deaths that had occurred years earlier. Madison was surprised when, after feeling like an outsider the entire semester because she had never lost a loved one, her grandfather unexpectedly died two weeks after the end of the term: the course suddenly took on a new meaning for her. They were surprised by their relatives' and friends' extreme reactions to the course, reactions that ranged from highly positive to highly negative. They were surprised that the course was helpful both to those who had lost a relative or friend and to those whose lives were not yet touched by death. Perhaps most of all, they were surprised that the course heightened their appreciation of the living. They told me again and again in their response essays that after writing an essay they would call home and tell their parents how much they loved them.

Many of the surprises were positive, but a few were negative. One surprise—or rather, shock—occurred during a discussion of the Book of Job when a student angrily started shouting in class and then, denouncing me as a "false prophet," stormed out of class—only to return a few minutes later, still agitated. Everyone was startled. This was the first time in my thirty-three-year teaching career that a student lost control. Many students later told me in emails that they were terrified at the possibility of violence when he returned to the classroom. The incident dramatized the incendiary nature of religion in the early twenty-first century, an age in which religious mistrust, intolerance, and violence threaten to engulf the world.

Chapter 1 focuses on the structure and requirements of Love and Loss, including the syllabus and writing requirements. Chapters 2 and 3 discuss how students wrote first an obituary of a classmate and then a eulogy of a living or deceased relative or friend. This was the first time most of them had written an obituary or a eulogy, and they learned a great deal from the assignments. Chapter 4 explores the challenges of teaching the Book of Job, a work that proved unsettling to everyone. Chapter 5 investigates how students wrote about the relationship between religion and death. Chapter 6 reveals how students imagined young Cathy Linton in Emily Brontë's novel *Wuthering Heights* might have felt about her deceased mother. I asked them to write a letter to Cathy's mother, who died while giving birth to her. This essay was an effort to understand maternal loss, perhaps the most wrenching loss anyone can experience. Chapter 7 relates how my students and I responded to the second anniversary of Barbara's death, as well as how I handled another "student problem," albeit of a different kind, and how the students "evaluated the evaluator." Chapter 8 examines what turned out to be the most unusual writing assignment of the semester. I asked the students to imagine that they were told they were terminally ill and had only a few months to live. What were the ten things they would attempt to do before they died? This was overwhelmingly their favorite writing assignment, filled with serious and comical imagined activities. Chapter 9 analyzes their essays on euthanasia and physician-assisted suicide, a subject that is at the center of *One True Thing*, which we were reading in class. Chapter 10 shows how my present students responded to my former students' writings on love and loss in *Empathic Teaching*. They learned that loss can take many forms, including the loss of one or both parents as a result of divorce. Chapter 11 offers a "teacher's self-eulogy": how I would like friends and students to remember me. The appendixes consist of an essay on death education written by my teaching assistant, Richard Bower; an extended discussion of how Breanna wrote about her father's death, which occurred when she was fifteen; an essay by Sara E. Murphy, an undergraduate who discusses how the course helped her to come to terms with her recent diagnosis of multiple sclerosis; and a copy of the syllabus, midterm, and final exam for Love and Loss.

To speak personally about death is to speak about our emotions as well as our thoughts. Academics are famously reluctant to acknowledge the power of emotions or to express their own emotions in the classroom. As Peter Elbow observes in his foreword to an edited volume on emotions and composition studies, "Emotions often yield good insights and intuitions that are only much later confirmed by thinking and evidence. When we ignore emotions and go only for logical thinking, we are liable to miss crucial things—not just in us but in the world" (vii). I can give an example of how my emotions were more insightful than my thoughts. I vividly recall one therapy session Barbara and I had shortly before her death. Our therapist, Ed Dick, spent most of the hour talking with Barbara about her fear of death. I remained quiet, listening attentively. Ed turned to me shortly before the end of the session and asked me how I was doing. I exploded into tears before I could say the word "fine," my body convulsed with emotion. My tears were a more accurate indication of how I was feeling than the word that could not escape from my lips. As the philosopher Martha Nussbaum would say, my tears were "geological upheavals of thought" (90), testimony to the tempestuous force of feelings. Or as Miriam Greenspan suggests, tears are "grief's natural lubricant" (99), making possible the promise of healing. Our emotions often reflect a deeper truth than our thoughts. My tears demonstrated to Barbara and Ed that I was not doing fine, that what was happening to both of us was unspeakable. I felt better when I stopped crying, affirming the twelfth-century Jewish philosopher Maimonides' observation that "those who grieve find comfort in weeping and in arousing their sorrow until the body is too tired to bear the inner emotions" (qtd. in Moffat 100). Barbara and I left the therapy session shaken but determined to do the best we could in an impossible situation. I shared this experience with my students, reminding them that to speak or write only about our thoughts is to express half-truths.

Remembering the Dead

Teachers who are interested in adopting or modifying my approach to death education should be prepared to receive emotionally charged essays, as many of the writings in this book demonstrate. They should also be prepared for emotionally charged responses. Most teachers believe that intense self-disclosures are best left to psychotherapists. I agree with Michelle Payne's recommendation: "It is important that we, as writing teachers, stop seeing emotion, pain, and trauma as threatening, anti-intellectual, and solipsistic, and instead begin to ask how we might, like therapists, feminist theorists, and philosophers, begin to recognize them as ways of knowing, not signs of dangerous pedagogies or teachers who are acting as therapists" (30).

Some of the essays in this book produced tears, mainly in the form of teary eyes. No one wept openly or uncontrollably in class. I realize that many teachers will feel uncomfortable crying in the classroom, but tears indicate that we are moved by another person's loss. Tears may also indicate an essay's rhetorical power. In *Empathic Teaching* I recall the response of a student who was absent during a class in which I cried while reading an essay by a young woman named Matilda about her father's death: "I know that I would have been very shocked to see my professor lose his/her composure during class time. I probably would have felt like I wrote a great, yet poignant essay if it was my essay you were reading" (242). Tears may function not only as a safety valve for pent-up emotions but also as an outlet for harmful substances in the body. Lynn Caine cites a research study conducted at the St. Paul–Ramsay Medical Center in Saint Paul, Minnesota, which suggested that "crying, like perspiring or any other excretory process, cleanses the body of toxic substances. One of the theories is that emotion stored inside the body can produce chemical changes, or an imbalance, resulting in people being sad, depressed, or angry, and crying is a natural way to correct the chemical imbalance" (58). The study also found that emotional tears are different in chemical composition from tears caused by irritants, such as onions, lending further evidence to the theory that emotional tears have a purging effect.

Echoing Freud, Michael Bernard-Donals and Richard Glejzer remind us that "teaching is an impossible profession." Nowhere is this more true than in death education. "We need to teach *that what we are supposed to know we do not know*" (174; emphasis in original). How can we teach about death, the greatest of all mysteries? The answer is that we can teach our own perceptions of death, our own experiences with the dying, and we can learn from others' experiences. Students who shared their essays on death also learned from their classmates' experiences, thus experiencing the phenomenon of "normalization" discussed by Martin and Doka. Students discovered that their anger, sadness, confusion, and guilt are part of the process of grieving.

Carolyn Heilbrun states in *Writing a Woman's Life* that "lives do not serve as models; only stories do that. And it is a hard thing to make up stories to live by. We can only retell and live by the stories we have read or heard. We live our lives through texts. . . . Whatever their form or medium, these stories have formed us all; they are what we must use to make new fictions, new narratives" (37). I believe that stories serve as models, but I also believe, as Heilbrun does not, that lives serve as models. Teachers and students can model empathy for each other, and they can also model strength and courage when responding to dying and death. The dying also serve as role models for the living. Barbara's life continues to inspire her relatives and friends.

In her 1977 book of essays *On Photography*, Susan Sontag concludes that overexposure to suffering and violence can make them less real to viewers. The same is true about an overexposure to death education. It is possible to be overexposed to death. But in her book *Regarding the Pain of Others*, published one year before her death in 2004, Sontag shifts position, now believing that "remembering *is* an ethical act, has ethical value in and of itself. Memory is, achingly, the only relation we can have with the dead. So the belief that remembering is an ethical act is deep in our natures as humans, who know we are going to die, and who mourn those who in the normal course of things die before us—grandparents, parents, teachers, and older friends. Heartlessness and amnesia seem to go together" (115). Many of the students whose writings appear in this book would agree with Sontag's view that remembering the dead is, achingly, the only relation we can have with them. We mourn not only those who die in the "normal course of things" but also those who die far too young. We write about the dead to remember them, to celebrate their lives, to memorialize their deaths, to affirm our living connection with them, and to enable those in the future to remember us.

About six months after Barbara's death I received from hospice a list of "elements of healing," several of which can be applied to death education. Writing about a dead relative or friend compels one not to forget but to remember. Good memories are especially important. To acknowledge the limitations or imperfections of the deceased is to affirm that they are not saintly but human. One of hospice's central assumptions is that "learning about the experience of others gives insight into your own story." Such learning may arise from plays and novels about death, or the learning may arise from hearing about a teacher's or student's experience with death. The more one learns, the more one recognizes the difficulty of bereavement. People grieve differently— there are many cultural, historical, and religious differences with respect to death customs. Nevertheless, there are many commonalities of bereavement that students can share with each other, including the difficulty of understanding and coping with dark emotions. Sharing death stories creates a special bond among the members of a class, teacher and students alike. Shared stories about dying and death support another hospice tenet: "Assume whatever you are going through is normal." We never offered clinical advice to each other, never pretended we were psychologists. Students can derive strength and courage from others who have dealt successfully with loss: "Persons who have been down the road before you can be symbols of hope." Finally, one's experience with death may cause others to make significant changes in their lives.

"It is only when death touches the writer in real life," remarks Daphne du Maurier in her essay "Death and Widowhood," "that he, or she, realises the full impact of its meaning." When her husband died, "it was as though the sheltered cloudland that had enveloped me for years, peopled with images drawn from my imagination, suddenly dissolved, and I was face to face with a harsh and terrible reality. The husband I had loved and taken for granted for thirty-three years of married life, father of my three children, lay dead." The death of my wife of thirty-five years, mother of my two children, shattered my own sheltered cloudland. Du Maurier's motive for writing about her husband's death characterizes one of my own motives for writing about my wife's death. "If by writing about it now I expose myself and my feelings, it is not from a sense of self-advertisement, but because by doing so I may be able to help those readers who, like myself, have suffered the same sense of shock" (271–72).

Death education is becoming increasingly important for health professionals, who must confront dying and death every day, but to my knowledge, *Death in the Classroom* is the first book of its kind written by an English professor. Like my other books on teaching, *Death in the Classroom* is a student-based text, filled with students' writings. Students have given me permission to use their writings, and I have also received permission from my university's Institutional Review Board, which must approve all human research. I have not edited my students' writings except to correct misspellings and obvious typographical errors, and to maintain their anonymity. They supplied their own pseudonyms. They have also seen and approved the ways in which I have contextualized and commented on their writings. Several of them have read the first draft of the manuscript, offering comments and suggestions that I have incorporated into the final draft. *Death in the Classroom* may be read as a companion volume to *Dying to Teach*, but it can also stand alone. During the first full class of Love and Loss I read aloud my eulogy of Barbara, which appears in *Dying to Teach*, and on the last day of the semester I read aloud the final two paragraphs from the chapter "Life after Barbara." I include both passages in the present book.

Love and loss may be the oldest theme in literature and mythology, but it is unusual for teachers and students to share their own experiences with death. Literary scholars "theorize" death all the time; why should they not be permitted, indeed, encouraged, to speak personally about death? "Why does the professor teach / the geography of death?" Pablo Neruda asks in one of his koans in *The Book of Questions* (7). Neruda does not answer the question, nor can I, except to say that we cannot escape from the geography of death. Sooner or later all of us will be in the position of the dying person, and the sooner we talk honestly and openly about death, the more prepared we will be for the inevitable. Death education will be helpful for those who have not yet suffered a major loss—and for those who have. It can ease the way for the caregivers and for the dying. To talk about death is to talk about life, as E. M. Forster suggests in *Howards End:* "Death destroys a man: the idea of Death saves him" (239). None of us can predict when losses will occur. As Madison observes in her email, "I knew that contemplating death would prepare me for loss in the future; however, I never imagined that I would be tested so soon after the course ended."

1

~

Getting Started

Sunday, January 22

Classes begin tomorrow, and over the weekend I read Irvin Yalom's wonderful novel *The Schopenhauer Cure*, which Sophie Freud had recommended to me. It's about a psychoanalyst, Julius Hertzfeld, who finds out that he's dying from melanoma and has only a year to live. Wondering whether he has made a difference in his patients' lives, he contacts a man named Philip Slate, whom he had treated twenty-three years earlier for a sexual addiction. Arrogant and unlikeable, Philip has become a philosophy professor and a disciple of the nineteenth-century German intellectual Arthur Schopenhauer. Philip identifies strongly with Schopenhauer, a dazzlingly original thinker who was notoriously gloomy, embittered, and misanthropic. Philip, who claims that he was not helped by his analysis with Julius, is now training to become a psychotherapist, and he agrees to enter Julius's therapy group for six months in exchange for the analyst's clinical supervision. The two men clash over everything, including the value of human attachments, trust, and openness. Both explore their feelings about life and death, and both have an impact on the other members of the group.

Yalom is a distinguished "existential psychiatrist" who has written several classic psychiatric textbooks as well as one of my favorite novels, *When Nietzsche Wept*. He seems to know continental philosophy as well as he knows psychotherapy, and he understands that the former can teach us as much about self-healing as the latter. (One of the achievements of the novel is to show us how Schopenhauer's writings influenced Freudian theory.) Many passages from *The Schopenhauer Cure* are relevant to Love and Loss. Yalom's awareness of the centrality of the therapist-patient relationship parallels, in my view, the teacher-student relationship. "*It's not ideas, nor vision, nor tools that truly matter in therapy,*" Julius tells Philip. "If you debrief patients at the end of therapy about the process, what do they remember? *Never the ideas—it's always the*

17

relationship. They rarely remember an important insight their therapist offered but generally fondly recall their personal relationship with the therapist" (62–63; emphasis in original). Yalom makes a similar observation in his celebrated book *Love's Executioner,* which contains fascinating clinical narratives of his relationships with ten patients: "It's the relationship that heals, the relationship that heals, the relationship that heals—my professional rosary" (98). The same is true about education. As I suggest in *Empathic Teaching,* students remember best those teachers who have made a difference in their lives, who have encouraged and supported students rather than simply imparted knowledge to them.

Several passages in Yalom's novel affirm the importance of death education: "Death is always there, the horizon of all these concerns. Socrates said it most clearly, 'to learn to live well, one must first learn to die well.' Or Seneca, 'No man enjoys the true taste of life but he who is willing and ready to quit it'" (69). One of the best descriptions of "death denial" appears in *Love's Executioner:* "As we grow older, we learn to put death out of mind; we distract ourselves; we transform it into something positive (passing on, going home, rejoining God, peace at last); we deny it with sustaining myths; we strive for immortality through imperishable works, by projecting our seed into the future through our children, or by embracing a religious system that offers spiritual perpetuation." To those who insist that they do not deny death, Yalom responds, "The truth is that we know but do not know. We know *about* death, intellectually we know the facts, but we—that is, the unconscious portion of the mind that protects us from overwhelming anxiety—have split off, or dissociated, the terror associated with death" (5–6). Yalom might have quoted Montaigne's observation that we should spend our lives preparing for death rather than confronting it only when it approaches us.

Yalom realizes that the therapist-patient relationship becomes more authentic when each feels able to self-disclose to the other. Thus Julius muses: "Jung had other things in mind when he said that only the wounded healer can truly heal, but maybe honing patients' therapeutic skills is a good enough justification for therapists to reveal their wounds" (252–53). While reading *The Schopenhauer Cure,* I recognized for the first time that I am a "wounded teacher" and that I am exposing my wounds to my students. Yet these wounds, while still raw, are also healing, and I hope my students can see that reading and writing help one to survive a grievous loss. As D. H. Lawrence observes in a letter, "One sheds one['s] sicknesses in books, repeats and presents again one['s] emotions, to be master of them" (90). Yalom's awareness that therapists heal themselves when they heal their patients describes perfectly the feeling of exhilaration I have when I am teaching, how I seem to be magically released from whatever is troubling me:

One of the major side benefits of leading a group—a fact never stated in the professional literature—is that a potent therapy group often heals the therapist as well as the patients. Though Julius had often experienced personal relief after a meeting, he never was certain of the precise mechanism. Was it simply a result of forgetting himself for ninety minutes, or of the altruistic act of therapy, or of enjoying his own expertise, feeling proud of his abilities, and enjoying the high regard of others? All of the above? Julius gave up trying to be precise and for the past few years accepted the folksy explanation of simply dipping into the healing waters of the group. (95)

Other passages from *The Schopenhauer Cure*, expressed by both Julius and Philip, offer insights into confronting one's terror of death. Thus Philip says, "Spinoza was fond of using a Latin phrase, *sub specie aeternitatis*, meaning 'from the aspect of eternity.' He suggested that disturbing quotidian events become less unsettling if they are viewed from the aspect of eternity. I believe that concept may be an underappreciated tool in psychotherapy" (101). I'll want to discuss with my students the value of trying to develop and maintain this cosmic perspective, something I need to work on myself. I haven't read Schopenhauer since taking an introductory course on philosophy in college. Yalom quotes a passage from the essay "On the Doctrine of the Indestructibility of Our True Nature by Death" that strikes me as containing the highest wisdom, an insight that will help me deal with my own fear of death: "If in daily intercourse we are asked by one of the many who would like to know everything but who will learn nothing, about continued existence after death, the most suitable and above all the most correct answer would be: 'After your death you will be what you were before your birth'" (210). Yalom makes only one observation in his novel with which I disagree: "Schopenhauer had one further method of keeping death-anxiety at bay: death-anxiety is least when self-realization is most. If his position based on universal oneness appears anemic to some, there is little doubt about the robustness of this last defense. Clinicians who work with dying patients have made the observation that death-anxiety is greater in those who feel they have lived an unfulfilled life. A sense of fulfillment, at 'consummating one's life,' as Nietzsche put it, diminishes death-anxiety" (340). Barbara's death-anxiety was intense throughout her life, and it rose to panic levels after her diagnosis, but all who knew her would agree that she had a deeply fulfilling life in her family and career until her death at the age of fifty-seven. Perhaps this death-anxiety would have diminished had she died in her nineties, like her parents and grandparents. Despite this one disagreement with Yalom, I would have included *The Schopenhauer Cure* on our reading list had I known about the novel a few months ago.

Monday, January 23

This morning I spoke on the phone with James Peltz, the interim director of SUNY Press. He told me that *Dying to Teach* will appear in both cloth and paperback editions and that I can include up to 20 photographs of Barbara and our family. I'm elated, for this will be my most important book. I'm sad it's finished—it was easier writing about her every day than *not* writing about her. Nevertheless, I'm delighted that others will soon be able to read about Barbara and her impact on her family and friends. I feel almost as much joy over the book's acceptance for publication as I did when my granddaughter, Talia, was born last week. I had little doubt that Jillian would give birth to a healthy baby, but I had a great deal of doubt that my book would be published, mainly because it's so personal.

A few hours after speaking with James, I met with the students in my Love and Loss course. Most of them had read the description appearing in the English Department's spring 2006 booklet of course offerings:

Love and Loss in Literature and Life

Love inevitably ends in loss: this is one of the oldest themes in literature. In this course we will focus on the ways in which writers portray love and loss and seek to find consolation through religion, art, or memory. The reading list includes selected eulogies and elegies, several Emily Dickinson poems, the Book of Job, C. S. Lewis's *A Grief Observed*, John Bayley's *Elegy for Iris*, Emily Brontë's *Wuthering Heights*, Ernest Hemingway's *A Farewell to Arms*, Anna Quindlen's *One True Thing*, and Jeffrey Berman's *Empathic Teaching*. There will be several short essays (which will constitute 50 percent of the final grade), a midterm exam (25 percent), and a final exam (the remaining 25 percent). This course will be emotionally challenging without, I hope, being depressing.

I knew from experience that some students do not read course descriptions: they sign up for courses that fulfill distribution requirements, meet at convenient times, or have interesting titles. Consequently, I wanted to be as specific as possible on the first day of the semester. I told them that I've never taught this course before and that I am teaching it because of Barbara's death. I also mentioned that I will be reading aloud passages from *Dying to Teach*: both the course and the book are part of my effort to celebrate Barbara's life and memorialize her death. I anticipate that teaching the course and later writing a book about it will help me to grieve her loss. But there are other less personal motives as well, including helping students learn more about a subject that surrounds us daily but that is rarely discussed in the classroom. There is a world of difference between fictional and real death. The course will be an experiment in "death education," I added, and like any experiment, we can't predict whether it will succeed or fail.

Part of the experiment will be to see how everyone reacts to the intense emotions surrounding death. Students in other courses—especially my Expository Writing course—tell me that they have never seen anyone cry in the college classroom except for events such as the assault on the World Trade Center and the Pentagon on September 11, 2001. Before Barbara's diagnosis, I can recall crying only once in the classroom (see *Empathic Teaching* 234–47), though over the years I have sometimes found myself misty-eyed when discussing an emotionally charged essay or story. There seems to be an unwritten rule that teachers do not cry—and, therefore, students are also reluctant to cry. But why should we be ashamed of being "moved to tears" by powerful events and words? Why should it be appropriate to laugh in the classroom when something is funny but inappropriate to cry when something is sad? Most people regard me as "intellectual," but I would characterize myself as 99 percent emotional. Academics fear the "sentimental" (excessive emotion) far more than they fear the "cerebral" (excessive intellect). Ideally, there should be a balance between emotion and reason, but generally the scales are tilted toward the latter in the college classroom. If any subject demands to be taken emotionally, it is death education.

I passed out the syllabus [see appendix D] and the course packets. Everyone listened attentively and respectfully as I spoke about the requirements of the course and the emphasis on writing assignments that personalize death. As usual, I was self-disclosing, acknowledging that I have become a "crier" as a result of Barbara's death and that there may be moments during the semester when some of us will become teary-eyed. I wanted to indicate to them from the beginning that this will be an intense course, with seven unusual writing assignments: writing an obituary of a classmate; a eulogy; an essay on how their religious beliefs (or disbeliefs) affect their attitudes toward death; a list of "Ten Things to Do before I Die"; a letter from Cathy Linton to her mother who died in childbirth in *Wuthering Heights*; an essay on euthanasia; and an essay on my former students whose writings appear in *Empathic Teaching*. Since the writing topics are highly subjective, with no right or wrong answers, I will be grading not on content but on quality of writing.

I knew that some students might question why I was teaching one of my own books. The reason, I told them, was because I wanted them to read how students their own age, studying at their own university with their own teacher, have written about different forms of loss, including the loss of one or both of their parents as a result of death or divorce. Realizing that some students might object to buying one of their professor's own books, I told them that I have given up all my royalties from the book to keep the price as low as possible. I also informed them of my unusual "refund" policy: if students tell me after I have submitted final grades that they have found the book disappointing, I will refund the purchase price. But first they must look me in the eye and say, "Jeff, your book sucks." The class laughed when I said this, but I was serious: I want them to believe that the book was worth buying.

I'll try as hard as I can to make this course meaningful to my students. I want it to be as powerful for them as I anticipate it will be for me. I believe, with Henry Adams, that "A teacher affects eternity; he can never tell where his influence stops" (300). I know that this course will make a difference in my life, and I hope it will make a difference in my students' lives.

Is There Anything Worse Than Death?

During class I spoke about the emotional resistance that we feel toward death. Most people intellectually accept the inevitability of death but remain emotionally in denial about it, especially when they are young. As Tolstoy's masterpiece *The Death of Ivan Ilych* reveals, we can accept others' mortality but not our own. Sometimes this denial is healthy, while other times it is not. "Is there any subject that awakens more terror in you than death?" I asked rhetorically. After a few seconds of silence, one woman said that she was more frightened of rape than death. "This is a terrible question to ask, but would you rather have your mother raped or murdered?" She said that she never thought about that question but agreed that murder would be worse than rape. A male student said that working with brain-damaged children has convinced him that losing one's memory or mental functioning is worse than death. I hadn't expected this answer, but I immediately agreed with him, for I fear Alzheimer's disease more than I fear death. I ended class by predicting that there will be more smiles than tears in the course. I hope this is true.

I thought the introductory class went well, and I'll be curious whether many people drop the class. [Three students dropped the first week.] Even though the course closed at sixty students, there were several people trying to add the course, including Baxter, who came to my office before class and pleaded to get in. "I've taken three courses with you and got A's in all of them. I know this will be the highlight of college for me." I didn't give him a definite answer, but I told him to come back on Wednesday, when I would have a better idea about the class size. [I did allow him to add the course.] Two graduate students, Gladys and Ava, both of whom took my Thomas Hardy/D. H. Lawrence course last year, are also taking Love and Loss as independent studies. I'm happy to have them. And I'm delighted that Richard Bower will be assisting me. A doctoral student in our program and a tenured assistant professor at Cayuga County Community College, Richard took my Age of Freud course last summer. He will be attending every class, offering me his own insights on Love and Loss, teaching two classes, and interviewing several students to learn about their perspectives on the course. Richard observes in his opening diary entry that "first days are often survival days for students and professor":

> "The personal experiences are those that are interesting." This is one of the tenets by which Jeff makes his classrooms matter, and certainly there is much importance for individual students to be allowed a space where they can investigate personal experience—their own and each other's. In all the organizing that must occur in this large class of sixty people on the first day, it is not the newness or nervousness that people remember. First days are often survival days for students and professor. What people may likely remember is not the syllabus or introductions, not the awkwardness of the room or artificial lighting, not the initial noise or roll call. They may not remember exactly how large and long the class is. . . . Many will not remember how the class is mostly female—I count twelve males and must note how many are attending by the course's end. [There were eleven men at the end of the course.]
>
> What people may likely remember from this first class are two answers to Jeff's question: Is there anything worse than death? He asks this as a claim to the usefulness of taking this course, how he is glad there are so many people interested in what he confesses will be the most challenging teaching experience of his career. When he asks the question, he rises on his toes, wondering if there could be anything worse. For me, it's unclear if Jeff has thought through such possibilities; I admit that I cannot think of anything worse. But then, two students surprise me. One woman says "rape." And there is a moment when the class's importance may be undercut before it starts. Jeff asks apologetically what he says is a terrible question, would you rather have your mother raped or murdered? Truly, it is a terrible question, and a question most would not ask. In fact, I think most would avoid answering such a question. The student admits she'd prefer to have her mother alive. This is a genuine and gutsy response. It's honest and what we would all prefer, though we ardently wish something terrible like rape never to happen at all. It's a terrible fear with which many women in the class probably live, yet all are likely to agree that this is not worse than death. David Foster Wallace has commented on this in his book *Brief Interviews with Hideous Men*.
>
> Another student tells how he worked with a person who is mentally disabled and how he can't imagine living this way. The young man paints the sadness of experiencing life this way with a few words and the weight of experience; his opinion doesn't come across as self-serving at all, only sincere and serious. No one says much, and Jeff lets everyone make their own conclusions in respectful silence before using a personal anecdote about his classroom to move the material back to the course.

"What would your dying words be?" One doesn't often get the chance to answer this question, but Jeff has asked us to think about it as we'll be expected to write them next class. Caring is maintained in his voice as he moves to issues and hopes for retention, how he will not grade on content of one's ideas, only their written presentation. Most of the students appear "sold" on the course; they are interested in the logistics of how class will work, but not just those. They seem to genuinely care about being there. Are they engaged?

Jeff comments on how crying may be a part of this course. Invariably, he says he will cry when it comes to his wife. "Hope it won't freak you out," he says.

Students had no questions in the end, but the explanations of what to expect seem to prepare them well for what is to come. After class, Jeff comments on how the two student answers have given him much to write about in his journal. He says before leaving, "Yes, there are things worse than death."

Wednesday, January 25

Today was the first full class, and I began by asking the students to fill out an anonymous questionnaire:

Why I'm Taking Love and Loss in Literature and Life

I'm interested in knowing why you are taking this course—both the academic and personal reasons. Please spend a few minutes responding to the following questions. Write your answers in the space below each question. (Use the back of the sheet if you need more space.) Be as truthful as possible—and don't sign your name. I'll read some of the responses aloud next class. Please write legibly.

1. What are the academic reasons you're taking this course?
2. What are the personal reasons you're taking this course?
3. What do you hope to learn from the course?
4. Do you have any special fears or concerns about the course? If so, how can I help you to deal with these fears or concerns?
5. What if anything should I know about you?
6. What if anything should you know about me?

I have never asked students to indicate in a questionnaire why they are taking a particular course with me, so I can't compare the results with those of other questionnaires. Nor do I know whether these students are representative of others who are enrolled at my university. Nevertheless, the results are interesting. Students cited several academic reasons for taking the course. Many chose the course because they needed to fulfill requirements for being an English major or minor, and this one looked attractive. One person wrote that "the course covers a theme that I've never had the opportunity to explore." Another found the reading list appealing: "I feel this class offers the opportunity to explore a great sample of seminal works in literature through a unique, interesting, and valuable perspective for both the personal and academic worlds." Another registered for the course, decided to drop it, but then chose to remain: "I need to satisfy a few English requirements. I actually was planning on dropping this course and taking creative writing next year, which would instead satisfy 2 course requirements rather than this one class satisfying only 1, but after you talked about the class on Monday I've decided to keep it." Another offered an explanation that combined flattery and pragmatic convenience: "I heard the teacher's really good and it's a Monday/Wednesday class, so I don't have any classes on Friday." Another student, presumably a junior or senior, registered for the course over the objections of his or her adviser: "Although I needed to take one more '200–400' level course, members of advisement tried to persuade me not to take this course, their reason being that as a 200 level course it wouldn't be 'challenging' enough." Fourteen students—nearly one-quarter of the class—stated that they had taken one or more courses with me before and felt comfortable with my teaching style.

The personal reasons for taking the course were more unusual and varied. Six students were taking the course because of the recent death of a relative or friend. "The course description caught my eye because as I was reading it it made me think of a very close friend that was killed in a car accident in September, his 21st birthday was 5 days ago." Wrote another, "One of my friends passed away in October, and I felt this class would be interesting and emotionally challenging." Another: "I lost a person I loved to an illness. I have bottled up my feelings and emotions and I feel like this class can help me confront these feelings." Another: "My grandmother recently passed away. I hope this class will help me deal with her death. Death, grief, and euthanasia are also topics I am considering for my thesis." And another: "I love to write and have always dreamed of some day being a published author. My style of writing comes from my own life experiences and dreams, so the topic of this class is 'right up my alley.' My father and I were in a car accident a few years ago in which he died and I almost died. This experience, as well as other traumatic and emotional losses in my life, color my writing and I want to learn how to harness my emotion in my writing." Another spoke enigmatically about a near-death experience: "Death is an intimate topic as in the past few weeks I have been face to face with the idea of my own death. These experiences have been drug induced but have brought to my attention the requirement in my own life to deal with these important issues."

What did the students hope to learn from the course? The following comment is representative: "A deeper understanding of loss, death, and the grieving process as a means to accept death more fully." Several wanted the reassurance that they were not the only ones worried about death: "I hope to learn that other people are as scared about dying as myself." Some were taking the course because they hoped it would lead to self-improvement: "I hope to become a better person and open my mind to as many new things and people as possible." One person hoped the course would make it easier to console others who have suffered a loss: "I hope to learn how to relate to other people when they lose a loved one. I personally do not have a problem with the loss of a loved one, but when someone else loses someone they love I never know what to say to them or how to act." Another sought a "greater appreciation for the dead and those they left behind." Many expected the course would teach them how to become more effective writers: "Better writing skills—I haven't taken an English course in a long time, and I'm not sure what I remember!"

To question 4, whether they had special fears or concerns about the course, more than half the students wrote the word "no" or left the question blank. A few expressed academic concerns about the amount of writing. "Both my parents are journalists," one person quipped, "but I didn't luck out enough to get the English writing gene! I've avoided taking English for one and one half years here in Albany, so I hope this one works out." Others were concerned about the amount of reading, which they feared might be excessive for a 200-level course. The remaining twenty students were afraid that they might cry in class. "I'm worried I may get emotional during class," one student admitted. "I don't want to cry too much," acknowledged another, "but I hope it will be more smiles than tears like you said on the first day of class." One person anticipated that discussions of love and loss might be painful because of a dying relative. "My grandmother whom I am very close to is dying from fibrosis of the lungs. My family and I take care of her. We prepare all her meals, take her to the bathroom and much much more. We understand that she may not be with us much longer. I am worried that I may begin to tear up and might have to leave the room for a bit when we discuss death." Another person recently lost a grandparent and was apprehensive that the course might evoke sad memories. "I am nervous that this will be emotionally taxing on the heels of my grandmother's death." Others expressed more generalized fears. "While I am very open with my friends and family about my feelings, fears, and emotions, confronting the idea of loss and pain in an open forum is somewhat intimidating. I plan on facing my fears head on, but I don't quite know where that will take me."

Question 5—"What if anything should I know about you?"—produced several responses. "You already know me fairly well," wrote someone who had taken an earlier course with me, ending the sentence with a happy face. Another declared, "I don't like to show my weaknesses, so I do not like for other people to see me cry." Several students admitted that they have little experience with loss. Others made the opposite statement. "I have a great deal of experience with traumatic loss. Death has been all too prevalent in my life so far. I also have firsthand experience. In my car accident, I was technically dead for a brief time, so I have 'issues' with death, but I am open about my experiences to a degree." Several people are taking the course to work through grief and master fears of death. "I have dealt with the loss of many family members and perhaps this class will help me to deal with these losses." Another made a similar comment: "I have had many people pass away in 2005, and to hear others' experience will help." Another: "The only major losses I've experienced (besides pets) were my great-grandfather and, a few months ago, my stepbrother who was terminally ill with a genetic disorder (he died at the age of 6 but was only expected to live until 2)." Another: "My grandma is very ill and will die soon." Another: "I am completely terrified of dying before I succeed and accomplish what I desire from life." And another: "I was diagnosed with MS while taking your Hemingway course last summer and am more terrified of losing my dignity one day than I am of dying."

About half the students did not respond to the final question: "What if anything should you know about me?" They may have left the question blank because they ran out of time—or because they agreed with the person who wrote, "Nothing. I don't like to pry." A few asked me silly or playful questions: "Favorite color? Shoe size? Blood type?" Others asked me general questions—"Why did you become an English professor?"—which I could answer easily: "Because I love to read and talk about literature." The remaining fifteen students wanted to know why I was teaching this particular course. "What are your objectives in teaching this class, and what do you *hope* students will take away?" Another asked a related question: "How do you feel teaching this class and [do you believe that] letting us in your life will help us (because I think it will)?" Three people asked "coping" questions. The first wrote, "I would like to know what helped you cope with the death of your wife. I was only with the person I loved for 5 years, but to me it was a lifetime, so I feel like I am in a similar situation." The second wondered, "after seeing death firsthand, what do you do to get out of bed in the morning?" And the third asked me why I wrote a book about my wife's death: "What did you think writing about your wife's death would do for you—did you do it to cope with what was going on or for other reasons?"

It will take me an entire semester to answer these questions, but I will try to give brief answers in the next week. Since there is never enough time in class to answer all of the students' questions, I may have to provide answers only in my diary, to which I can return later in the semester if I have time. Surely one of my objectives in teaching this course is to help students learn more about the enigma of death and its impact on our lives. "All fiction takes as its great central mystery death, mortality," Anna Quindlen writes in *One True Thing* (145). To speak effectively about these mysteries is to speak *affec-*

tively, acknowledging the power of emotions. Throughout the semester we will be talking and writing about these stories of life and death. Nearly every modern student of thanatology has remarked that death remains the most taboo subject of the twentieth—and, we may add, the twenty-first—century. In the foreword to Marie de Hennezel's book *Intimate Death*, Francois Mitterand raises the question, how do we learn to die? "We live in a world that panics at this question and turns away. Other civilizations before ours looked squarely at death. They mapped the passage for both the community and the individual. They infused the fulfillment of destiny with a richness of meaning. Never perhaps have our relations with death been as barren as they are in this modern spiritual desert, in which our rush to a mere existence carries us past all sense of mystery. We do not even know that we are parching the essence of life of one of its wellsprings" (vii). Mitterand, the former president of France, was terminally ill when he wrote these words, and thus he speaks about death with a special urgency. I hope my students will take away from Love and Loss an increased understanding of both death and life, along with a heightened appreciation of how beautiful and fleeting life is. This is an "objective" behind all my teaching—the belief that literature can make us more aware of what we have. Now that I have lost my wife, I am painfully aware of how little time we have with loved ones.

I see no contradiction between teaching students how creative writers reflect on love and loss and talking about my own experiences. To use an anthropological term, I teach from the point of view of a participant-observer. To separate literature from life, limiting classroom discussions to the former but not the latter, strikes me as impoverishing both. Nor do I see a contradiction between talking about how I have been able to deal with grief—in large part, by reading and writing about it—and helping my students with their own grief. The theme of love and loss affects everyone—except perhaps the unlucky few who have never loved or been loved. One of my relatives asked me, while I was writing *Dying to Teach*, why I wanted others to read the book. The question surprised me, and after a moment of silence I replied, "The short answer is because writers want to be read; the long answer can be gleaned only by reading the entire book." I am both the teacher of Love and Loss and a student of grief: all of us are learning about the joy and sorrow of human existence.

What helps me get out of bed in the morning—apart from my dogs, who demand to be taken for a long run? For the first eighteen months following Barbara's death, my main incentive to get out of bed was to write about her, and when I completed *Dying to Teach*, my incentive changed to thinking about my new course, Love and Loss, and the book I knew I wanted to write about it. I'm sure that I'm not the only writer for whom death is the undying muse of art.

Dying Words

I asked students to write down on a note card what they would like their "dying words" to be. Their responses offer insight into their lives, particularly what they hold most dear. Of the fifty-seven people who responded to the question, twenty-seven expressed love and gratitude for relatives and friends. The word "love" appears in nearly all these dying words:

> I'm going to miss the people I love, and the people that loved me.
> We're birds, I'll see you soon. I love you with all my heart.
> Thank you to everybody who has touched my life. I will miss being here with you. I love you.
> I love you, I'll miss you. Don't worry and spend too much time in sadness, we'll be together again later.
> I have led a fulfilling life. I have no regrets. Thank you for sharing this life with me. I love you.
> Love and appreciate everything dear to you. I have.
> I love you, always remember me, but move on soon.
> I finally feel at peace. Do not feel sad. I will love you and be with you forever.

These responses are remarkable not only for the students' love and gratitude for relatives and friends but also for their lack of bitterness, disappointment, or anger with life. They are protective of those who survive them: the dying want the living to move on with their lives rather than dwell on loss. The dying wish to be remembered but not in a morbid or depressing way. The emphasis on love and gratitude in these "dying words" affirms the students' attachment to their relatives and friends. They are connected securely to these people, and in the final moments of their lives they desire to acknowledge the life-sustaining importance of human relationships. I imagine that one of the most terrifying aspects of death is the dying person's feeling of disconnection from those with whom he or she is closest, along with the perception that the living are abandoning the dying. Expressing one's eternal love helps to offset the loneliness and grief experienced by both the dying and the living.

The dying words of an additional eleven students contain explicit or implicit references to God or heaven. These dying words vary strikingly in tone and diction, ranging from solemn and devout, on the one hand, to light-hearted and bantering, on the other:

> Lord forgive me for the sin that I have committed; I am ready to move on.
> I'm going to be with my dad again.
> This isn't the end, it's only another beginning.

I believe that Jesus Christ is the son of God and he died on the cross for my
sins. I accept him into my heart and as the Lord of my life. I love my
family and friends with all my heart. This is only a reaffirmation of my
faith.
Keep your head up. I'm only dying physically.
Meet me at the stoplight after the gate.

Most of the remaining eighteen students imagined upbeat or funny
dying words. They testify to the importance of remembering the dead, enjoying life to the fullest, living a good life, embracing love, and accepting the joy
and sorrow of existence:

Move on, for if you don't, you're as useful to this world as I am right now.
(Dead)
I'll be back.
Teddy
Just because I'm gone, doesn't mean I'm not going to be here. What's lost
shouldn't be forgotten.
This sucks, give me a beer.
Make sure there's an ice cream cake at my funeral for Lisa and play Jeff
Buckley's "Last Goodbye" & "Grace" at the ceremony.
When you have to go, you gotta go!

It is impossible to know whether many of my students will remember
their imagined dying words when they are actually dying. Nor can we say
whether anyone will be around to hear their dying words, which represents,
paradoxically, a dying genre. [As John Updike remarks in the *New Yorker*,
"Last words, recorded and treasured in the days when the deathbed was in the
home, have fallen from fashion, perhaps because most people spend their final
hours in the hospital, too drugged to make any sense. And only the night nurse
hears them talk" (7 and 14 August 2006).] Nor can we know whether many
will remember their Love and Loss course when death overtakes them. But we
can say that their imagined dying words reflect the wish for a fulfilling life that,
for most of my students, centers around family, friends, and God. One can infer
that these are the dying words of young people who believe they have many
good years ahead of them, and who therefore do not worry that they will soon
be at death's door. These are, to be sure, idealized dying words, uttered by
college students who are generally young, healthy, and in the prime of life.
That many of these statements are expressed in complete sentences—some of
them quite lengthy—reveals their assumption that neither physical nor mental deterioration will prevent them from communicating with loved ones. I
suspect that the dying are unable to communicate with the living in many or

most cases, either because they are too weak to speak or because no one is around to hear them. Richard makes this observation in today's diary entry:

> My own final words would not be composed of words but of facial expressions that look to gesture and imply everything I may have said to my audience over the years. It seems to me that by the time of my dying words I would have said everything I was going to say. If I could choose, I would not rush into some kind of capstone statement. I'm sure I would only get much wrong, possibly leave sentiments out for people or most probably not capture what my life could mean for them. I'd hope to speak with a smile, which some students did indicate, some facial gesture of reaching out to touch whichever loved one is at my side, and a hand grasping my wife's. In thinking about it now, I think I'm brought back to these decisions by my grandfather's death with the exception that he clenched my hand in panic. I don't know that my eyes will show anything more than his that were mixed with fear.

To illustrate how much difficulty the dying have in expressing themselves, I gave everyone a photocopy of Barbara's last written words to me, on the occasion of my fifty-ninth birthday, less than three months before her death. Several of the words were almost illegible, indicating her unsteady hand, and there were many words crossed out, misspelled, or repeated twice: "This is such a special day that I couldn't let it pass without writing. It's so difficult for me to combine letters and words. We've shared a spectacular life together, a love for one another that has only strengthened by time." In sharing with my students Barbara's last written words, I was trying to illustrate, as Richard suggests in his diary entry, a life in the process of self-extinction: "Jeff shares his wife's last written words. Meaning making was passing out of Barbara's control; for students to see this disclosure is paramount to witnessing mortality. Unbelievable! Expressions matter, first, last, and all the words in between matter. It's just that we forget sometimes how much. The sharing of the last words is dramatic for some students—a curiosity to witness mortality; for others like myself, the last words reveal how life is an act of writing that matters to those we can get to listen. We need caring to be able to complete this rhetorical act; we need empathy in order for any communication to matter."

I saved the last twenty minutes for the reading of my eulogy of Barbara:

Eulogy for Barbara

Barbara and I met in the fall of 1963 in our freshman English class at the University of Buffalo. She was not yet seventeen years old. For me, though not for her, it was love at first sight: I couldn't take my eyes off her long flowing hair, green eyes, high cheek bones, olive complexion, and delicate nose. She had a natural, unself-conscious beauty that never faded, not even after her illness. Two of the black-and-white photos I took of her in 1967 now hang on my office wall at the university; students who walk into my office invariably comment on her exotic features. Barbara and I could not have been more different in class: I spoke incessantly, enraptured by my own words, while she remained silent like the sphinx, which only increased her mystery to me. I was annoyed that she received higher grades on her essays than I did. Early in the semester I told our English teacher, Len Port, how much I liked her, and not long afterward he summoned us to his office. I didn't realize it at the time, but he was a matchmaker: he deliberately failed to appear, and she and I were forced to speak to each other for the first time while waiting for him.

Our relationship began inauspiciously. Our first date was November 22, 1963, a day that no one of our generation will ever forget. After classes were canceled because of President Kennedy's assassination, we decided to see a movie; we were among a handful of people in the theater as we watched Laurence Olivier play Heathcliff in Emily Brontë's *Wuthering Heights*. On our third date I walked her back to the dormitory and asked if I could kiss her goodnight. "No" was her immediate reply. I turned around and left, vowing never to ask her out again. A few months later I broke that promise, and we began seeing each other. When I later told her how hurt I was by her rejection, she replied, "It was a stupid question: you should have just kissed me."

We dated throughout college and were married in August 1968. Barbara's only precondition for marriage was to have a dog. I had been bitten by a German shepherd when I was a child and therefore agreed reluctantly, hoping she would forget my promise. Barbara never forgot anything in her life, and within a few months we acquired the first of five Belgian sheepdogs. I remember little about our wedding except that I didn't want to be there: I wanted to be married but did not believe in marriage rituals. I should add that this was during my adolescent rebellion stage, a stage which continues to this day; I enjoyed our daughters' weddings far more than our own, and I still have not looked at our wedding photos. The one detail that I remember about our wedding is that I asked the bandleader to play the Barbra Streisand song "Never Will I Marry" for our first dance, but he ignored my request, perhaps because he did not appreciate my wry irony.

Two weeks after our wedding I received a phone call from Len, telling me that he was in the process of committing suicide; Barbara and I were devastated by his death. A month later we were in Cornell's graduate library, where I spent most of my time studying. Though she rarely read the *New York Times*, and never the obituary page, a premonition compelled Barbara to do so, and she saw the obituary of Len's wife, Phyllis, who had died, perhaps by her own hand, on his birthday. This was the first but not the only time that Barbara felt the existence of a supernatural force shaping her life.

Barbara began her career as a first grade teacher, but she never liked teaching, and she resigned after receiving tenure. She felt that if she continued teaching, she would never want any of her own children. She believed at the time that she could never love a child as much as she loved our dog Cybele. The night before she gave birth to Arielle in 1973, she started crying, fearing that she had made a great mistake by becoming pregnant. As soon as Arielle was born, however, Barbara felt an immediate and intense maternal bond, which only increased over time. Her devotion to her children and her dogs never wavered. I soon realized that if I were foolish enough to give her an ultimatum between choosing her husband or dog, I would be the one sleeping in the doghouse. She would have loved to be reincarnated as a dog and cared for by a person like herself.

Unlike me, Barbara could do almost everything well, and she had a multitude of talents, interests, and hobbies. Not only did she excel at her professional work, first as a teacher and then as a computer analyst, but she loved arts and crafts. She created a magnificent stained glass chandelier that would have delighted Tiffany, and no one was better at crocheting blankets or knitting sweaters. She made Arielle's exquisite wedding gown, and after finishing it, she sewed into the back of the dress a label with the following words: "For Arielle on her wedding to David Albert, October 7, 2000. Every stitch sewn with love by her mother Barbara Berman, with support from her mother, Jean Lederman Kozinn, and with spiritual guidance from her mother, Sarah Seliznick Lederman." In her diary she wrote: "I think it was a spiritual experience sitting on the bedspread that my grandmother spent two years hand crocheting for me thirty-five years ago and working on Arielle's gown and veil. She would have been proud. So many memories of my grandmother were involved with sewing and making things. I can hear her needle piercing the hatforms as she was working on her millinery. They were works of art."

Everything Barbara made was a work of art, and she was meticulous to a fault. Her eye invariably spotted misweaves and imperfections, and she demanded of others what she expected of herself, which was nothing short of perfection. Once she became upset with a stone mason because he repaired our garage wall without lining up the mortar pattern of the bricks. No one but Barbara could see the difference, but that did not stop her from taking him to small claims court. To support her argument, she took photographs of the other houses on the block, demonstrating that all their mortar patterns lined up perfectly. She won the case. Later she said that she regretted not becoming a lawyer, an ambition our younger daughter Jillian has fulfilled. It is not easy living with a person whose standards are so high; she was as mechanically inclined as I am mechanically declined, and I became dependent upon her ability to fix anything. She could repair faulty wiring, broken toilets, temperamental boilers, cracked floor tile, and leaky faucets. By contrast, I was hopeless. Her favorite story about me was the time I spent two hours replacing a head light in our car, only to discover that I had replaced the wrong light. Once in exasperation I said to her, "You're such a perfectionist that I don't understand why you married me." Without hesitation she replied, "I didn't think about it very much." Lucky for me that she didn't.

Barbara was a good person. She befriended nearly everyone with whom she came into contact, and she never forgot to wish a relative or friend happy birthday. Mentioning Barbara's name would invariably bring a smile. If you were Barbara's friend, you were a friend for life, and several credit her for turning around their lives by encouraging them to end abusive relationships or by finding employment for them when they lost their jobs. She was never too busy to bake cookies for friends who were ill or send cards to cheer them up.

Barbara saved everything she received, regardless of whether it had intrinsic value; each object was a treasure that reminded her of a person or an experience. Many married couples argue about money; we argued about whether I was allowed to throw out what I considered junk but what she cherished as family heirlooms: a desk that she had used in elementary school, an unused tire for a car that was now rusting in a junkyard, or a broken typewriter or adding machine that her father used forty years earlier. She saved all her report cards from elementary school; marbles from her childhood; the letters her parents sent to her when she was in college; old AAA tour books; maps and globes that are now out of date; rocks and seashells from our trips; and even a bath towel, now filled with holes, which her parents gave us when we became engaged. As our children were cleaning out her closets, they noticed bags of dog hair that Barbara intended to weave into a sweater. She was thrifty and self-sacrificing to a fault and preferred to buy gifts for relatives or friends than for herself.

Barbara's worst quality was that she was a worrier, and here we were unfortunately similar. For decades she worried about the health of her mother and father, who are now eighty-nine and ninety, respectively. She worried about events that happened and those that did not. She was grief-stricken when we had to put a dog to sleep, and one of her dying wishes was to have the cremated ashes of her beloved dog Ebony placed in her burial casket. In therapy I learned a new word—catastrophizer—and it immediately resonated within me. Perhaps we were catastrophizers because of our parents, who had difficult lives during the Depression; perhaps we were catastrophizers because we are Jewish and therefore keenly aware of persecution and suffering. For whatever reason, we spent too much time fearing the worst. Both of us were blessed in so many ways—with our children, relatives, friends, work, and with each other.

Catastrophe finally struck on August 12, 2002, one day after our thirty-fourth anniversary, when she was diagnosed with metastatic cancer. No one can explain why Barbara, who could have been a poster child for living a healthy life, and who comes from a long-lived family without any history of cancer, was stricken by such a virulent disease. We were fortunate to have the best medical treatment. No one could ask for a more devoted oncologist than Dr. Fred Shapiro; and we were equally fortunate to have the loving help of my cousin, Dr. Glenn Dranoff, through whose influence Barbara was accepted into a clinical trial for an experimental pancreatic cancer vaccine, which almost certainly prolonged the quality of her life by several months.

Shortly after Barbara's diagnosis I received a letter from my dear friend Randy Craig's brother, David, whose wife had died recently after a long battle with breast cancer. David wrote that the last months of their marriage were the happiest of their life, the time when they felt the greatest understanding, contentment, and intimacy. I think that Barbara would agree with me that as close as we were before her diagnosis, we became even closer afterward. Scarcely a day went by without declarations of our love for and devotion to each other. We had always been close with our children, who have also been our best friends, but we became even closer, and our admiration for their husbands became even greater. For the first time in our lives, our children began to parent us. Arielle and Jillian took turns coming home every weekend, as did their husbands, Dave and Alex, and all four unselfishly put their lives on hold in order to prolong Barbara's life. No parents have been prouder of their children than we are of ours.

In one of the most quoted lines of twentieth-century poetry, Sylvia Plath observed in "Lady Lazarus" that "Dying / Is an art, like everything else. / I do it exceptionally well." It is impossible to take comfort in a loved one's suicide: the legacy—or illegacy—of suicide is lifelong anger, guilt, confusion, and sorrow in family and friends. By contrast, dying with courage, strength, and dignity, as Barbara did, makes it easier for loved ones to grieve their loss. Barbara's acceptance of death was her final gift to her family, allowing us to take comfort in a life that was extraordinary to the end. She remained fiercely protective of her children; she would often tell me that she was being tortured by physical pain, but she never expressed this to Arielle and Jillian. She wished to spare everyone from the grief arising from suffering and death. She always had a grateful smile for the nurses in the chemotherapy room, who came to feel a special affection for her. She would bring photographs of our new grandson to show the nurses, and equally important, she would admire the nurses' photographs of their own grandchildren. She always appreciated the help I provided and told me repeatedly that it is more difficult for the caregiver than for the dying person. She never gave up on life, even when life gave up on her.

Barbara and I did not spend much time talking about the unfairness of her illness. We had no regrets about anything except that we did not have more time together. She felt little anger and no bitterness. She died during what would have been the best time in her life, when her children were grown up, happily married to wonderful men, successful in their careers, and beginning families of their own. She delighted in our new grandson, Nate the Great, who filled her heart with joy.

Premature death always raises the most fundamental religious and existential questions, and each person will answer these questions differently. Amid tragedy, those with strong religious faith may have emotional resources lacking in those without religious faith. I wish I could believe that Barbara is now in a better world, that there is a reason for her death, and that one day I will be reunited with her. What I do believe is that she will always be alive to those of us who were privileged to know her. I want to end by quoting a passage from Charles Dickens's novel *Nicholas Nickleby:* "In every life, no matter how full or empty one's purse, there is tragedy. It is the one promise life always fulfills. Happiness is a gift and the trick is not to expect it, but to delight in it when it comes and to add to other people's store of it." Barbara was one of those rare people who increased the store of happiness in the world.

I read the eulogy for several reasons: to show my personal involvement with love and loss; to describe my love for Barbara; to allow students to see me not simply as a teacher but also as a person; to demonstrate that one can survive a devastating loss and still find life worth living; to affirm the power of language to memorialize loss; to reveal that a eulogy can be both funny and sad; and to offer my students an example of a eulogy that may help them in the future when they are called upon to memorialize a relative or friend. I've discovered, along with other researchers, that self-disclosure begets self-disclosure, and I hope that my willingness to talk about my experience with love and loss will encourage students to share their experiences with the class.

I hadn't read the eulogy aloud since Barbara's funeral, on 9 April 2004, and I was surprised that I was able to read it so easily. When I read the eulogy to my Expository Writing students in March 2004, shortly before Barbara's death, I was so choked by emotion that I could hardly complete the reading. Now, however, I had little trouble maintaining my composure. I guess this is what happens when grief begins to diminish.

Coincidentally, today I received a letter from Amanda, who was in that Expository Writing course. The letter describes her response to reading *Dying to Teach*, and I'll include it in the appendix to the memoir, along with her classmates' responses. The letter comes just in time, for this week I sent the final manuscript to SUNY Press. Amanda's response to the entire book is different from her response to the eulogy when I read it in class. She now writes: "When my friend's mother died in March 2004, the semester I took your course, writing about it was soothing. At least that is how I feel about the process now, but when I was writing the essay it was painful and complicated. I can only recall my emotions at the time because I still have that essay, that time capsule of sensations. I remember writing it in the open basement of my dormitory, streaking the ink with my uncontrollable tears. I remember how my sinuses felt like they were imploding, and how grateful I was that no one bothered me." Like Amanda, I can now reread my words without my voice breaking, my body convulsing with emotion. The emotions at the time were raw, like a festering wound that cannot be touched. Now the wound has largely healed, covered by scar tissue. Not a good metaphor, since the memory of Barbara can hardly be compared to scar tissue. Nevertheless, I continue to be surprised by the ease with which I read the eulogy.

In their anonymous responses to a questionnaire I asked them to fill out in class, most students in Love and Loss felt moved when they heard me read my eulogy, and they could begin to understand my feelings for Barbara. "I felt sad for you, and listening to you speak I could tell the amount of love and respect you had for your wife." Another appreciated that I wanted to share something so personal. They could feel the depth of my love for Barbara and hoped they would have the same kind of love when they married. They believed the many concrete details I used in the eulogy helped to bring her to life for them. They didn't use the word "art," but they responded to the eulogy as a highly crafted essay. Like other eulogists, I tried to reproduce in words the undying beauty of a loved one's life. "[I was] amazed that you read it without needing to stop and impressed and touched that it was so heartfelt and beautifully detailed. I felt that on some levels I knew your wife." Many of their comments characterized precisely what I tried to convey in the eulogy: "It was sad and beautiful at the same time. Your words gave her life. She seems like someone I would have liked to know." They identified with me and realized that one day they might be in the same situation. Most of the comments were positive, but two students made statements that might be considered negative: one wrote, "I was shocked that you allowed us to hear something so personal"; the other wrote, "I thought it was a little weird."

Many people said it was painful to hear the eulogy, but no one said it was too painful. The following characterizes most of the responses: "I had thought it would be painful, and was prepared for emotions, etc. Rather I almost felt happy to know that kind of love & relationship can exist in real life, never having been given such an example by my own parents or relatives." Another person felt that the eulogy "sounded like a beautiful story with a not-so-happy ending. I greatly appreciated hearing the eulogy." Those who empathized could picture themselves at the funeral, mourning Barbara's death: "It was painful in that I felt like I was at her funeral & painful because I imagined I was there & could picture everyone there & their feelings of sorrow."

Twenty-six of the fifty-five students did not believe that hearing the eulogy changed their relationship to me. They did not explain why; they simply wrote the word "no." The remaining students believed that their relationship to me had changed, if only slightly. "I think hearing it will help me understand you better, understand why you're teaching this course, and feel a bit closer to you since you shared something so personal." They appreciated the opportunity to see me as a person rather than only as a teacher. "Too often students do not have the chance to get to know the instructors as people. The act of sharing such a personal act of your life was a refreshing change." They believed my willingness to share my feelings with them made it easier for them to share their feelings with me.

Twenty-seven people did not think that hearing the eulogy would change their feelings about the course. The remaining twenty-eight believed that their feelings had *already* changed. "I think for me, it reiterated the fact that this was the class for me. Loss has been a very central theme in my life, and part of who I am is exploring this." Does this statement imply that hearing the eulogy affected mainly those who have also suffered a major loss? There is some evidence to indicate this. "Yes, because now that you have openly shared with me your emotions and tragedies, I will be more at ease sharing mine." And another: "It will definitely make me reflect on the people I lost in my lifetime." Others also believed that hearing the eulogy changed their feelings about the course, even though they did not refer to any specific losses in their lives. "Yes, it made me understand that love and loss is a theme in literature that affects everyone & which everyone can relate to." Another person took the course more seriously because I read the eulogy. The eulogy surprised several students and made the course different from their other high school and college courses. "The second I heard that, I knew this class would be very different from any other class I've taken." Wrote another, "I will enjoy it more."

A large majority believed that hearing the eulogy encouraged them to reflect on relatives' and friends' deaths. "I spend a great deal of time reflecting on the losses of loved ones in order to keep them part of my life. Hearing your eulogy to your wife gave me another opportunity to do so." My eulogy reminded several students of their own specific losses. "Your eulogy made me think a lot about my great-uncle's death because I read a eulogy at his funeral." Another: "I attended the funeral of my grandmother just this weekend, so in a way, hearing the eulogy was of some comfort to me." Another: "My aunt just passed away in December so it allowed me to think back on pleasant memories of her." And another: "Very much. I lost a great friend at 18 and since your reading have been thinking about the experience a great deal." Those who have not yet suffered loss reacted differently to the eulogy. One observed: "I haven't had someone very close to me pass away. Hearing the eulogy scared me a little because I pictured someone close to me dying & what I'd have to write for their eulogy."

Fifty-two out of fifty-five people believed it was appropriate for me to read aloud my eulogy. They would agree with the following comment: "I think it was very appropriate for you to read the eulogy aloud. It gives us insight toward your intentions of the class and how you are 'qualified' to lead a discussion on the topic of loss." Another liked the fact that the teacher was doing what he wanted his students to do. "If we are expected to be thoughtful and honest in this course it is encouraging to know our professor also holds himself to this standard."

The final question—"What if anything did you learn from the eulogy?"—elicited many specific answers. "I hate death even more." Another: "I learned that eulogies don't always have to be sad. They can have some lighter moments to them." And another: "I learned to reflect on the happy memories of people who have passed on rather than on the fact that they are no longer here." One person was struck by how "human" Barbara and I were during the early years of our life together. "I thought it was amazing & reassuring in a way that your wife was scared the day before giving birth about her mothering abilities and I thought it was really great that your wife first turned you down for a kiss and that you told us your weakness regarding your inability to handle rejection."

Only one response disturbed me: "I learned how much you loved her and how you have not moved on since her death." In my view, writing about Barbara's life and teaching a course on love and loss demonstrate that I *have* moved on with my life. What can be more constructive than honoring the memory of a beloved spouse by writing a book about her and by devoting oneself to death education? It would be different if I withdrew from life, or if I couldn't stop weeping, or if I was so self-preoccupied with grief that I could not focus on other people, but I have remained involved with life, emotionally composed, and focused on my students. My sense of the course so far is that students find it meaningful and that they do not dread coming to class. Perhaps the person who wrote that comment believes that the only way to move on after a person has died is to stop talking and thinking about her. If that's true, I never want to move on.

I'm pleased that the students responded so positively to my eulogy of Barbara, as did Richard:

> Before reading the eulogy he read at his wife's funeral, Jeff comments on how he held the fantasy that he would predecease his wife and how this was comforting. I think we all take to this kind of image of our deaths with a trail of accomplishments and mourners in our wake. Though some students are perhaps embarrassed by the "emotion" present in such a reading, most are moved, including me. It's almost like I phase out of my body while listening. I'm more than myself, and afterward I feel more motivated to accomplish things because I'm lucky enough to be alive and healthy, with most of my family intact.

I want my students to see my personal as well as pedagogical involvement in love and loss. Like many of them, I'm struggling with loss, and they derive comfort from the fact that I don't claim to have omniscience or omnipotence. I believe that the vast distance separating most teachers from their students can be narrowed without eroding the respect each has for the other. Students will see my vulnerability when my voice becomes choked up or my eyes watery, but I hope they will also see the resources that one calls upon in a time of sadness. It is always risky to speak or write about one's vulnerability, but one becomes *less* vulnerable in doing so.

As the students were leaving class today, someone turned in a handwritten note that conveys the emotionally challenging nature of this course:

> I am writing this just to give you a more true understanding of my feelings about this class. The fact that you shared something so personal like your wife's eulogy made me want to share something as well. I am only 20 years old and very scared of dieing or seeing someone close to me die. I have to admit everytime I walk into this class I am a little scared because it makes me think a lot about dieing and also growing old. It's like when you think about something so grand like an Eternal End—it just makes me sad. Even things like my father's death. I try not to think about it out of fear. Which also scares me because my grandmother I pray does not pass away may pass away soon. I really don't know how to handle these things and I am hoping I get a better way of thinking about death rather than shove it off to the side or not dealing with it from this class. Like I said I like the fact that you was honest and willing to make this course meaningful and that I may actually gain something from this class. Rather than just be here to get 3 credits.

I find the note moving despite its grammatical and spelling errors. One can see the depth of the student's anxiety in the sentence, "I pray does not pass away may pass away soon." I'll do whatever I can to keep the course from becoming depressing or morbid.

Monday, January 30

I read some of the "famous last words" appearing in a thin volume compiled by Ray Robinson, which I bought a few months ago at the New York Historical Society. I was particularly interested in artists' last words: "Lift me up, for I am dying. I shall die easy. Don't be frightened. Thank God it has come" (John Keats); "I don't know which is more difficult in a Christian life—to live well or die well" (Daniel Defoe); "Maria, don't let me die!" (D. H. Lawrence); "I shall hear in heaven!" (Ludwig van Beethoven); "I am dying. I haven't drunk champagne for a long time" (Anton Chekhov); "I have just had 18 whiskeys in a row. I do believe that is a record" (Dylan Thomas); "I want nothing but death" (Jane Austen). There were several funny last words, including, "Good, a woman who can fart is not dead" (Comtesse de Vercellis) and a statement by Conrad Hilton that the ever-practical Barbara would have enjoyed: "Leave the shower curtain on the inside of the tub." My favorite, and the one I could imagine myself making in the same situation, is Ida Straus's comment upon refusing the lifeboat offered to her so that she could remain with her husband on the sinking *Titanic:* "We have been together for forty years, and we will not separate now."

At the end of class today, when I paired each student with a partner for the first formal assignment, writing an obituary of a classmate, a collective roar seemed to emanate throughout the classroom, almost as if they were participating in a sporting event. I expressed amazement to Richard, who was also startled. I don't know how they feel about the obituary assignment, but it seems to have generated lively interest and enthusiasm. I've never given an assignment like this before, and I'm curious about the results.

2

~

Writing an Obituary

Wednesday, February 1

Three students came to my office today before class to discuss their personal reasons for taking the course. One said that though she had written that no one in her family had died, she now remembers two of her relatives dying a few years ago. She was surprised that she had forgotten about these deaths. Another said that he felt guilty that no one close to him has died. I told him he was indeed fortunate and reminded him of Dickens's observation that tragedy is the one promise life always fulfills. And the third student said that he was not affected by two of his classmates' suicides. I didn't say much in response to this except that suicide usually has a devastating effect on friends and relatives. Sometimes this effect may not be apparent for months or years.

Today the first assignment, writing a classmate's obituary, was due. These were the instructions I gave last week:

Writing Your Classmate's Obituary

For your first writing assignment, I would like you to write an obituary of a classmate, while helping him or her to write an obituary of you. To begin this assignment, determine the age at which you imagine yourself dying. (You might see yourself dying young or living to be a hundred, or anywhere in between.) Then imagine ten important events in your life that you would like to be included in your own obituary. Some of these events have already occurred, such as your birth and the birth of your siblings, religious identification, interest in athletics or the arts, hobbies and talents, graduation from high school, first boyfriend or girlfriend, and study at the University at Albany. Other events may not have yet occurred, such as military service, work experience, marriage, children, grandchildren. For each of these past, present, or future events, write a brief paragraph. ("I was born in New York City to John and Mary Doe. I was the second of three children. Growing up, I fought with my brothers, but now we are close friends.") Bring these ten paragraphs to class next Monday, January 30. Toward the end of class I will pair you with a classmate: you will interview your classmate and he or she will interview you. You will then write your classmate's obituary, and he or she will write your obituary. The obituaries are due on Wednesday, February 1. Give me one copy of the obituary and your classmate another copy. I'll read some of these obituaries aloud the following week.

I've never given this writing assignment before, and I'm not sure what to expect. In planning the assignment, I decided to have students write a *classmate's* obituary so that they could learn more about another person's life. Students could compare their own lives with others' and perhaps feel kinship with their classmates. It might also be easier and more instructive to write about a stranger's death than one's own. All the students would choose the material for their own obituaries, learning more about themselves *and* others. I believe that hearing me read aloud several obituaries will expose them to different points of view, including different attitudes toward death, thus expanding their knowledge of love and loss.

It was fascinating to read the obituaries, and they contained many surprises. The first was how optimistic most of the students were about their lives. To begin with, nearly all imagined living to an advanced age. With the exception of two students who imagined dying in car accidents at the ages of 18 and 22, and another who died at 32 in a skydiving accident, they viewed themselves as exceptionally long-lived and remarkably healthy. They apparently believed that life in their 40s would be trouble free, because no one died during this decade. Three people died in their 50s, three in their 60s, seven in their 70s, twelve in their 80s, sixteen in their 90s, and four people in their hundreds. (The oldest was 130.) Nine people did not specify an age—either they forgot to answer this question or ignored it.

Most enjoyed a peaceful death, with many dying in their sleep, as can be seen in the 90-year-old Hannah, who was still teaching English at the University at Albany at the time of her death: "Although 90 may seem to be an intimidating age for some, she remained lively and vigorous right up until the end. She taught four classes a week, including Contemporary American Literature, Advanced Creative Writing, and the Major Works of Shakespeare." (I can't resist pointing out that the wizened professor must have done something to incur the wrath of her chairperson or her dean, for she had a much heavier teaching load than do any of my colleagues.) Most students imagined dying from "natural causes" or from cancer or heart disease. Nearly all lived a healthy, active life to the last moment. Curiously, not a single person predicted death from Alzheimer's disease or other neurodegenerative diseases like amyotrophic lateral sclerosis (ALS, or Lou Gehrig's disease). If my students' obituaries are an accurate prediction of the future, no one needs to purchase long-term medical insurance because chronic, debilitating diseases will no longer pose a threat to one's physical, psychological, or financial health.

Another surprise is the number of students who suffered from life-threatening illnesses in early infancy or childhood and whose survival they ascribe to a miracle. Dean is the most dramatic example. "Born three months premature and weighing only 2 lbs, Dean spent the first three months of his life in the hospital. While in the hospital he underwent over fifteen blood transfusions. He also endured hernia surgery. The odds did not seem in his favor and his parents were told to prepare for their child's death. Fortunately, Dean surpassed all odds and grew to be a healthy child and successful adult," dying at the age of 90. Another dramatic example is Krystal, who was born two months prematurely and spent three weeks in an incubator until she was strong enough to go home. At the age of 1 she suffered another medical crisis: "She contracted meningitis, which resulted in high fevers that subsequently caused her to suffer three seizures. Her heart also stopped for a brief time because of the virus. Though the doctor's prognosis was gloomy with an expectation of her going deaf or blind, she persevered through her illness and thankfully made a complete recovery without any complications. After her respiratory failure and struggle with meningitis, she lived a very active and healthy life until the end." Brooke also nearly died from the same disease:

> Less than ten days after she was born, she came down with what some doctors believed to be the flu, but mother's instinct took over, and her mother insisted that it was not the flu. After rushing her to the hospital, the doctor was called and made the discovery right away. She did not have the flu, she had spinal meningitis. The diagnosis was grim, and survival of spinal meningitis at such a young age was not expected. The doctors told her mother that if by some miracle she did survive, she would probably have numerous health problems because of the disease. By some miracle, she did survive and the only effect of the meningitis was nystagmus, a shimmering of the eyes, which to Brooke is not even noticeable.

Other students survived life-threatening complications arising from premature birth. Interestingly, in nearly every case, those who experienced close encounters with death believed that their survival was either a "miracle"—a word that is often repeated in their obituaries—or a "blessing in disguise." Students who suffered a serious injury made a full recovery, largely because of what they perceived to be courage and fortitude. "An incident that exemplifies Madison's great strength was one that happened her freshman year of study at SUNY Albany. She was hit by a car and broke her pelvis and experienced internal bleeding. This injury caused her to drop her first semester in order to recover fully. Although this was a great setback in her ultimate plan, it did not stop her. Nothing was going to stop her from doing what she wanted."

Two other students wrote about surviving a psychologically traumatic childhood. It is harder to write about this kind of trauma because unlike physical illness or injury, psychological trauma is often stigmatized and may arouse shame. Both students were each other's best friend, and each wrote the other's obituary. They shared many experiences in common, including being born in another country, separated at an early age from mothers who left for the United States, and then reunited with their mothers in this country only to discover that they missed their relatives back home. Connie's obituary focused on her feelings of abandonment as a result of these painful separations. "Connie was the first child of a fifteen-year-old who was not ready to face the responsibility of bringing another life into this world. Her mother did not receive any support from her family and was forced to immigrate to the United States with the hopes of a better life for her and her child. She was four years old lying in the street crying as the taxi drove away her mother." Nor were the child's difficulties resolved when she was reunited with her mother in the United States. "On the day they were reunited Connie said, 'My hands were sweaty, my legs trembled.' This was not only because she would see her mother, but because she realized at this moment that her life had taken a different turn." Life in her new environment was unsettling. "She struggled with the language and the fact that her mother was very unstable. Her mother moved constantly making it very difficult for Connie to establish herself and make close friends." Nevertheless, she overcame her difficult adolescent years, and through the help of a strong support system, she was able to commit herself to marriage, children, and work.

Clarissa also felt sorrow when her mother departed for the United States to "provide her daughter with the opportunities she was not able to obtain in her own country." We learn little else about Clarissa's life until she is seventeen years old, when her world falls apart as a result of her boyfriend's death. "She had survived the experience of watching him die, watching him cry—watching her one true love fade away while losing grip of his life. She had become isolated, lost sight of reality, sight of her own life and had to be placed under the care of a therapist as well as put on medication. For her, her world had collapsed in pieces—and it was through these moments that those around her showed their love and care. Her sorrows and questions toward God became her everyday ritual—and it was through these doings that she spent most of her days."

Two women wrote about the death of their fathers, and a man wrote about the death of his mother. All three students wrote about these early losses not as victims but as survivors. Breanna's father died when she was fifteen (see appendix B). Lily also lost her father when she was a teenager, nearly perishing in the same auto accident, but she refused to allow the tragedy to embitter her:

> While most of her childhood was nothing out of the ordinary, Lily suffered a great tragedy at the age of thirteen. She was in an unfortunate and freak car accident that claimed the life of her father and almost took hers as well. The emergency responders who came upon the scene could not believe that she had survived. Around the police station she was known as the "miracle child." After that she always credited her life to two "angels" who rescued her from the accident. Her only regret was not being able to thank them properly. Although many people would find it hard to recover from such an event, Lily took it as a second chance at life and took advantage of every opportunity that came her way.

Lily was one of two students who revealed information in her obituary that she had first disclosed in the anonymous questionnaire on the second day of the semester. When asked to explain in the questionnaire her personal reasons for taking the course, she wrote, "In my car accident I was technically dead for a brief time, so I have 'issues' with death." Sara was the other student. She mentioned in her obituary that she had multiple sclerosis, information she also revealed in the anonymous questionnaire: "I was diagnosed with MS while taking your Hemingway course last summer and am more terrified of losing my dignity one day than I am of dying."

Elijah suffered two major losses. First he lost his mother shortly after he was born, and soon after that his father vanished:

> He was born to a mother and father who struggled with drug-related problems. The drug abuse impacted both his life and the life of his parents. His mother died shortly after his birth and his father was sent to a group home, unable to raise his son. This left Elijah with no other option than living with his aunt and her six children. Because of his mother's use of drugs during her pregnancy, he suffered health problems until the age of three. Constant hospital visits and blood work not only affected his life at that time, but a fear of needles and hospitals remained with him for the rest of his life. Despite the problems that life threw at him, he rose above expectations and had a goal to make something wonderful out of his life.

I suspect that Lily, Sara, Breanna, and Elijah will return in their later writings to these life-transforming events. Their essays will be especially noteworthy in describing love and loss. Other students disclosed in their anonymous questionnaires but not in their obituaries information about beloved grandparents' deaths or caring for dying grandparents. This information may appear in the next assignment, writing a eulogy.

Seven students focused on another form of loss: the breakup of their families as a result of their parents' divorce. Four of these students write about having little or no contact with their fathers. Sometimes, as in Kitty's situation, growing up without a father is described in neutral language, at least initially: "She was raised along with her brother by her mother after a divorce led to the departure of her father. From four years old on, Kitty never knew her father, and relied on her mother's strength as a source for her own." Later, however, we learn about the consequences of the divorce: "Kitty always claimed to have had bad luck with dating as an adolescent and into her adulthood. It was difficult for her to trust men after her father disappeared." Baxter also lost his father at the age of four, and one can infer the painful consequences of this loss. "Soon after he left with his mother and siblings, but his father had not gone with them. After this, he never maintained a relationship with his father, and although this hurt him, he managed to make the best of it and grew up having a very strong sense of integrity. This is what made him such a wonderful person to be around, as was said by family members and friends alike." Baxter believes that the absence of a male authority figure in his life may have motivated him to seek a divine surrogate. "While growing up, Baxter had a strong faith in God and believed that God was the source of strength in difficult times. He began to see God as his father to replace the unhealthy relationship he had with his own biological father. At the age of fifteen, he made a personal decision to be a follower of the Christian faith, and he became a very devout, what could be considered 'born-again' Christian."

Two other students wrote about the problems arising from their parents' divorces. "Chad suffered strong depression throughout his adolescence, as a direct result of his parents' bitter divorce, leaving him in reluctant and limited contact with his father. Although it helped him to learn to be independent at a young age, good for the long run, at the time he began to rebel against any authority, giving his mother and teachers the difficult challenge of controlling him. Finally, as high school neared, he realized the difficulties he had been presenting everyone around him with, most specifically his mother, and made a deliberate attempt to turn around his entire image." Of the seven students who wrote about divorce, Scotty was the oldest when his parents separated, but it was still wrenching for him. "His parents have been married for twenty-five years and all of a sudden, like the snap of his fingers, it was as if it never happened. Scotty always described these times as probably the worst times he has ever been through. It was both physically and mentally exhausting to him, but he would tell himself and everyone around him that he would overcome and get through it. This is exactly what he did. He would always tell himself that there are worse things in life and that 'I should be grateful because I will still have two loving parents that love me very much.' His optimistic outlook on everything got him through a lot, and something that he never expected that would come from this divorce did."

Surprisingly, nearly all students, including those who wrote about their parents' painful divorces, believed they would escape the "sins of the fathers or mothers"—the family conflicts that shattered so many of their parents' marriages. Only one of the fifty-five students imagined getting divorced—and in her case, it was largely conflict free: "Like so many, she split up with her first husband. As evidence of her composure and great kindness, they parted amicably." What makes the absence of divorce in my students' projected lives more striking is that nearly all of them wrote about getting married and having children and grandchildren. Most described marriages that were little short of perfection. In an age when nearly 50 percent of first marriages and 60 percent of second marriages end in divorce, it's interesting to see how my students thought they would defy statistics. Nor was there mention in the obituaries of students having drug or alcohol problems in their later lives, despite conceding that their parents and siblings have these problems.

Nearly all the students who wrote about painful events in their childhood or adolescence believed that these misfortunes helped to strengthen them. They would agree with Nietzsche that "Whatever doesn't kill you, makes you stronger." In some cases, students imagined devoting themselves in later life to eliminating those injustices or illnesses that affected them or relatives years earlier. After his retirement, for example, Elijah created his own community center "so the local children could have something positive to do in school while learning things and building relationships. Not only friendships were built in his Community Center, but parental relationships as well. Many of the children were not brought up with strong or healthy relationships with their parents so they would go to the center to talk to someone about their problems and spend time doing positive activities. The children's well-being was always the uppermost concern for him and he did everything in his power to reach out and have an impact on the lives of children all over Houston." Elijah's classmate Jo chose a job after college in pharmaceutical sales, "where she sells drugs for cystic fibrosis and other lung conditions. This was due to the fact that her brother was diagnosed with cystic fibrosis at birth, and she wanted to do everything in her power to help the cause." After marriage, she and her husband take over the Cystic Fibrosis Foundation and donate all their time to finding a cure for the disease.

As we saw with the "dying words," the obituaries reveal that many students have strong religious faith. Breanna's obituary begins with angelic imagery: "At first there was birth. Then the golden gates of heaven swung free on October 15 of the year 1986 to let a single angel free from heaven to bless the earth." Another student's death evokes similar Christian imagery: "Her death was victorious; when she turned 100 years old, her Lord and Savior Jesus

Christ took her up in a cloud." I have already noted that Baxter "began to see God as his father to replace the unhealthy relationship he had with his own biological father." Religion helped another person turn her life around. "Esther described herself as very rebellious in her teenage years. As a result of this behavior, which left her estranged from her loving parents, she learned the true value of family and found the grace of God. Through Him Esther was able to restore her relationship with her family owing to a better understanding of herself and forgiveness." Religion also transforms Belle's life. "As a young adult, struggling between atheism and skepticism, Belle's life was profoundly changed when she came to accept the existence of God and the power He had in her life. She explained that it wasn't in finding God but in accepting Him into her life as an omnipresent force that she was saved." And Jean is described as a "devout Roman Catholic, her love for God radiating from choir singing and Ukrainian folk dancing. She believed that these activities brought her closer to her heritage and to God."

Perhaps the major surprise for me about the obituaries was how many students predicted they would become high school or college English teachers. Of the fifty-seven students, seventeen imagined themselves as high school teachers, many of them English teachers, and another eight saw themselves as English professors. It's true that some of them later made career changes, becoming restaurateurs, for example, but most remained lifelong educators and derived great satisfaction from their work. I was delighted to learn that so many of my students later became distinguished writers, in large part, I would like to believe, because their writing skills improved so dramatically in my course. Ava was awarded the Nobel Prize for Literature and was said by many to be the "single most important female novelist of the twenty-first century." A classmate wrote two *New York Times* bestsellers and was awarded the Nobel Peace Prize for her work on poverty and AIDS in third world countries. Other writers (either full time or part-time) included a best-selling novelist who also won two Oscars for Best Actress and an Emmy Award; a former lawyer who wrote a novel that remained on the *New York Times* best seller's list for more than a year; a journalist who authored a memoir called *Mommy-Mode*; another journalist who penned a Pulitzer Prize–winning book called *A Step in the Left Direction*, a "fictional piece about a young artist struggling as a drug dealer in modern suburbia"; an educator who published a book called *Special Kids and You*, a textbook on teaching students with disabilities; another educator who turned his doctoral dissertation in philosophy into a book called *Death and the Existentialist Works*; a novelist whose book *Life in a Pleated Skirt* was made into a film; a literary scholar who wrote *Etruscan Erotica*, a critical study of D. H. Lawrence; a writer who authored a book called *It's Not What You Know; It's Who You Know*; another author who completed a book called *Ethics without God: A Philosophical Discussion*; and a writer who published six novels, "though none of them reached beyond number forty on the *New York Times* best-seller list."

I was particularly struck by the last writer, Sara, largely because of her reasons for writing. "For those privileged people that knew Sara, it was clear that she did not write these novels for money or fame; she wrote them because they provided her with a feeling of comfort in the eternity of the written word." Most books will not last for a century, let alone eternity, but like Sara, I want to believe that my book about Barbara will last forever. This was perhaps my main motive in writing *Dying to Teach*. I suspect many writers are comforted by the knowledge that their books will exist long after the authors are gone.

Most of the women imagined themselves as having both families and careers. Eleven women decided to put their careers "on hold" in order to be with their young children, a sacrifice that, tellingly, none of the men made. The women appear to make this sacrifice willingly, without resentment. There is no mention of conflicts between family and work in any of the obituaries, nor of serious economic struggles.

Many of the obituaries quoted philosophers' and novelists's statements about death. One obituary begins, "The wise and knowledgeable Socrates once said, 'Death is really a change: a migration of the soul from one place to another.' Cassie has traveled through many stages in her lifetime, ultimately migrating to a better place where she is free of pain. In this new place, she is reunited with her loving parents." Another obituary ends with an appropriate passage from a Greek philosopher: "Anna would often quote Plato, saying to those she loved, 'To fear death, gentlemen, is no other than to think oneself wise when one is not, to think one knows what one does not know. No one knows whether death may not be the greatest of all blessings for a man, yet men fear it as if they knew that it is the greatest of evils. And surely it is the most blameworthy ignorance to believe that one knows what one does not know." Still another obituary ends with dying words that have a literary ring to them: "What strangeness, that human kind would feel themselves capable of knowing enough to name death."

The obituaries also cited many twentieth-century writers. One begins, "Brendan Behan once said, 'There is no such thing as bad publicity except your own obituary.' Scarlett knew all about positive publicity from grade school until the day she retired as the vice president of the Universal Marketing Company and all the way up to May 6, 2079." Ava, the Nobel laureate in literature, died in an appropriately literary way: "She was found clutching her collection of quotes. One reading, 'Now what,' the final words of Gregor Samsa in Kafka's *The Metamorphosis,* was marked." Two students cited the same Native American proverb: "You came into this world crying, and those around you were smiling. Live your life so that when you leave this world, you will be smiling and those around you will be crying." Popular culture is also represented: one obituary ends, "He was loved by all who knew him and was self-sacrificing till the end asking nothing for himself except to be buried with his acoustic guitar and a copy of J. R. R. Tolkien's *The Lord of the Rings*."

However unrealistic these imagined writerly accomplishments may be, they suggest that many students had fun in imagining their own obituaries. I hope their literary ambitions are indeed fulfilled. Some may have felt existential dread when contemplating their own mortality, but others, such as Joy, enjoyed fantasizing lives of epic heroism. After graduating from the University at Albany and then completing graduate work at Stanford, Joy is sworn in as the forty-fourth president of the United States—"recorded in history books as the first woman president and the first of mixed race and nonspecific religion." She serves two full terms but instead of living the rest of her life in quiet retirement, her real accomplishments begin. She and her research team solve the global climate change problem; she helps to eliminate world hunger; and then, when the earth is attacked by extraterrestrial beings, she defeats the evil robot King and saves the planet. Not even death defeats her, for when she is struck by an incurable illness at the age of ninety-seven, she chooses to be cryogenically frozen "in hopes that sometime in the near future there would be a cure. It was agreed that her knowledge and outstanding reasoning should be passed on to future generations."

Monday, February 6

Today I read aloud selections from several obituaries, some sad, others funny, and I asked the students to write anonymous responses telling me their feelings about the assignment. The topic was emotionally demanding for them. "It shocked me honestly. This was probably the most unique assignment I've ever gotten but I greatly enjoyed writing this." Most expressed positive feelings about the assignment, using words like "excited" or "intrigued" to describe how they felt. Writing the autobiographical paragraphs was hard for some students and easy for others. "It was difficult to imagine a future from which to draw on the as-yet-fictional paragraphs; it was also somewhat strange to imagine a future family." One person felt that it is unwise, even dangerous to attempt to predict the future: "It was a little weird to write the paragraphs. I felt like I was 'jinxing' myself by forecasting my future." Others thought it was an imaginative assignment. "I enjoyed this greatly. It got me to organize my thoughts and goals for my future and look at what I've accomplished thus far." Another enjoyed the opportunity to indulge in wish fulfillment. "It was easy because I was given complete control of my destiny. I was able to do literally whatever I wanted with my life. So I chose to be a hero of the world."

Nearly everyone enjoyed learning about classmates' lives. "I felt like I got to know a lot about the type of person she was, and I was intrigued by the person she planned to be." Many were struck by their classmates' hardships. "I felt that not everyone's life is so easy. There are drug addictions, problems with the law, and so much more. The thing is that the person went through some of these hardships but overcame them with the strength of his family." Indeed, many students commented on their classmates' ability to overcome adversity. "My partner had a hard childhood—I found it enlightening because I had an enjoyable childhood. I was impressed that he wanted to grow up and offer to help children in his situation." Some people felt that it was more difficult writing a classmate's obituary than writing their own. "It was *much* harder than I originally thought. I felt like I had their life in my hands and I didn't want to mess it up. I felt responsible to write a good obituary for her." Many identified with a classmate's life. "I learned a lot about my partner's ideas of life and death. I almost felt as if I was traveling through her stages of life with her." Several spoke admiringly of their partners and commented on their religious faith. "I learned a great deal about her life and am honestly in admiration of her strong faith that seems to temper her feelings about life. Originally, it felt a little invasive." Significantly, no one spoke negatively about a classmate's life. Learning about a partner's life—and imagined death—was uplifting. "I felt optimistic while reading my partner's paragraphs. Even though death can be morbid or depressing, thinking about the good in my partner's life made the assignment positive."

Twenty people said that the obituary assignment did not heighten awareness of their own death. The remaining thirty-five students felt that it had. "Writing my paragraphs and my partner's obituary did cause me to think about my own death. I have always had a fear that I will die younger than I would like and in a more tragic way than I would like, since this has been the majority of my experience with loss, but I chose to plan my imagined death in a way that I would find more comfortable." Those who lost a close relative, however, knew that real death is always more unsettling than imaginary death. "When my father died of cancer it was a shock because we were all told of his amazing improvement and I think we would all like to plan our death but it will inevitably shock everyone." Some implied that heightened self-awareness of death was a positive experience. "I have started to think about my own death, and the death of those I love. I think it's a good heightened awareness because once in a while you need to remember that life isn't forever." For others, however, heightened self-awareness led only to heightened anxiety. "It kind of scared me. I was forced to think of everything in my life and choose my death. It was disheartening." Two people found their obituaries so unnerving that they did not read them. "It was a little eerie to read my own obituary. As a matter of fact, I haven't read it completely through. I am not comfortable with reading this fabricated life story with my death as the commencement." The other student's reaction was more extreme: "It is sitting in my desk drawer, but I refuse to read it. I think it would depress me."

Students were split over whether they preferred to write their own or a classmate's obituary. Twenty-one wished they could have written their own obituary, mainly because they would have had more control over the final copy. "I think that as much as I enjoyed hearing and reading my life's story as told by another, I would have liked to have written my own, simply because I know my own thoughts and feelings, which would most likely create a different feel to the obituary." A few were disappointed by what their partners had written. "I didn't feel my partner conveyed my experiences and life the way I would have liked." One person complained that the writer did not go into sufficient depth in the obituary. "I would always rather write from within. It makes for better writing when nothing is held back." A woman who wrote her own obituary because she was absent the day I paired everyone with a partner made a surprising remark: "I did write my own, and my first thought was how morbid it was. My boyfriend agreed. But my parents cheerfully said, 'Oh, we both wrote ours in college.'" The remaining twenty-six students preferred writing a classmate's obituary, largely because they felt that they took the assignment more seriously than if they had written their own obituary. They also enjoyed learning about a classmate's life. Several people believed it would have been traumatic to write their own obituary: "I'm not sure I would have been able to kill myself off! I probably would have had myself live forever."

Most students felt that the obituary assignment taught them more about life than death. "I learned a lot about my life's goals and what I expect out of my life." The idea that death heightens our appreciation of life is not new, of course, but many students seemed to realize this for the first time. The assignment also increased their understanding of classmates. Many would agree with the person who learned that "most of us aspire to be great." So would they agree with the statement that "I learned that there is much more to most people than I give them credit for in passing." Some students responded to the question with ironic humor: "I'm glad that the next time I have an obituary written about me, I won't be alive to read it!" Everyone took the assignment seriously, but several found the obituaries unexpectedly playful. "I just learned that obituaries are not always completely sad, they can have lighter moments to them." Another discovered that the "world is going to be threatened by an 'evil robot King' and I'll get to say I took a class with our savior ex-president!"

The class was equally divided over whether hearing my eulogy of Barbara influenced their obituaries. Those who were not influenced believed that a eulogy has nothing in common with an obituary. Nor did they believe they could write with emotional depth about a stranger. Others, however, felt that my eulogy did influence their obituary. "The eulogy made me want to praise my partner and show them in a positive light more to emphasize their strengths and accomplishments." Another stated that my eulogy affirmed the importance of honoring another person's life, a statement that recalls Emmanuel Levinas's belief that each of us is responsible for the other. And still another said that the eulogy "influenced us to write about the little but important things in life rather than look at the huge events, for those little memories shape who a person is remembered as."

Finally, thirty-eight people believed that I should use this assignment again, with no modifications; twelve thought I should use it again but allow students the choice of writing their own obituary or a classmates's; and one person recommended not using the assignment again.

I think the obituary assignment was a resounding success and helped us to begin the course on a positive note. Everyone wrote about "real" death—or at least the death of a real person—and there was a good balance between seriousness and playfulness. The obituaries are fascinating from a cultural studies point of view, offering snapshots of contemporary college students' lives and their expectations of the future. I suspect, however, that the next assignment, writing a eulogy, will be harder, for many of them will probably write about a beloved relative or friend who has died. Will the tone of the eulogies be darker than that of the obituaries? We'll see.

3

~

Writing a Eulogy

Today we continued our discussion of Emily Dickinson's poems, focusing on "Dying" and "After Great Pain." (We discussed "The Chariot" on Monday.) I told my students that this is the first time I've taught her poetry and that I feel like a novice. I didn't have time to make this observation in class, but I'm aware of a split in me with respect to death. While Barbara was dying, I did everything I could to ease her suffering. I tried to domesticate death, taming and demystifying it so that she and I would be less terrified of its approach and more accepting of death as the natural end of life. This is precisely why our psychotherapist, Ed Dick, and Barbara's hospice nurse, Geraldine Breitenstein, were so helpful: they enabled us to talk about our specific fears of dying and death to alleviate our anxiety. We always felt better after speaking with them.

Ironically, I value Dickinson's poems precisely because she doesn't allow us to domesticate death. Her poems are ironic, ambiguous, and unsettling, compelling us to confront the enigma of death without taking comfort in platitudes or certitudes. Contrary to Nietzsche's dictum that we "possess art lest we perish of the truth," death is sometimes more frightening in literature than it is in life. I think Barbara would have been upset if she had heard me talk about Dickinson's poems. Poets, novelists, and playwrights often refuse to resolve conflicts and tensions within their writings, whereas physicians and mental health professionals seek "cures" or at least symptomatic relief for their patients. Yet perhaps there is less difference between the artist and the psychotherapist than I have implied; both aim to strengthen our will to live and assist us in finding ways to cope with death. As Donald Hall observes in *The Best Day the Worst Day*, a memoir of his poet-wife, Jane Kenyon, who died in 1995 from leukemia, "Poetry gives the griever not release from grief but companionship in grief" (118). "Companionship in grief" is an intriguing expression, and I plan to use it as the title of my next book, a study of memoirists who write about their deceased spouses.

Had I known about Dickinson's aphoristic poem "A Word," only nineteen words long, I would have quoted it in *Dying to Teach* to show how our language outlives us: "A word is dead / When it is said, / Some say. / I say it just / Begins to live / That day" (23). Public speakers fail to realize that we would not remember momentous events in history were it not for the words that describe them. This is why I asked my students to read Lincoln's Gettysburg Address. Was he being ironic when he said that the "world will little note, nor long remember, what we say here, but it can never forget what they did here"?

Reading Dickinson's other poems compels me to wonder about Barbara's dying moments. Would she have agreed with the speaker's assertion in "The Inevitable" that "While I was fearing it, it came, / But came with less of fear, / Because that fearing it so long / Had almost made it dear" (26)? I think Barbara would have agreed with the poem "The Mystery of Pain": "Pain has an element of blank; / It cannot recollect / When it began, or if there were / A day when it was not" (10). And I would agree with the first stanza of a poem in *Time and Eternity:* "They say that 'time assuages,'—/ Time never did assuage; / An actual suffering strengthens, / As sinews do, with age" (234).

Wednesday, February 8

We spent much of today's class talking about John Donne's poem "Death, Be Not Proud" and Dylan Thomas's villanelle "Do Not Go Gentle into That Good Night." We haven't had much class discussion this semester, partly due to the size of the class but also because I spend so much time reading aloud student essays and responses to the writing assignments. Nevertheless, today I asked them to offer their best observations about Thomas's poem. No one volunteered. "OK, make an obvious comment about the poem and we'll go from there." One person obliged by saying that the poem was about death, and then a classmate said the speaker didn't want his father to die. We continued for a few minutes, and then I asked whether "Do Not Go Gentle into That Good Night" was a young or old person's poem. That's when we began to talk about how the poem can be read as a youth's fear of letting go of an aging parent or grandparent. I told my students that when my grandmother was dying in 1985, at the age of eighty-three, when I was forty, I implored her not to die, but she said she had lived a good life and was ready to leave. I couldn't understand her statement then, but I can now. I also told my students how our family's attitude toward death changed when Barbara was dying. Death was a feared and hated antagonist upon her diagnosis, and we did everything we could to prolong her life, but nearly twenty months later, when she was in unendurable pain, death became a welcome ally that could not come fast enough for us.

Monday, February 13

Malechi came to visit me today before class. I had asked him to speak to me because his first assignment was poorly written. Far from being angry or defensive, he thanked me, saying that he had turned in carelessly written essays at his previous college, SUNY–Stony Brook, where he received A's from his professors. He is not the first student to tell me that receiving a poor grade motivated him to work harder in the future.

The other reason for Malechi's visit was more unusual. He said he had great difficulty completing the eulogy assignment, which was due today, because of a persistent migraine headache, from which he has never previously suffered. Writing the eulogy, he speculated, forced him to confront the inevitability of his own death, resulting in the migraine. He told me he was the person who wrote that three weeks earlier he had nearly died as a result of taking a hallucinogenic substance. He had a "bad trip," and his friends warned him that he might not awake if he fell asleep. This was his first close encounter with death, and he was scared. Writing the eulogy was the second time in less than a month he had been forced to confront the specter of death. He viewed the migraine as a response to his death anxiety: he remained in bed this morning for an hour, knowing that he had to finish the assignment but unable to move. I asked him if the obituary assignment was also difficult to write and he said it was not, mainly because he was writing about a death that did not seem to affect his own life. (No one in his immediate family has died.) I gave him an extra two days to complete the assignment and asked him if he would be willing to write an additional optional essay evaluating the eulogy assignment. He agreed. I don't think he fabricated a story simply because he didn't turn in the assignment on time. I'll be curious to read his response essay. I wonder if any of his classmates had the same difficulty with the eulogy assignment.

The Death of Ivan Ilych is not on our reading list, but I spent a few minutes today discussing one of the most famous stories about dying and death. I pointed out how darkness turns to light during the epiphanic moments preceding the protagonist's passing, an observation on which Richard elaborates in his diary entry:

> I found it interesting how Jeff defined epiphany as the moment when God appears and how it now means any moment of insight. With this new definition in mind, the correlation between literary studies, character, and religion is stronger than I imagined. I understood how the preacher-like qualities overlap

with the pulpit, but studying epiphanies now has an entirely new meaning for me. The idea that death is associated with light is quite interesting, as this then implies death is another form of knowledge; at least metaphorically, we may look at it this way. Elisabeth Kübler-Ross mirrors this idea with her five stages for the terminally ill: (1) shock, denial, isolation; (2) anger at God, nature, healthy people, parents; (3) bargaining: I will die if———. The person may not know he/she is bargaining; (4) depression; (5) acceptance, resignation. This process could be read as a process toward insight/knowledge and enlightenment.

∾

Today the eulogies were due. The assignment was as follows:

Writing a Eulogy

For your second assignment, which is due on Monday, February 13, please write a eulogy for a person who is either living or dead. Try to describe the special qualities of the person you are eulogizing. See if you can use words to bring the deceased back to life. Remember that showing is better than telling. The eulogy is usually the most important part of a funeral, so make your language as heartfelt as possible.

I consulted several books while writing my eulogy for Barbara and found two especially helpful, *The Book of Eulogies*, edited by Phyllis Theroux, and *Inventions of Farewell*, edited by Sandra M. Gilbert. Theroux reminds us that the "eulogy, or 'funeral praise,' is the oldest and, in some ways, least valued of our literary forms. It is practiced by amateurs. When someone dies, it is customary for a member of the family or a friend to 'say a few words,' composed under great duress, about the deceased. Mourners are not literary critics; we will accept any words at all, as long as they are not mean-spirited or self-serving, and if a particularly moving or graceful tribute is delivered, we are grateful for the balm" (13). Gilbert observes in her anthology that sooner or later most poets must confront bereavement: "Aesthetic assumptions and poetic styles have altered over the centuries, yet the great and often terrifying themes of time, change, age, and death are timeless, even though cultural imaginings of them may differ radically" (25). Gilbert admits in her more recent book *Death's Door* that following the unexpected death of her husband during what should have been routine surgery, she has become preoccupied with the "poetics of bereavement," writing with a "testimonial passion" that took her by surprise (xviii–xix). Like Gilbert, I feel compelled to bear witness to a beloved spouse's death: that's why I have become a student and teacher of sorrow.

I have never previously asked students to write a eulogy, and I suspect it was more difficult than the obituary assignment. I doubt that many students have actually eulogized relatives or friends. Consequently, this was a new type of writing for them. My eulogy of Barbara may have been the first one to which they were exposed. How did they react to a new genre of writing that poses unique emotional challenges? Was the assignment too wrenching for them? Of the fifty-six people eulogized, twenty-eight are deceased and twenty-seven are still living. The former include one mother, one father, six grandmothers, six grandfathers, two distant relatives, and twelve friends. The latter include eight mothers, six fathers, four siblings, one future husband, five friends, and three self-eulogies. One student eulogized her dog.

No one mentioned a grandparent's death in the obituary assignment—such information rarely appears in an obituary—but many eulogies focused on these deaths. Richard showed me an email he had received on a composition listserv in which a teacher who claims to value "expressive" writing nevertheless refers to students' "well-intentioned but trite narratives about how grandpa's death broke their hearts." I find such pedagogical cynicism offensive. It's true that any type of writing can become stale, but I was struck by how many of my students' eulogies of their grandparents are fascinating character sketches that would bring a smile of approval to the most jaded literature teacher. Witness, for example, Chad's eulogy of his grandfather:

> Saint Augustine once said, "No eulogy is due to him who simply does his duty and nothing more." I would like to think that he was foreshadowing the life of my grandfather. He was a man who would give to his family, his colleagues, and his county before he ever thought of giving to himself.
>
> "Papa Tom" was always one to have a playful violence shadowed in his aura. He was a bold and solid man with a near impenetrable exterior. But as we all found out, if you broke through the shield, he was the most loyal and most caring person you could ever meet. Not a day would go by without him threatening to beat me over the head with a two by four with a spike in it, which was immediately followed by a loving bear hug. I never saw him pull out that legendary piece of wood; something deep inside tells me, he didn't actually have one. He did have a clenched right hand though. I would watch a vein pop out from his skin as he smiled and offered me "Irish punch." I would consistently tell him that I liked Hawaiian Punch. Nevertheless, I went along, blissfully drinking my juice box.
>
> I was not able to see Papa Tom as much as I would have liked to. Since I live in New York and he lived in Florida, I could never go around the block and knock on his door for a good time. My biggest regret was not cherishing his time enough. I was a competitive little kid; I wanted to win every game I played and he was always there for a game of anything. I will never forget the day he beat me

in table tennis. Instead of a congratulatory hug, I greeted him with a kick in the balls. That was the only day I ever lost his trust. I learned to never disrespect my grandfather in such a way again and to make more of when I saw him. I look back and feel fortunate that he didn't respond with his patented Irish punch.

He knew how to play off of my competitiveness though. During a week's vacation at his home in Florida, Papa Tom placed a wager between Michael, my brother, and me. He knew that we loved to annoy each other; better yet, I loved to annoy him. My grandpa reached into his wallet and took out a twenty dollar bill. As he placed it on the table, he looked both of us in the eye. He told us that whoever behaved better, would win the twenty dollars. Since I was a competitor, I bit my tongue for five days. I could have given my brother some pokes and prods, but decided against it. On the sixth day, I started an argument and a bitter fight broke out. We both had our share of blame and felt our prize slip away from us. An hour before we left for the airport the next day, he took two twenty dollar bills out from his wallet and gave one to each of us. I was shocked. I almost felt cheated; I hate ties. But it shows you the type of man he was. He did not expect perfection nor did he look for miracles. He knew how to make his loved ones smile. For the record, I lost the twenty bucks on the plane and cried when I realized it. On the other hand, my brother went out and bought baseball cards. In the end we did not tie after all.

Papa Tom and my grandmother had a long-running tradition with their grandchildren. On their thirteenth birthday, they could fly down to Florida on their own and spend a week with them; we could choose anything we wanted to do. My brother and my older cousin jumped on this opportunity. Michael was able to travel to Universal Studios and Disney World. I was not as lucky. I turned thirteen a year and a half earlier. At the time, Papa Tom had just had surgery and was told he had to be in a wheelchair for a while afterward. I was told we would not be able to do as much as their grandchildren had done before me. Nanny and I struck a deal. Instead of a week in paradise getting spoiled, she wrote me a check for eight hundred dollars. With that money, I bought a stereo for my room, a printer for my computer, and I wasted the other four hundred and fifty dollars. Right now, I would give back the stereo, printer, and everything else in my room to spend six more days with him.

All we need is one more monkey joke between the two of us. To this day, I don't think anybody knows how it started. There was a special bond between Papa Tom and me. I was his little monkey. Every holiday, we would both give and receive little gifts involving monkeys. Sitting in my room at this moment are over a dozen stuffed animals, dolls, figurines, and miniature statues pertaining to monkeys. This does not even include the numerous birthday and Christmas cards. Two days ago, my family went to the local mall near my grandparents' house. I went into a store that had a wall of fifteen different types of monkeys. I picked a certain one up; I didn't know what compelled me to choose that one. I went to buy it as a tribute to Papa Tom, but my mom told me to put it back. When I returned to their house, my grandmother pulled the exact monkey I almost bought from her closet. She told me he had bought it for me and was planning to give it to me on my next birthday.

When I go back to my home on Long Island, I will have a brass coffin on a gold necklace filled with a few of my grandfather's ashes. Something drew me to that monkey in the store and my necklace will grace the neck of my stuffed animal that will sit on my nightstand. Papa Tom, you were an amazing grandfather and an even better person. If I ever get the chills and wake up in the middle of the night, all I will have to do is look on my dresser into the eyes of my monkey and I will feel the warmth of your hugs all over again.

Chad brings his grandfather to life in scarcely more than one thousand words, capturing his oxymoronic "playful violence." His home-made bludgeon may have been apocryphal, but his clenched hand and bulging vein are menacingly real. The eulogy offers us a portrait of a grandfather who is fully capable of delivering "Irish punch" and a portrait of a grandson who, unfazed by real or rhetorical violence, insists that he prefers "Hawaiian Punch"—all the time drinking "blissfully" from his juice box. One senses that grandfather and grandson are adoring opponents, each challenging and being challenged by the other.

As with all eulogies, time is the relentless antagonist in Chad's tribute to his grandfather. He offers us two visions of himself, that of the young child who is unaware of the passing of time and that of the young man who has sadly discovered that love inevitably ends in loss. He never sentimentalizes his grandfather or himself. Nor does he tell us why he kicked his grandfather "in the balls" after losing to him in ping-pong. Was this an act of oedipal emasculation or simply adolescent immaturity? (Recall the statement in his obituary that he acted out throughout adolescence as a result of his parents' bitter divorce.) He never tells us, but he allows us to imagine the horror-stricken expression on the combatants' faces. It was probably not easy for Chad to recall such a shameful memory in a eulogy, but he is unflinching here and elsewhere.

Every eulogy is a double portrait of both the eulogized and the eulogizer. Chad tells us that his grandfather knew "how to make his loved ones smile." So does Chad. He delights in undercutting himself, as when he reveals how he let the prize of a twenty dollar bill slip out of his grasp—twice. He could have withheld the detail that he was the one who instigated a fight with his brother, but he has no desire to soften this aspect of his personality. Nor does he conceal his ferocious competitiveness, his preference to win or lose a contest rather than to reach a tie. It's as if Chad doesn't care how the reader views him—he will tell the truth, as he sees it, no matter how unflattering it may be.

Ironically, in acknowledging these questionable character traits, he earns the reader's sympathy and admiration. He describes himself as competitive, aggressive, materialistic—a gambler who prefers taking money from his grandmother to spending a week "in paradise"—yet he is also fiercely loyal, devoted, and caring.

Chad ends the obituary with an "insider joke" that testifies to the special relationship with his grandfather. It is uncanny when he picks out the same stuffed animal that his grandfather had bought, presumably in the final months of his life. Like the stuffed animal, the eulogy captures the ways in which grandfather and grandson delighted in monkeying around with each other. The last paragraph is masterful in its imagery, tone, and voice. It is startling enough to imagine a gold necklace with a brass coffin filled with his grandfather's cremated ashes, but Chad goes a step further by placing the necklace around the neck of a stuffed animal sitting on his nightstand. Somehow this image seems appropriate. So does the final sentence of the essay, in which Chad predicts that the stuffed monkey will allow him to feel the warmth of his grandfather's hugs—a warmth that is conveyed no less effectively throughout the eulogy. The quotation from Saint Augustine that begins Chad's essay— "No eulogy is due to him who simply does his duty and nothing more"— characterizes not only Papa Tom but also Chad: his eulogy is a tribute to both his grandfather and himself.

Other students also wrote memorable eulogies of grandparents who, like Papa Tom, were psychologically complex and concretely described. "I will never forget her," writes Belle at the beginning of her eulogy and then supplies us with the details that explain why her grandmother was the strongest woman in her life:

> The smell of her perfume still lingers in my memory. When I was young, I would occasionally spend the day or the weekend with her and my grandfather. She would bring me to her club where I was subjected to endless hours of watching her play "May I?" At the time, I could not wait to leave the hot stuffy club and return to the house where my grandfather could be found in his beautiful garden. I longed to be outside with my grandfather, and to spend time with him. However, as I look back I would give anything to spend even another minute in that club with my grandmother and her friends. I would give anything to see her young and vibrant again. I want to see her blond hair curled and her nails polished a brilliant red.
>
> She was an amazing woman; I have so many wonderful memories of her. Sometimes I drive past her old house, and I cannot help but smile. So many memories of my grandma lay within that white house with red shutters. It was within those walls that I learned how to make Italian cheesecake, play rummy-o, and how to make sauce. My grandma was an amazing cook. I can still taste her

amazing sauce and scrumptious cakes and cookies. We would sit in the kitchen for hours during the holidays and bake. I would grind the figs for the cookies that my mother still loves to this day and grandma would roll the dough to make the honey-balls. I hated grinding those figs, but I love memories that I have left over from the hours of grinding them. My grandmother was a permanent figure in that small kitchen. When I close my eyes I still see the round table with the glass top, the hutch that had cups of her change and jewelry stuffed in them, the small radio nestled on a shelf above the sink that was always tuned to one talk program or another, and the spider plant that hung by the door.

Most people, especially Italians, believe the kitchen is the heart of the home. I know it is not the kitchen that is the heart of the home; it is the woman that lovingly prepares food in it that is the true heart of the home. I can remember running down the short hallway to the back room with my sister and greedily eating sprinkles or sneaking to the china cabinet and indulging in the endless amounts of candy my grandma always had on hand. We never wanted to be caught because we knew that meant a scolding from grandma, where I would inevitably be called a brat. However, we could eat all the candy we wanted from the candy dish on the coffee table in the living room.

I still find it funny that my grandma was so stingy with candy but overly generous with everything else. It is hard to imagine that a woman who yelled if you ate her baking sprinkles would buy us a computer, or take us to Italy for several weeks. I will never forget that trip; I do not think my mother or sister will either. It was an amazing few weeks. My grandma was happy to be able to expose us to our culture. I do not remember seeing my grandma happier than when we walked down the streets in Sicily. She was truly in her element.

When I look back at all the time I spent with my grandma, it is not hard for me to pick my favorite times with her. Most precious to me are the simple times: the mornings when we would sit on the deck at her house while she drank the first of her three cups of coffee, the evenings after dinner when we went for walks with my grandfather and she would pick fruit from the tree of a neighbor, and the nights she spent playing rummy-o with me and my sister.

My grandma was the strongest woman I knew. She loved fiercely, lived strongly, and fought for herself and her family. She never let anyone break her down and she taught me to do the same. I credit most of my personality to my grandma. I am strong, thick-headed, and tough because of her. She never gave up, not even as her health began to fail.

As we sit here saddened by our loss we must remember that "seeing death as the end of life is like seeing the horizon as the end of the ocean" (David Searls). Death is just a beginning of another journey, the journey to a perfect existence in the presence of God. The bible says in John 3:16–17, "For God so loved the world that he gave his only Son, so that everyone who believes in him will not perish but have eternal life. God did not send his son into the world to condemn it, but to save it." I can remember grandma saying, "I'll outlive you all," and she was right. My grandma will outlive us all because she will live on in the hearts and memories of her family and friends.

Chad and Belle offer heartfelt testimonies to grandparents who have made an indelible impression on their grandchildren's lives. The eulogies are more about life than death and contain many more smiles than tears. They both reveal grandparents who are human rather than idealized and whose zest for life remains part of their undying legacy to their grandchildren. Both essays fulfill the main purpose of the eulogy: to comfort the bereaved and to speak the grief that might otherwise break the heart. As Shakespeare observes in *Macbeth:* "Give sorrow words. The grief that does not speak / Whispers the o'er-fraught heart and bids it break" (4.3.208).

Those students who could not attend relatives' funerals expressed regret and, in some cases, guilt. Brooke wrote about gradually losing touch with her beloved great-aunt in high school. She admits toward the end of her eulogy that she now reproaches herself for not attending the funeral:

> I received an alarming phone call, three days after I was initiated into my sorority. My mother told me my Annie had died. She said that she had died five days earlier, but she did not want to tell me because I was pledging; I had not spoken to my family a lot, while pledging. I felt angry because my parents had not told me she died; my parents knew I would have driven home, immediately. The woman who had been my second mother was gone. I did not get to say goodbye. I wanted to attend her funeral, but my parents refused and sternly advised me not to come home. I cried for two days straight. I did not attend any of my classes and I went to church, for the first time in Albany. My roommate was involved within the Christian church, so she gave me information because I had no knowledge of religious services on campus.
>
> The way I adored and admired her, will never be the same for anyone else in my life. She was a person I looked toward as a role model, a person who I could trust and one of the best friends I could ever imagine having. Her countless stories and life experiences have helped shape me as a person.

Anna also regretted not being able to say goodbye to a cherished relative, in her case, her grandfather, whom she calls "Papa." Like so many of her classmates, she found herself growing apart from a relative during her adolescence, and this distance made it difficult for her to grieve his death. Writing a eulogy more than a decade after a relative's death is no substitute for saying goodbye to him while he was still alive, but writing about one's feelings is never too late, as she implies in the last paragraph:

The last years of Papa's life were a hard time for me. I was becoming a teenager, full of angst and questioning every belief my parents had tried to instill in me. This included religion. I stopped going to church, stopped attending Sunday school. I was trying to create my own identity, and doing so meant being the opposite of everything my parents had expected me to be.

It seemed like not enough time had passed for me before that Sunday morning in December. It seemed like everyone knew, without having to talk about it, that this was Papa's last day with us. He had not been able to eat for the last few days, but somehow managed to eat a full dinner the night before, from his bed of course. Almost everyone was in the apartment. His wife, his children, his grandchildren. Nana had called for a priest. I sat on one side of his bed, holding his hand even though he could not hold mine. I listened to his irregular breathing, and searched his eyes for something to calm me. They looked frightened, and I was frightened too. I sat by his side until the end. The priest was praying. My sister was screaming. The rest of us were silent.

The priest lit a candle, and he told us all to hold it, say a few words to Papa, and then pass the candle along. I would like to say that I can remember what anyone said, but I cannot. When the candle came to me, I said nothing. I only paused before passing it to my mother. I did not believe Papa could hear me. I did not believe that the candle was some sort of spiritual microphone.

More than eleven years have passed since that terrible morning, and not a day goes by that I don't wish I had said something, anything. This is my way of reaching out. This is my spiritual microphone. When I was little, when it was time for me to retreat up the back stairs and go to bed, Papa would watch me to make sure I climbed the stairs safely. We had a tradition of saying goodnight. It became scripted; I can never forget it.

Papa, goodnight, sleep tight.
Don't let the bed bugs bite.
See you later, alligator.
In a while, crocodile.

Eleven students eulogized deceased friends, and their writings contain many poignant memories. Some students implied that premature deaths were so shattering that they called into question the value of human attachments or the existence of God. Baxter wrote about his friend Jesse, whom he met in 2002 at a campus Christian group. "It didn't take long for us to become good friends. We had similar interests. Both of us played the guitar; we considered the same girls hot; we worshiped the same God. One big difference was that his kidneys were failing and he was on dialysis every night." After several months a kidney from a "perfect donor" was offered to Jesse, but he unexpectedly turned it down. "What Faith!" writes Baxter. "What foolishness? I don't know. He explained that transplant patients are on medicine for the rest of their life that gives them the immune system of an AIDS patient. But a stronger reason was that he/we were holding out for a miracle." For a time the miracle looked like it was occurring, especially after he broke his hip and arm and appeared to be recovering, but then his condition deteriorated. After Jesse's death, Baxter wondered whether he didn't pray hard enough for his friend's recovery. "I wish I could visit his grave. Rather than go to his funeral, I drank alone. I believed that something had given up. I cannot process the suffering and death of Jesse." Baxter allows Jesse to speak for himself near the end of the eulogy with words that his friend sent to him via instant messenger: "whats kewl about speedbumps in our walk with Christ is that when we get to the top of them, God always shows us a little bit more of His nature, our path, and His plan, ya know? And then you walk down the other side of the speedbump and go on, stronger and wiser than you were before u hit it"—to which Baxter then responds, in closing, "I don't know, Jesse, I just don't know. But I miss you, Jesse, school isn't the same without you."

There were two other memorable eulogies of deceased friends. For Scarlett, the unusual spelling of her friend Mollie's name suggested her singular character. "Mollie was the only 'Mollie' I have ever known who spelled her name with an 'ie' instead of a 'y.' She would correct people over and over until they had ingrained into their head the correct way her name was to be spelled; she was different, and would make sure people knew it." Scarlett never tells us how and when her friend dies, but she ends the eulogy with a sentence that captures her friend's uniqueness: "Mollie left imprints on the lives of all she encountered, and she will continue to serve as an inspiration for all of us to live 'selflesslie,' 'memorablie,' and 'completelie'—all spelled with an 'ie.'"

Also memorable is Gladys's eulogy of her friend Hans, who was mysteriously shot to death in his apartment. Once he discovered she was a creative writer, he always encouraged her to write poems and stories. One of the highlights of their relationship was when he took her to a film festival to see a screening of a documentary on the influential French philosopher and literary critic Jacques Derrida. "I had no idea who Derrida was prior to that night; now I am constantly reading his work and constantly being brought back to the memories of that night." She concludes by describing Hans's impact on her life and how she now sees traces of him everywhere:

> For the past few years it hasn't been Hans's memory, but the memory of his death, that has haunted my thoughts. The way he died was violent and tragic, and opened up so many questions for those around him, questions that will never be answered. Hans's murder has never been solved, and I doubt the case will ever be

picked up again. I've just begun to put away the questions and learn to remember him the way we were with each other, instead of letting his death and the rumors around it taint my memories of him.

In the past few months so many things have come back to Hans. Little coincidences keep popping up in my life that all lead to the same place. I don't know if I believe in fate as much as I find comfort in unexplained coincidences. I recently found the movie flyer from the Derrida film tucked into an old book in the attic. I heard a new song mourning the loss of a friend named Hans. Every line of the song alludes to some memory I share with Hans. The song brings me back to the times we sat listening to Jeff Buckley or discussing my writing. On New Year's, I met a Northeastern alumnus named Hans who, out of the blue, mentioned that he remembered seeing Hans and me around campus.

Hans was twenty-one when he died, the age I am now, yet he always seemed so much older and more mature. Maybe I was just young and immature. Then again, I seem to remember the talk of old souls over coffee, and stories of a young boy offering sage advice to his mother on the facts of life. What I know of Hans's life is little and scattered, but the impact of that life on mine is anything but little. I only knew Hans for five months, but his memory, and our time together, will stay with me forever.

Not surprisingly, the eulogies of deceased relatives and friends are generally psychologically richer than those of living people, if only because real loss generates more intense feelings than imagined loss. But two eulogies of living people are especially lively. Dean, the "miracle child" who weighed only two pounds when he was born three months prematurely, wrote a eulogy that portrays his mother's unwavering pride in her son's achievements—a pride that at times strikes him as excessive:

There are many moments in her life when she showed how dedicated a parent she was. She would watch sports and try to pretend she knew what was going on, just because I had a love for sports. She knew that I would appreciate this, so she did it to make me happy. My father was often working during the day, so my mom would attend my sporting events. One moment in particular stands out. It was during my first Little League game. I ran over to the car to get a bottle of water; as I approached the car I saw a giant smile on my mother's face. She was ecstatic; she rolled down the window, and clapping her hands she asked if I scored a run. I then told her that the dirt marks on my pants were from falling in the dugout. This didn't put a damper on her mood. Throughout my school career, she made the effort to make it to all of my games. Something I greatly appreciated, but never took the time to tell her.

Chuck's wry eulogy of his older brother reveals not only the sibling rivalry between them but also his gratitude for his brother's unappreciated act of heroism:

> Apparently, I became very annoying to my brother in my early childhood. Once when we were out in the yard with our mother, who was busy gardening, my brother decided to smack me in the nose with a spade. As if that wasn't bad enough, the injury caused the capillaries in my nose to be unusually sensitive, and any future trauma would easily result in nose bleeds. Unfortunately for me, my brother was always willing to provide me with the necessary punches to cause me to bleed. It became such a routine that he was even punished for saving my life. I was riding a tricycle on our driveway with my brother standing on the back. For whatever reason, I decided to ride down the fairly steep slope toward the road. As I was picking up speed, he caught sight of an oncoming car and pulled me off the tricycle. When my mother came upon the scene, she saw me lying on the driveway and my brother checking on me. She, therefore, logically concluded that he had once again beaten me up.

I read selections from several of the preceding eulogies to the class, but there was one that I could not read aloud because it was turned in late. It was written by Elijah, who observed in his obituary that his mother had died when he was a young child. The eulogy is filled with grammatical, stylistic, and proofreading errors. Nevertheless, I found it powerful and unforgettable:

> When asked to do this eulogy I questioned myself and wondered if I would even have the strength to write it without breaking down. Then I thought of the daunting task of saying it in front of friends and family. That is when I realized how much of an honor it would be to say the eulogy of my mother who has always been the most important person in the world to me.
>
> I still remember the last day I saw you. The last day we spoke. The last day I felt your embrace. I know I was only a child but the memory has remained fresh in my mind. I play back the same scene over and over again. Nobody had the heart to tell a four year old the truth. Everybody just told me, "mommy is in the hospital still" or "mommy is in a better place" well after you had passed away. If I would have known that was the last time I would have seen you I would have snuggled up next to you and never let go. My mother, Gail, was one of the strongest people I have ever had the privilege of being in association with. I know this because I ended up becoming a very strong willed and accomplished individual and I got every ounce of strength from you. I see you every time I look in the mirror and it makes me smile every time. My mother was a person without any prejudice. She came from a very racist family but she was always different. She loved everybody no matter what they looked like. Her spirit, generosity and warmth reached

through barriers of race and class. One of the biggest challenges she ever faced was from her family who hated the idea that she was involved with a black man. They became even more furious when they found out she was having a child with a black man. But if she would not have had that strength than I would have never been created. I owe my existence to her courage and determination.

My mother had a myriad of friends, many of which are here today. She could go anywhere in the world and turn it into home because she was so receptive to everyone and everywhere. Her favorite thing to do was to get everybody that she knew together, put the needle on the record of her favorite Bee Gees album and dance the night away. I remember that on the nights where all of her friends would come over and dance, I used to get to stay up late and watch. Those were some of my most memorable times. Her gift was the ability to make something out of nothing. She was like my miracle worker, never in my life have I seen someone make the best situation out of the worst resources. It didn't matter where we were; on Christmas she always made sure Santa came by and managed to leave something for everybody. On birthdays there was always a home made cake, a card and whatever it was that I had been whining about that I wanted. Even in those tough times when we were struggling and didn't have any food or the necessities needed to maintain a family she always made something happen. Even if she had to walk 10 miles to a welfare office she always had a way to provide for me. I know it was hard for her and even though I was only a young child I could still appreciate all of the sacrifices she made. It was not until I became older that I realized how much of a struggle it was for her.

I wish I could go back in time. I wish she could have another chance. I wish that I could just see her again. My mother was a victim of the virus known as HIV. Back in the 1980s in my neighborhood almost every household lost a member of their family to HIV or AIDS. Many people lost cousins, brothers, sisters, aunts, fathers and mothers. It was a very sad time for a lot of minority families. To make matters worse there was not a lot of information on AIDS or the virus that causes it. I love my mother very much and I always feel that ever since she left she has been like a guardian angel that has been watching over me. But I know she wasn't perfect and every angel has flaws. Growing up I often had mixed feelings about her and everything that happened to us. Part of me blames my father but part of me blames her. My father was the one with the drug addiction and my father was the one that introduced my mother to drugs and alcohol. My mother contracted the HIV virus after I was born by sharing needles when using drugs. I remember her fighting with my father about how they both needed to leave drugs alone for my sake and how much she hated when he would bring drugs into our house and get high in front of me. She was fighting demons on the inside and the outside and it became too much for her.

The last memory I have of my mother was not a good one. It was December, two months before my fifth birthday and she and I were lying down. She had already been very sick for some months now. I had not seen my father for a couple of weeks and she did not know where he was either. I remember she was in bed and as a result of her sickness she had lost control of her bowels. She managed to get to the bathroom but she was very weak. While in the bathroom she asked me to get her a change of pants and underwear from the bedroom. I was only four years old and the dresser that the clothes were in was very tall. I remember looking at that mountain of a dresser and it seemed like the tallest thing in the world to me. And as fate would have it the pants and underwear drawer had to be the very top drawer. I couldn't reach the drawer or get it open. And I just felt like I failed her. I started crying and she kept telling me it's okay but in my mind all I remember was her being so sick and weak and asking me to do something as simple as get some pants and I couldn't even do that for her. I felt like the worst person in the world. She eventually came out of the bathroom, cleaned up, changed clothes and went to bed. We went to sleep and when I woke up there was an ambulance and cop cars and all these lights everywhere. That was the last time I saw my mother and that was the night she passed away.

I know she only wanted the best for me, and ever since she passed away I have always felt like their was somebody watching me. I must have been in some really serious situations and on a few occasions a voice or some sort of power has spoken to me and made me make the right decision. I know it's her and whenever I am alone with my thoughts I always tell her I love her and she has nothing to worry about because I will be all right.

I find Elijah's eulogy remarkable for many reasons. First, he recalls with clarity and vividness events occurring in early childhood, a time in my own life of which I have only a few dim and isolated memories. Second, though he acknowledges the agonizing difficulty of eulogizing his mother, he considers it an "honor" and does everything in his power to pay tribute to her memory. And he succeeds despite often cumbersome language. Third, he conveys his mother's strength of character and love while at the same time admitting her drug and alcohol dependency as well as her struggle with internal "demons." Yet he never demonizes her or his father, despite the fact that the latter was the one who introduced her to drugs and alcohol. Finally, he recalls a scene of heartbreaking pathos in which he cannot fulfill what turns out to be his mother's final request, to bring her a change of clothes. "I felt like the worst person in the world," he informs us, and then he reveals that she died a few hours later.

Elijah's obituary reveals only a brief, unemotional reference to his mother's death, but he now provides the details in his eulogy. He also conveys his feelings about a traumatic childhood. We now have a better understanding of why he imagined in his obituary devoting his entire life to creating a community center in which children could talk about their problems and receive help from trusted counselors: "The children's well-being was always the uppermost concern for him." Central to Elijah's life is the desire to provide love and comfort to those who, like himself, found childhood to be a time of shattering loss and heartbreak.

One senses, to use Dominick LaCapra's term, that Elijah is writing trauma, "acting out, working over, and to some extent working through" a traumatic experience (Writing History, Writing Trauma 186). I don't know whether it was difficult for him to write the eulogy, but unlike speakers, writers can pause if they find their words or thoughts emotionally wrenching, returning to writing when they feel more in control. Terry Martin and Kenneth Doka call this process dosing: "that is, if the griever finds something too painful or difficult, he or she can set it aside for a while" (148–49).

How does one grade a eulogy solely on its grammar and style? I had no choice but to give Elijah a "check" instead of a "plus" despite the fact that the eulogy powerfully affected me. I circled every grammatical and stylistic error and rewrote several sentences. To emphasize the importance of compression, I shortened his sentence, "My mother, Gail, was one of the strongest people I have ever had the privilege of being in association with" to "My mother, Gail, was one of the strongest people I have known." After making these changes, I concluded with the following comment: "This is a *very* moving essay, Elijah. Your love for your mother is apparent in every paragraph."

Elijah ends his eulogy with the statement that there was "somebody watching" him. It's unclear whether this has spiritual significance, but religion figures prominently in twenty of his classmates' eulogies, including those by Belle and Baxter, both of whom identified themselves in their obituaries as born-again Christians. Two other students quote a well-known passage from Corinthians that is often used for wedding services: "Love is patient, love is kind. It does not envy, it does not boast, it is not proud. It is not rude, it is not self-seeking, it is not easily angered, it keeps no record of wrongs. Love does not delight in evil but rejoices with the truth. It always protects, always trusts, always hopes, always perseveres." Jean, a devout Roman Catholic, begins her eulogy for her grandfather with a passage from Ecclesiastes—"To everything there is a season"—and ends with the following: "Until we are reunited in Heaven, we say goodnight. Sleep well, pleasant dreams, we'll see you in the morning." Hannah ends her eulogy by describing her friend's faith in her parents and God: "Every time I think of Christine, I find comfort in the fact she always lived her life to the fullest and died riding horses which was third only to God and her parents on her list of things she loved most." In a section of his eulogy that I have not quoted earlier, Dean remarks that his mother's "devotion to her faith is a reason why I am able to read this eulogy today." Several students end their eulogies by observing that an angel has left earth to return to heaven where he or she belongs—an angel whom many students believe now watches over them. Sometimes students believe that this angel has saved a relative's life, as Jackie describes in a eulogy for her father:

> When my father was 21 years old, he lost his father, and when I was 21, tragedy almost repeated itself. On December 19, 2005, my father was driving home from work, and from Christmas shopping for me, and was involved in a car accident that could have taken his life. The nurses and police told my mother and me how lucky he was to be alive. For a short while, I agreed with them, I also thought luck was on his side. But soon, I came to believe it was not luck, but an angel on his shoulder that protected him that day. I never met my grandfather, but after seeing the wreckage, I was convinced that something, or someone, was in that car watching over him. He saved my father, and made us all realize how important family is.

An additional eight students eulogized relatives or friends who had strong religious faith. Ava does not indicate whether she is religious, but her grandmother was: "Her abiding faith was shown each day as she began her morning by reading the Bible. There is a verse of scripture in the book of proverbs that captures her essence. It reads: 'Strength and dignity are her clothing.' Nanny lived a quiet life; she was an amazing woman who never advertised the fact that she lived her life for others." Some students who are not themselves religious, such as Malechi, nevertheless end their eulogies by implying that the dead are still watching over the living: "I know you're listening. Good night." The remaining twenty students make no reference to religious or spiritual faith in their eulogies, though this does not necessarily imply absence of faith. The next writing assignment—describing how one's religious beliefs influence one's attitude toward death—will encourage students to explore this important question.

Evaluating the Eulogy Assignment

I once saw a sign on a fire station commemorating one of our country's most solemn holidays: "Every Day is Memorial Day." Eulogizing the dead is one way to pay tribute to those who are no longer here. Writing a eulogy proved to be one of my students' most unusual and compelling assignments, as they indicated in anonymous questionnaires. About half of the students said that writing the eulogy was painful. The following is representative of the many who became tearful while writing the eulogy: "I felt like crying as I wrote incidents that myself and the person I wrote it on shared. Several times my eyes watered. It was painful to think that I would even have to do that for my best friend. As I write this now, my eyes watered." One person "cried three times, but it wasn't painful. I cried about the good stuff." Another experienced intense joy and sorrow while writing the eulogy: "While writing it I would either be laughing so much I had to stop writing (having remembered good times) or crying so much that I could not see the screen to type (when I remembered all the things we had planned but never did)."

Some expected the assignment to be difficult and were surprised when it was not. "I decided to write about my dying grandmother. I was having second thoughts about doing this because I was afraid that if I wrote about her, she would die sooner. I understand that this may sound unrealistic, but in a way I felt I was deciding her fate sooner. Surprisingly, it wasn't painful. It actually brought me comfort. Seeing all the memories I had shared with her on paper brought comfort to me." Others had the opposite response. "I felt fine writing it. It made me remember a lot of great times with my grandma. It wasn't until I read it aloud to myself that I felt the hurt. I broke down crying and could barely speak. I don't know if I will give the eulogy at her funeral." One grandmother not only gave her grandchild permission to eulogize her but also made an unanticipated request: "It was very hard to write because my Gran is still alive and I felt as though I might be jinxing her and found myself knocking on wood. I called Gran for permission to write it. She wanted a copy."

Nearly everyone was moved by the eulogies I read aloud, and the comments were overwhelmingly positive. Several students expressed sadness that so many classmates had lost a parent, grandparent, or close friend. "The eulogies were powerful. I am so amazed at how people write. I think a lot of these students are English majors who have an advantage over me since I am a business major and am taking this course as an elective." Indeed, many were impressed by the verbal power of the eulogies. "They were *amazing*. I was glad I could hear them." Several were distressed by their classmates' losses. "I was saddened by the depth of loss that so many of these young people have already experienced." Many stated that the eulogies were affirming as well as sad. "It was uplifting to hear all the heartwarming tales of loved ones, and I was inspired by the love and dedication." Some noted a powerful identification with classmates that at times became disturbing. "I had goose bumps all over my body—the eulogies led me to thinking that just like many of my classmates, I am bound to have someone die, a situation I do not want to imagine." Others were comforted that they were not alone in their fears and problems. "Some were sad. I find myself looking around the class, wondering where some of the phrases and images originated. I feel as though I am surrounded by people like me—people with problems."

Nearly two-thirds of the students believed that the assignment heightened their awareness of both life and death. "I noticed that I am more accepting of the reality of death and that it is easier for me to talk about it in conversation. When my mother brought up our friend with cancer, it was easy for me to discuss death as a likelihood in the near future for her. This shocked my mother." Another made a similar comment. "It did heighten my awareness. I felt as though I fear death more so now, because I guess I was in denial. I never really thought about it. Now I talk of death all the time." Some students believed that heightened awareness of death leads to heightened appreciation of life, and they expressed gratitude that their closest relatives are still alive. "The assignment heightened my awareness of my mother's death, which hasn't happened yet. It made me appreciate the fact that she is still living." All but four students believed that the assignment will help them write eulogies in the future. "Absolutely. There is a pretty good chance that I will use this eulogy someday at my grandmother's funeral."

Students praised the eulogy assignment for many reasons. "It makes you realize how important that person was to you. Also, when you're writing it, you definitely realize *all* the memories you two have shared. It puts your relationship into perspective." And another: "It is a chance to say goodbye. A chance to honor your loved one. An emotional outlet for grief." Several felt that writing a eulogy is therapeutic. "It's an important tool in the grieving process, as it allows one to play some role in the aftermath of death. It's one of those things you probably never regret having done." Another implied that writing a eulogy enables the writer to internalize the dead. "It allows you to put them somewhere in yourself that you wouldn't otherwise be able to do. Also, it lets anyone who hears it remember how much they loved them." The eulogies were particularly valuable to those who have lost relatives. "Personally, it helped me cope with my dad's death and remember all of the little things in our past together." For others, writing the eulogy was a psychological tool for introspection. "It allows you to delve into areas of your psyche and unearth new emotions." All of these benefits, I should add, I experienced myself when writing my eulogy for Barbara.

I was delighted that the students found the eulogy assignment so helpful. The assignment seemed to have a negative effect only on Malechi, who believed he suffered a persistent migraine headache as a response to it, but as promised, he turned in his eulogy two days late. He also submitted the additional essay I had asked him to write, titled "Writing about Sorrow," in which he explained his difficulty in completing the eulogy and how he overcame writer's block:

> I consider myself a well-versed writer. I have been crafting stories for years with topics ranging from the dangers of smog to adventures of fantasy. I have taken numerous writing classes, penned many short stories, and even began a journal with my craziest ideas and most insightful poetry. Writing has become a cornerstone of my life, even if my current career aspirations don't include it. When it came to college, often times I wowed the professor with my writing style so much so that they gave me grades I didn't deserve. In one particular instance I

wrote a paper inside of 20 minutes for a class. When I got the 3-page paper back and I had received an A minus on it, I was so angry that I burned the paper in frustration. Aside from those small disturbances college was almost too easy. No assignment was too complex, no page length too imposing, until the death and dying class in the spring of 2006.

Death was not a new or unfamiliar topic for me. I had many brief moments where death came and stared me straight in the face. My best friend of 10 years had attempted suicide at least 3 times in the span of 8 months and had been institutionalized for depression twice in that same time. That had been in the summer and fall of 2003 and the spring of 2004. My grandfather, who I was never really close with, had passed in early spring of 2005. In the summer of 2005 I ran into some troubles on my trip to India and became so violently ill that it taxed me psychologically to the point where I believed I was going to die. And finally I had been put face to face with death on a psychedelic trip that I had experienced in January of 2006. This last experience was illusionary, but also sudden, adding another dimension to an experience that I had already seen was impersonal and certain.

The writing assignments in class have been both challenging and harrowing. I have found myself challenged more than ever when put to the task of a simple two- or three-page paper. Unusual stress, the likes of which I have never seen before, has been associated with each paper in different ways.

The first paper was relatively easy to write, simply crafting the information given to me by my partner held no real emotional baggage. Putting together the things I wanted said in my obituary was, however, far more difficult. It took about 2 hours and eventually was a cathartic experience. It forced me to look back on my life and find things that I was proud of that I could expand upon in the future. For a self-declared existentialist, the future is a difficult topic to approach; however, this assignment helped me to approach it with a sense of inherent character and irreproachable honesty that I was amazed at myself.

The second writing assignment was much more difficult. I have been living with my girlfriend for almost 6 months now and have been dating her for 2 years. I chose her as the close person that I would write my eulogy about. I chose her instead of my best friend Eddie because I had already had many experiences trying to deal with close encounters with death. These were not experiences I wanted to revisit. When I went to begin this assignment, I was suddenly struck with writer's block. Writer's block for me was uncommon, but it was easily dealt with. I found that I simply had to write every word that came to mind, quickly they would become sentences about something and I could simply direct my thoughts. Eventually, using this technique I would find myself writing effortlessly about anything I wanted to in minutes. This time, as I sat down at the keyboard, I felt something I had never felt before. It was a constant pressure behind my forehead that was later explained to me as a migraine. I had never had one of them before, and I started to investigate the possible reasons. Eventually I found that it was the paper itself. I found the pressure increased most when I thought of the paper. I decided to go to sleep, not wanting to hurt myself for the sake of a paper. I found myself the next day a bit more comfortable and began writing the paper out by hand on the bus. Eventually I did finish the paper in the school computer lab. I had to hold back tears throughout writing the paper, and when I was finished I met a friend on campus who immediately exclaimed, "Why are your eyes so red?" I consulted a biology major or two for confirmation and found that your eyes can become bloodshot when you hold back tears for more than half an hour.

The writing assignments have shown me many things about myself. How even after repeated encounters with death, and the confrontation with the fact that it may be at anyone's doorstep, at anytime, we can still be terrified of it. It showed me that you could only come to terms with death after talking about it, or expressing it some way. Expressing those beliefs changes the way that you interact with death. It makes death something that only you can understand to something that can be talked about. Understanding that everyone else, at one point or another, feels the same fear, the same anxiety, and the same pain helps people deal with death.

I think this class, although it may not do exactly that, strives to accomplish as much of that as possible and so is a worthwhile class for anyone. I have already had an excellent experience in this class, and I look forward to writing on the other topics this year.

4

∼

On Teaching the Book of Job—
and Being Denounced as
a "False Prophet"

Monday, February 13 (continued)

We began the Book of Job today, and I asked my students whether they thought one could read the story "more or less objectively." About twenty people raised their hands; another twenty felt that it was not possible to read it objectively; the rest were not sure. I said I would bet anyone in the class one dollar that I could prove an "objective" reading of the story is impossible. Chuck accepted my challenge. I asked him a "factual" question: did he agree with his classmate Baxter that two of the main characters in the story are "God" and his rival, "Satan"? "Yes," said Chuck, falling into my trap. I smiled and pointed out that although in the original Hebrew the name is *ha-satan*, translated in the King James version of the Bible (which we were reading) as *satan*, there is a fundamental difference between the early Jewish and Christian conceptions of the name. As the editor of *The New Oxford Annotated Bible* writes, "In the book of Job, *Satan* is not yet the personal name of the devil, as in later Jewish and Christian literature. Rather, the Hebrew (with the definite article) simply means 'the adversary' or 'the accuser'. . . , a reference to one of the members of the divine council who served as a sort of independent prosecutor" (728). Dating the Book of Job as written between the seventh and fourth centuries BC (before Christ) instead of BCE (before the Common Era) reveals the same bias.

I gave another example of Christian bias: the assumption that the Old Testament anticipates the New Testament. As Harold Bloom notes in his book *Jesus and Yahweh*, "Though all of Christian theology, as well as the formidable Dante and his devoted exegetes, avers otherwise, nevertheless no later text ever has 'fulfilled' an earlier one, or even 'corrected' it. Plato's *Republic* battles

Homer's *Iliad*, and Plato gloriously is defeated. Joyce's *Ulysses* boldly engages both Homer's *Odyssey* and Shakespeare's *Hamlet*, and sublimely loses. Historically, both the New Testament and the Qur'an have pragmatically eclipsed the Hebrew Bible, but these successes are neither aesthetic nor necessarily spiritual, and Yahweh may not yet have spoken his final words upon this matter" (27). Jewish readers bring their own bias to the Bible, as do agnostics and atheists. Every interpretation reveals something about the interpreter—and no book is more hotly contested than the Bible. Chuck came up to me after class and graciously handed me a folded dollar bill. Later I made a one dollar wager in my writing class that I promptly lost.

Wednesday, February 15

I began class today by talking about the many surprises in the Book of Job. One surprise, I pointed out, is that the story is not about Job's *patience*, as most people believe, but about his *persistence* in maintaining that he does not deserve the calamity that befalls him and his family: the loss of his seven sons and three daughters, the loss of his animals and servants, and the loathsome boils that afflict his body. Another surprise is the intensity of Job's rage toward God and his demand to take Him to court to prove his innocence. Job's anger disappears only at the end of the story, when God, the voice from the whirlwind, overwhelms him with a series of rhetorical questions demonstrating humankind's inability to understand the nature of the universe and the reason for suffering. Another surprise is that God rewards the contentious, defiant Job at the end of the story by restoring his lost fortunes, giving him twice as much as he had before, and by blessing him with ten new children and a long life. And still another surprise is that God's wrath is kindled against Job's "friends" for expressing conventional religious pieties.

As I was talking about these and other surprises, along with the differences between Jewish and Christian readings of the story, I found myself surprised—stunned, to be more precise—by what was happening in class. Raymond, a student who has always seemed bored and restless in class, was becoming increasingly agitated and disruptive. At first he appeared to be mumbling to himself and to a small group of students sitting near him. Then he started singing and chanting, and finally—despite my repeated requests for him to remain quiet—he rose from his seat, started shouting "Shut up!" to me, denounced me as a "false prophet," and stormed out of class, slamming the door so hard that he sounded like the "whirlwind" in the story we were reading. Everyone was shocked. "Nothing like this has happened in the thirty-three years I've been teaching at this university," I sputtered, trying to maintain my composure. I resumed talking about the story, noting that despite its happy ending, I would have remained grief stricken over the loss of my ten children if I were in Job's situation: new children can never replace deceased children.

A few minutes later Raymond returned to class, walking directly in front of me to get to his seat, and muttering to himself. I tried to avoid becoming confrontational, lest I demonize him. (A teacher's anger in the classroom, I discovered many years ago, is usually counterproductive.) He continued talking to himself, though I couldn't hear what he was saying. Ironically, I had decided before class to spend the last fifteen minutes reading "A Teacher's Self-Eulogy," which I intend to use for the conclusion of *Death in the Classroom*. As I was reading the self-eulogy aloud, I realized how hard it is for a teacher to remain empathic when a student is out of control. After I finished the reading, many students appeared shaken as they left the classroom, and Raymond walked past me, pointedly ignoring my request to speak to him.

Raymond's fulmination against me was extreme, but it illustrates how explosive religious discussions can be in a world inflamed by religious misunderstanding, intolerance, and violence. I told my students after he left the room that although there were no courses on "race, class, and gender" when I was an undergraduate in the early 1960s, now such courses are routinely offered in nearly every English department. Curiously, religion never finds its way into these cultural studies courses despite the fact that it is a powerful lens through which people see the world. Religion influences how we interpret nearly every aspect of life and death, including questions about God, death, the hereafter, morality, justice, and suffering.

The world was divided into two groups when I was growing up, Jews and non-Jews: I assumed that anyone who wasn't Jewish was Catholic, which for me was synonymous with Gentile. I'm embarrassed to admit that I still silently ask myself, upon meeting a person for the first time, whether he or she is Jewish, a habit I developed as a young boy. (I recall my mother always asking me this question when I told her that I made a new friend in school.) I suspect that the reason religion never finds its way into courses on "race, class, and gender" is that we live in an overwhelmingly Christian country, where most people, including cultural studies scholars, remain insensitive to Jewish perceptions of reality. Christian culture is negligent of other religious perspectives, including Buddhist, Hindu, and, perhaps now more than ever, Islam. In the chapter called "The Dark Side of Diversity" in *Risky Writing,* I suggest that it is easy to see ourselves as victimized by others' intolerance, but we must acknowledge our own intolerance toward others if we are honest with ourselves.

Why was Raymond so angry? He must have thought I was challenging his religious faith, which he was prepared to defend no matter what the consequences were. He saw me not as a literature teacher, trying to illuminate a complex biblical story, but as a Jewish atheist who was trying to destroy his belief in God. Perhaps he saw me as aligned with Satan. Ironically, a few minutes before Raymond's stormy departure I observed that Satan as God's enemy is a Christian rather than a Jewish concept. That I am Jewish and Raymond is Christian intensified the religious drama that was played out in class. If he saw himself as Job and me as Satan, perhaps this was his justification for disrupting class and challenging my authority. Or perhaps he saw himself following in the footsteps of Jesus.

Raymond's demand that I "shut up" is an extreme example of how people react to loss, in this case, the threat of losing one's religious certitude. For many people, the loss of religious faith is the most shattering loss of all. My own loss of religious faith, which was never strong to begin with, occurred not long after I was bar mitzvahed when I was thirteen, and I seldom think about how devastating this loss must be to those who have built their lives and belief systems around God and the hereafter. I was challenging everything that Raymond held dear in life, including his identity as a follower of Jesus, and he was not prepared to engage in a rational discussion. Nor could he remain quiet as I spoke. His response reminded me of a statement my friend Marshall Alcorn makes in his book *Changing the Subject in English Class*: "All of us, faced with profound loss, are tempted to deny loss and insist that what we love still survives. As everyone now seems to know, the first normal human response to loss is denial. If we are told about an unexpected loss, we deny the truth of the claim" (116). Certainly Barbara and I responded to the news of her terminal illness with shock and denial: we kept hoping that the CT scans were wrong and that her liver was not fatally riddled with cancer. Raymond must have seen me not as a teacher raising questions about the Book of Job but as a false prophet who was intent on destroying his God.

I wonder how Raymond would have responded to the opening page of Harold Bloom's *Jesus and Yahweh*, with its provocative assertion: "This book centers upon three figures: a more-or-less historical person, Yeshua of Nazareth; a theological God, Jesus Christ; and a human, all-too-human God, Yahweh. That opening sentence cannot avoid sounding polemical, and yet I hope only to clarify (if I can) and not to give offense." It is difficult to be provocative without giving offense, Bloom admits, especially when one challenges the central authority of the Western world:

> Almost everything that can be known about Yeshua emanates from the New Testament, and from allied or heretical writings. All these are tendentious: their designs upon us, as readers or auditors, are palpable and conversionary. If I call Yeshua "more-or-less historical," I mean only that nearly everything truly important about him reaches me from texts I cannot trust. Quests for "the historical Jesus" invariably fail, even by the most responsible searchers. Quest-

ers, however careful, find themselves, and not the elusive and evasive Yeshua, enigma-of-enigmas. Every Christian believer I know, here or abroad, has her or his own Jesus. St. Paul admitted that he himself had become all things to all men: that may be the single authentic affinity the great Apostle had with his savior. (1–2)

For the rest of the day I brooded over the incident, wondering if there was anything I could have done differently to have avoided igniting Raymond's wrath. Tonight I received an email from a student who offers another perspective on what happened in class:

Dear Jeff,

I'm in your Love and Loss class. I don't exactly know why I'm writing to you because I don't have anything specific to say, but I need to talk to someone about what happened in class today (Wednesday), when Raymond flipped out. I have very very similar views toward religion as you do, and it has always been a sore subject for me. I've always had certain prejudices toward people who place their faith in a God who they have no proof exists, besides a book with stories and rules written a long long time ago. I guess one could say I'm antireligious. But I don't try to make others think like I think. I respect their choices as much as I possibly can, and even though I really want to make them see things my way, I bite my tongue because I know that there is so much difference in the world, and I don't want to offend anyone.

I felt very discomforted after class today. It was like a mixture between being depressed, anxious, and angry at the same time. Some part of me wished you would have lashed out at Raymond for his cruelty and rudeness, but my brain realizes that you did the right thing. The whole situation was extremely ironic to me. I was raised christian, so I know most of their beliefs. Always I have heard people strive to be more "christ-like," which I thought meant being compassionate, caring, understanding, empathetic, kind, knowledgeable, etc., and all the other good qualities a person can have. Today, Raymond (who I know enough from previous meetings that he claims to be extremely "christ-like") displayed the very opposite of what I took his entire religion to be about, while you were the textbook example of "christ-like." I don't know how you did it, by the way. I would have definitely exploded. I greatly respect that you did not explode, and hope to one day be able to do the same. If I had any doubts about my choice as to question gods existence instead of have faith, they were destroyed today. His actions versus yours negated anything and everything he has ever said about Jesus and his religion to me, and his anger is something I never want to see or experience again. If only I were that lucky.

I guess I at least got this new respect for you during the experience. I feel like I know you a lot better than I did a few hours ago, and I'm extremely happy I have you as my professor. Sorry this email is going nowhere. I guess I just had to vent to someone.

Thank you so much, and have a good break.

Your friend and student,

Thursday, February 16

I read this unsolicited email with great interest, especially the observation that my behavior in class was "christ-like." I didn't feel frightened during class, but as I was falling asleep last night and trying to reconstruct the events of the day, I imagined Raymond pulling out a gun and shooting me in front of sixty horrified onlookers—an ironic confirmation of the above student's perception. My fantasy surprises me. I hope to teach until the end of my life, but until today I never imagined the possibility that my life might end by an angry student who regards me as a false prophet. It's a sobering thought.

It was also sobering to read Sam Harris's *The End of Faith*, a discussion of the gloomy implications of growing religious intolerance. "A glance at history," Harris opines, "or at the pages of any newspaper, reveals that ideas which divide one group of human beings from another, only to unite them in slaughter, generally have their roots in religion. It seems that if our species ever eradicates itself through war, it will not be because it was written in the stars but because it was written in our books; it is what we do with words like 'God' and 'paradise' and 'sin' in the present that will determine our future" (12). Harris adds that intolerance is central to every religion. "Once a person believes—*really* believes—that certain ideas can lead to eternal happiness, or to its antithesis, he cannot tolerate the possibility that the people he loves might be led astray by the blandishments of unbelievers. Certainty about the next life is simply incompatible with tolerance in this one" (13). Harris quotes Will Durant's observation that "intolerance is the natural concomitant of strong faith; tolerance grows only when faith loses certainty; certainty is murderous" (86). Harris is not opposed to religious faith; rather, he believes, or hopes, that spirituality "can be—indeed, *must* be—deeply rational, even as it elucidates the limits of reason. Seeing this, we can begin to divest ourselves of many of the reasons we currently have to kill one another" (43; emphasis in original).

Raymond and I were reacting in different ways to love and loss. I was teaching the course because of my wife's recent death, and I was trying to find comfort in the Book of Job, which explores with unrivaled poetic power the nature of undeserved suffering. The story affirms the value of questioning even if we can find no satisfactory answer to the enigma of innocent suffering. "Teach me, and I will be silent," Job implores God, "make me understand how

I have gone wrong" (*New Oxford Annotated Bible* 6:24). This was precisely the question Barbara and I asked as she lay dying. Job refuses to restrain himself: "I will speak in the anguish of my spirit; I will complain in the bitterness of my soul" (7:11). Steadfastly believing he is a "just and blameless man," he nevertheless feels like he is a "laughingstock" to his friends (12:4). Neither speech nor silence helps him. "If I speak, my pain is not assuaged, and if I forbear, how much of it leaves me?" (16:6). I identified with Job's heroic persistence rather than with his submission to divine authority at the end, when he concludes, "I had heard of you by the hearing of the ear, but now my eye sees you; therefore I despise myself and repent in dust and ashes" (42:5–6).

Raymond was also reacting to loss, not of a beloved wife but of a personal God, whom he saw endangered by my teachings. He was not interested in analyzing the ambiguities and contradictions in the story, as I was, and he had a ready answer to the question of why goodness may be punished and evil rewarded. He too may have identified with Job's refusal to remain silent in the face of adversity, but his Job was a man who, had he lived centuries later, would have been redeemed and resurrected by Jesus. Raymond apparently saw me as Satan, tempting him to turn away from his Lord. He may have also identified with Job's sarcastic rejoinder to his three friends, who fail to convince him that he must have done something to deserve suffering: "But I have understanding as well as you; I am not inferior to you" (12:3). Raymond must have felt justified in denouncing a threat to his religious faith. Had he carefully read the Book of Job, he might have quoted chapter and verse to defend his disruptive classroom tactics: "I hold fast my righteousness, and will not let it go; my heart does not reproach me for any of my days" (27:6).

February 16–23

This week I'm in Florida, on winter break, but I haven't stopped thinking about Wednesday's unsettling class. I asked two students in the Love and Loss course—one who had taken a course with me a year ago, the other who was also in my writing class—to offer their impressions of Raymond's behavior so that I can understand how his classmates felt. I'm reading their emails at the West Palm Beach Public Library:

> I was sitting near Raymond before class started and he was talking loudly to no one in particular about politics, the government, social inequalities. No one was really listening, one student was trying to joke with him, but it became evident that Raymond was not joking. When he stood up and started yelling at you during class, I was shocked. I have never experienced something like that in one of my college classes. I do not think he understood what you were talking about.

I was under the impression that you were pointing out the differences between how Judaism and Christianity interpreted the Book of Job. Raymond seemed to be looking for a way to make a scene. But I was frightened when he did stand up and start yelling. However, I thought you handled it very well and even relaxed my fears. You were able to smoothly continue the discussion without dwelling on his exit. But when he returned, I again became scared. I did not know what he was going to do, and of course, I assumed the worst. I did not expect him to return and spent the rest of class nervously looking at him, but trying not to make eye contact. But class did end after that without any other outburst. After talking to my classmates and friends about the incident, I did find out that Raymond is somewhat well known around campus as a crazy Christian guy. I think he attends open-mike events and speaks about Jesus and hands out Bibles. I have never seen him before, so I do not know if this is true. As a whole, I was appalled by his behavior. I do not think he fully understood your point or even wanted to. I thoroughly enjoy this class, and I was disappointed that another student would be so disrespectful and ignorant to the professor and the rest of the class.

The beginning of the class was like any other class; we signed the attendance sheet, and the professor spoke about the previous class briefly. The professor, Jeffrey Berman, also spoke about what he planned to do for the next class. He wants to read some of the eulogies aloud, and this was something I looked forward to because I put a lot of work into mine. On the course syllabus he added as one of our readings the Book of Job—a story from the Bible. On this particular Wednesday Jeff began to discuss the story. The class before this one, Jeff presented us with a very compelling argument—That there is no way we can read this story objectively. I agreed. During this class he began to elaborate on this point. He brought as an example the fact that in the Hebrew version of this story the word Devil is not used. He said this was a Christian word. This is when one of the guys began to get upset, and asked Jeff a question. I thought Jeff was trying to bring us closer to objectivity by not referring to the Devil but as the accuser, and by referring to the old version of the story. I was not really sure of what was going on because the class began to get out of control. One of the guys began to sing, religious songs. When Jeff tried to proceed and calm the class down the same guy said, "Shut up, don't talk about my Bible unless you have read it all." He also said, "Shut up, don't talk about my God." He got up and began to walk out. Professor Berman tried to ignore how rude this guy was acting and proceeded with the class. Every time Jeff began to speak the guy would say, "shut up." He left the room saying "Shut up, Shut up, Shut up." I was not really sure of what just happened. I always attended church as a child and as a result I have a bond with God, but I did not feel like there was any reason for me to be insulted. We proceeded to discuss the story, and disagreeing at times but taking into consideration that everyone has a right to their opinion.

Until I read the email from the first student, I hadn't realized that Raymond's behavior must have frightened some of the members of our class. Both students were distressed by what happened in class, and I suspect their classmates felt the same way. And both believe that Raymond was disrespectful not only to me but also to them. Richard also emailed me his diary entry:

Today exemplified my "nervousness" over teaching religious texts as literature. I documented over three pages of notes to capture what happened, but I think the notes mislead me as they are too heavily influenced by emotion. The class started very well. Jeff was soliciting written feedback and organizing when I arrived late from my earlier commitments. Then he asked the students what they found surprising about the Book of Job. Students commented on how Job did not grieve for the loss of his children, how his wife says "curse god and die." Throughout this warm-up to thinking about the Book of Job, Raymond—who I've noted before as confident to the point of being overly so, full of smiles and a bit of a joker—is mumbling to himself again, leaning back in his seat, or shifting his hat like he's bored. Previously, I noted how he did not fill out one of Jeff's anonymous feedback forms but put a line where each response should be. At that time, he noticed how I saw his lack of responses, so I asked him if he felt strongly about those being the responses he wanted to give. He smiled and said they were. Apparently, he wasn't bored, putting up with the class, or particularly lazy as I might have concluded. My new conclusion is that he wants to stay within the realms of discourse (i.e., language, activities, beliefs, and values) that are comfortable and most likely have had a history of being personally helpful.

At one point Raymond began singing hymns that were disruptive, if beautifully toned. I believe he wanted to surround himself with the music of his own discourse. He was not necessarily looking to disrupt or play the attention-getting fool. Instead, he wanted to reject what Jeff was saying. And this point is very difficult for most in the class to understand (me included). Jeff, as a teacher, is exceedingly accepting and nonjudgmental of other's perspectives. So what happened when Raymond snapped, got up, and walked out while calling out "False Prophet!" Upon exiting, he bounced the door off the frame so hard I'm surprised the doorknob did not pop through the plaster wall.

While Jeff is opening students' understanding of how religion subjectively changes our reading lenses, some students can't accept the academic process that this requires. Like the form that Raymond filled in by drawing lines through the blank spaces, it appears he does not wish to know new things by questioning. He takes the academic process of questioning as challenging his belief systems, systems that have probably provided a great deal of guidance, hope, and confidence. To consider that, historically, the Old Testament is used by Christians to prepare the way for the New Testament supposes that Christianity is not the originating and "natural" force that some of its congregation sometimes pretends it to be. Of course, since one of my close friends went into the Ukrainian branch of the Catholic priesthood, I've long understood that part of the training to become well educated in theology is to study, question, and know all religions. Otherwise, the believer accepts the comforting aspects of his or her faith without the complex reality of the religious system and must continually be "on watch" for heretics, or even fair and nonideological driven academics.

After 15 to 20 minutes, Raymond returned. At times, students eyed him suspiciously. I probably did as well, for I did not know what he would do next. Yet, this reaction saddened me. I can count on one hand the number of times students have stormed out of my own classes. It's generally rare, but considering the difficult subject matter—religious readings that are even more challenging than the emotional worries of death—it's the reason I'm continually nervous over teaching religious texts as literature. Raymond commented in class that it is not "Job being set up but Satan/the Adversary being set up." Certainly, this is an opportunity for Raymond to explain, see, and address his comforting beliefs. But I don't think he's interested just yet.

After class he approaches me, and I ask him, "What's up?" in order to give him the grounds upon which he might choose to speak. He reads a verse from Proverbs 12.1 (I think this is what's quoted). Then says, "Not many people may correct me." He looks away from my eyes, taps his mini-Bible, and walks quickly away. I know there is an opportunity here, but frankly, I'm too nervous to make it happen. And so I let Raymond walk toward Jeff and the exit while I field questions from other students. There are opportunities everywhere today.

Richard's recognition that there are "opportunities everywhere" reminds me of Shoshana Felman's statement that teaching "takes place precisely only through a crisis: if teaching does not hit upon some sort of crisis, if it does not encounter . . . vulnerability or . . . explosiveness it has perhaps not truly taught: it has perhaps passed on some facts, passed on some information" (55). The crisis about which Felman speaks arose in response to her graduate students' horror upon viewing a Holocaust documentary, but her statement applies to other crises as well. We cannot predict when these classroom crises will occur, nor can we predict how teachers and students will respond to them, but we can try to learn as much as possible from emotionally charged situations.

If I had had more time, I would have discussed Karen Armstrong's *A History of God,* one of the most brilliant books I've read on comparative religion. Armstrong, who spent seven years as a Roman Catholic nun before leaving the order to become a teacher, writer, and lecturer, gives us an encyclopedic history of the evolving views of Judaism, Christianity, and Islam. Noting in the introduction that human beings are inherently spiritual—"Indeed, there is a case for arguing that Homo sapiens is also Homo religiosus" (xix), she affirms another equally important truth: "if we look at our three religions, it becomes clear that there is no objective view of 'God': each generation has to create the image of God that works for it. The same is true of atheism. The statement 'I do not believe in God' has meant something slightly different at each period of history" (xx). Fundamentalists, she notes, who believe in an unchanging God and who therefore take an antihistorical approach to religion, would vehemently deny her claim, but she shows in painstaking detail not only how the "history of God" has changed dramatically over time but also how many of our unchallenged assumptions of religion have not always been historically true.

Armstrong is especially insightful in pointing out both the strengths and weaknesses of Judaism, Christianity, and Islam. She shows how the Israelites transformed God "beyond recognition into a symbol of transcendence and compassion," but she also observes that the God of the Old Testament is a "brutal, partial and murderous god: a god of war who would be known as Yahweh Sabaoth, the God of Armies. He is passionately partisan, has little compassion for anyone but his own favorites and is simply a tribal deity. If Yahweh had remained such a savage god, the sooner he vanished, the better it would have been for everybody" (19). Sympathetic to Jesus as the embodiment of love and forgiveness, she singles out for criticism Augustine's profound misogyny. Women's only function for Augustine "was the childbearing which passed the contagion of Original Sin to the next generation, like a venereal disease. A religion which looks askance upon half the human race and which regards every involuntary motion of mind, heart and soul as a symptom of fatal concupiscence can only alienate men and women from their condition. Western Christianity never fully recovered from this neurotic misogyny, which can still be seen in the unbalanced reaction to the very notion of the ordination of women" (124–25). And while she praises the Koran's belief that war is abhorrent—a belief that is tragically lost among today's terrorists—she states that as with Christianity, Islam was "later hijacked by the men, who interpreted texts in a way that was negative for Muslim women" (158).

Insights abound in A History of God, including the linguistic connection among the words myth, mysticism, and mystery: "All are derived from the Greek verb musteion: to close the eyes or the mouth. All three words, therefore, are rooted in an experience of darkness and silence" (211). She discusses with admirable balance and subtlety the advantages and disadvantages of a personal God.

Judaism, Christianity and—to a lesser extent—Islam have all developed the idea of a personal God, so we tend to think that this ideal represents religion at its best. The personal God has helped monotheists to value the sacred and inalienable rights of the individual and to cultivate an appreciation of human personality. The Judeo-Christian tradition has thus helped the West to acquire the liberal humanism it values so highly. . . . Yet a personal God can become a grave liability. He can be a mere idol carved in our own image, a projection of our limited needs, fears and desires. We can assume that he loves what we love and hates what we hate, endorsing our prejudices instead of compelling us to transcend them. When he seems to fail to prevent a catastrophe or seems even to desire a tragedy, he can seem callous and cruel. (209–10)

Armstrong also recognizes the fact that "All religions change and develop. If they do not, they will become obsolete" (84). In showing how the "mystical experience of God has certain characteristics that are common to all faiths" (219), she demonstrates the continuity between medieval mystics and the spirituality of twentieth-century thinkers such as Albert Einstein, who affirmed the compatibility of mysticism and science. She then quotes Einstein on religious belief: "To know that what is impenetrable to us really exists, manifesting itself to us as the highest wisdom and the most radiant beauty, which our dull faculties can comprehend only in their most primitive forms— this knowledge, this feeling, is at the center of all true religiousness. In this sense, and in this sense only, I belong to the ranks of devoutly religious men" (338). And Armstrong captures the contradictions of those who have lost their faith but who nevertheless remain devoted to God, as when she tells the story of a group of Jews in Auschwitz who decided to put God on trial. "They charged him with cruelty and betrayal. Like Job, they found no consolation in the usual answers to the problem of evil and suffering in the midst of this current obscenity. They could find no excuse for God, no extenuating circumstances, so they found him guilty and, presumably, worthy of death. The Rabbi pronounced the verdict. Then he looked up and said that the trial was over: it was time for the evening prayer" (376).

If I had had more time, I would also have discussed the book my dear friend Jerry Eckstein is writing, "An Old Man Contemplates Genesis," a commentary on the Pentateuch, the first five books of the Old Testament. Originally titled "An Atheist's Bible" (a title I prefer), the book explores the many contradictions, inconsistencies, ambiguities, and gaps in the Old Testament. Raised by ultra-Orthodox parents, Jerry lost his faith in a God that would allow the Holocaust to occur. Shortly before he was to be ordained as a rabbi, he felt he could not go through the process and decided instead to pursue a Ph.D. in philosophy, which he received from Columbia University. He spent most of his career teaching at the University at Albany, where he created the Judaic Studies Department, retiring in his midseventies. Jerry remains an atheist while at the same time acknowledging that Judaism is an essential part of his identity. He offers a powerful explanation of how an atheist can believe in the golden rule: "Atheists as much as believers require the Golden Rule, emotionally and politically. All who experience metaphysical loneliness need the Golden Rule, whether or not they are of the same race or species. A meaningless universe cries out for mutual love at least as much as God and a common origin do." Jerry is not what John Dewey called a "dogmatic atheist," one who is not open to rational argument and who is certain that God does not exist. A dogmatic atheist, Jerry writes, "is not merely biased— we are all biased, individually inclined toward positions—but he or she is prejudiced—prejudging positions with finality and without regard to evidence. I trust that such is not my way of atheism."

Jerry has written several books on Plato (his favorite writer), philosophy, love, and the meanings of life, writings that have influenced my own thinking. His close analysis of the Old Testament reveals a God who is neither omniscient, omnipotent, nor fair. "God's grace is unjust. That some are favored through no merit of their own while others are not thus favored, or are even disfavored, is an injustice experienced in most families with more than one child and in all societies. Even God favored Abel over Cain, without the Torah mentioning merit." Where is God's justice, Jerry asks, in creating a universe in which both nature and nurture continue to play favorites? Elsewhere in his book Jerry writes: "The problem of God's injustice arises throughout history and many times in the Bible, from Adam and Eve to Job. It is a main argument against the belief in an omnipotent and omniscient God who is absolutely just or absolutely merciful." Unlike many atheists who fail to apprehend the mystery of creation, Jerry sees mystery everywhere. "Why *this* universe? That is the penultimate question. Why anything at all, and not absolute nothingness? That is the ultimate unknowable" (emphasis in original).

A postmodernist before the term was coined, Jerry knows that no reading can be objective and that an interpretation may often reveal more about the interpreter than the object of interpretation. He is fond of quoting an observation by the late seventeenth-century Jewish philosopher Spinoza: "What Peter says of Paul tells us more about Peter than about Paul." He also reminds us of the wry insight of Xenophanes, the ancient Greek philosopher (sixth century BCE): "Mortals suppose that the gods are born (as they themselves are) and that they wear man's clothing and have human voice and body. . . . If cattle or lions had hands, . . . they would paint their gods and give them bodies in form like their own—horses like horses, cattle like cattle." A linguist as well as a philosopher and literary critic, Jerry argues against the fundamentalist position that Scripture's meaning is unambiguously available, and he cites the extremist view held by the teachers at his Yeshiva where he was educated as a youth: "If one letter of the Torah is false, then the entire Torah is false." He shows how throughout history the meanings of biblical words have changed, along with biblical customs and rituals; hence, he disagrees with fundamentalists who assert that they have an "infallible" understanding of the "inerrant" Bible. "Christianity, Islam, and Judaism have each undergone fundamental changes since their inception. To mention but one example: Although keeping the seventh day as the Sabbath is the Fourth of the Ten Commandments (Exodus 20: 8–11; Deuteronomy 5: 14–15), and although Jesus, his disciples, and the early Christians kept the seventh day as the Sabbath, Christianity, for the most part, later changed it to the first day." Jerry has taught me so much throughout our twenty-year friendship. Before I met him, for example, I often used the words "of course" in my teaching and writing. Now I am reminded of his caveat whenever I find myself becoming dogmatic about an interpretation: "I believe as a rule that when language like *of course, must, surely, stands to reason*, etc. is used, the matter is, at the least, questionable."

I wonder what will happen during our next class, when we end our discussion of the Book of Job and begin C. S. Lewis's *A Grief Observed*, which also questions the existence of undeserved suffering. I'm going to call the dean of student affairs to report Raymond's disruptive behavior and alert the administration to a situation that might become violent. I have never before reported a student for disciplinary action, and I feel uncomfortable doing so now. I don't want Raymond expelled from school, but neither do I want a replay of what happened last class. When I called Raymond to tell him that I wanted to speak to him in my office before the next class, I heard his voice with the following message on his telephone answering machine: "In the name of Jesus of Nazarus be loosed, In the name of Jesus Christ be set free." And his email address is "faithfulservantofGod." Next Monday's class should be interesting.

Monday, February 27

I spoke with the dean of student affairs this morning. He told me that I should ask Raymond to leave if he is again disruptive in class and that I should call the campus police if he refuses to leave. Today, for the first time, I brought my cell phone to class in case I needed to use it. Raymond did not show up. After class I received an email from the dean. "I'm dealing with Raymond on an unrelated issue right now. He may not be here much longer." [He never did return to class.]

Today I discussed the most common grammatical and stylistic problems in the eulogies. Many students still have problems with comma splices—and others now use semicolons when they should use commas. I've noticed this problem whenever I teach punctuation. Another common grammatical error was lack of agreement between noun and pronouns, especially with singular words such as "each" and "every." I'll use part of Wednesday's class to complete our discussion of Job.

Today's Love and Loss class proved uneventful, but I was startled this afternoon by an event in my Expository Writing course. We were doing the letters-to-and-from a parent assignment, which always produces emotionally charged essays, as I have observed both in *Risky Writing* and *Empathic Teaching*. I told my students that if anyone started to cry while reading his or her letters aloud, I would finish reading them, and that if I started to cry, as happened in the spring of 2001, then I would ask a classmate to complete the reading. I then said that my most memorable class occurred exactly twenty-three months ago, when I read aloud to my Expository Writing students my eulogy for Barbara, who was close to death. As soon as I said Barbara's name, the lights in the classroom suddenly went out, leaving us in the dark for about thirty seconds. Everyone was speechless. And then the lights went on. I know that for the past two years the classroom lights in the Humanities Building have been connected to a motion sensor. The lights automatically go out after a certain amount of time has occurred without motion, and they go back on when the sensor detects motion. But this is the first time that the lights have gone off while I was teaching. It's easy to explain why the lights went off, but it's harder to explain why they went off precisely when I mentioned Barbara's name—and then mysteriously went on again despite the fact that there was no motion in the classroom. (All of us were seated.) I was so startled that I choked up as I said, "I don't believe in signs from the dead; I don't believe in signs from the dead; I don't believe in signs from the dead." I looked around and noticed that I was not the only person who was teary-eyed. Afterward I thought of Hamlet's words to Horatio, "There are more things in heaven and earth than are dreamt of in your philosophy."

Wednesday, March 1

I began class today by making a few more observations about the Book of Job. Stephen Mitchell remarks in his translation that one of the "milder paradoxes that shape this greatest Jewish work of art is that its hero is a Gentile. Its author may have been as well. We know nothing about him, nothing about his world; he is even more anonymous than Homer." What makes the story particularly Jewish, Mitchell continues, is the theme of victimization. "This is what makes Job the central parable of our post-Holocaust age, and gives such urgency to its deep spiritual power" (vii). There is a vast body of commentary on the Book of Job, including Jack Kahn's psychological interpretation of Job's "illness," which emphasizes the dynamics of loss, grief, and integration. There are also intriguing feminist implications of the story. We don't learn the names of Job's seven new sons, his "replacement children," but we do learn the names of his three new daughters. Despite the fact that the Book of Job, like the rest of the Old Testament and the New Testament, is patriarchal, this last detail—along with the fact that Job gave his daughters an inheritance—is surprisingly feminist. I concluded with an observation by Moshe Greenberg: "The case of Job is a stern warning never to infer sin from suffering (the error of the Friends), or the enmity of God toward the sufferer (the error of Job). Although such a harmonization may offer some consolation to Job-like suffering, it is not spelled out in the book. With its ironies and surprises, its claims and arguments in unresolved tension, the Book of Job remains the classic expression in world literature of the irrepressible yearning for divine order, baffled but never stifled by the disarray of reality" (301).

I never thought about applying Elisabeth Kübler-Ross's stage theory of dying to the Book of Job until I read Richard's diary entry:

> How we put the dying process into form is something very interesting, poetic too! Plath's poem "Daddy" is a narrative shaped around how she dealt with her father's death. Which stage would Plath then fit? Anger and depression? The Book of Job is certainly a story centering around number 2—Job's anger at God. I was impressed to hear that only one-third of the students believed they could read Job objectively; it seems students have embraced postmodernity. I wonder what this does for their belief system as conservatives always fight against this state of mind. The students aren't overly questioning, which is what I would associate with postmodern ideals. Perhaps they aren't as critical in their thinking as they pretend.
>
> I also wonder if the students will be able to appreciate how Job moves beyond his anger to his acceptance of a possibly cruel God. I can't, but that's because I'm distressed about the children and wife that Job lost when God kills them. They cannot be replaced, even if they are replicated in the narrative's "happy ending." This seems Jeff's point: we cannot replace what is original. This is a fiction of loss no matter how we might want to believe that symmetry may be reached, justice done, or acceptance achieved. Wholeness or holiness is forever in question because we cannot know death.

After completing the story, I mentioned the two different conceptions of death in the Old and New Testament and quoted from Jacques Choron's book *Death and Western Thought*. "It would be vain to seek in the Old Testament comfort and consolation for the fact of death in terms of belief in immortality" (81). Choron adds that despite the fact that some scholars have found hints of immortality in certain Old Testament passages, including Job, the dominant view is expressed in Ecclesiastes: "Go thy way, eat thy bread with joy, and drink thy wine with a merry heart; for God now accepteth thy works. . . . Whatsoever thy hand findeth to do, do it with thy might; for there is no work, nor device, nor knowledge, nor wisdom, in the grave whither thou goest" (81). By contrast, Choron asserts, the "New Testament proclaims victory over death. The essence of the answer to the problem of death in the New Testament is that death is the last and greatest enemy, but that this enemy is already conquered. The Christian doctrine teaches the resurrection of the dead on the Last Day of Judgment. The graves will be opened, saint and sinner will stand before the Son of God and be judged. It is the resurrection of the body, and not the immortality of the soul; this latter is not Christian, but pagan" (84). Choron quotes Gilbert Murray's observation that audiences initially mocked Saint Paul's insistence on the resurrection of the body. "They were familiar with the doctrine of the immortality of the soul, but when this eloquent Asiatic tent-maker began to explain that the dead bodies would get up and walk, they could not take him seriously" (84).

In the remaining minutes of class, I read aloud selections from Mark Twain's satirical study *Letters from the Earth,* an iconoclastic work that made a great impression on me from the moment I read it as an undergraduate. "The two Testaments are interesting, each in its own way," Twain writes with disarming earnestness. "The Old one gives us a picture of these people's Deity as he was before he got religion, the other one gives us a picture of him as he appeared afterward. The Old Testament is interested mainly in blood and sensuality. The New One in Salvation. Salvation by fire" (44). The first time the Deity came to earth, Twain continues, he brought death—a merciful end to life's many tortures. Soon the Deity perceived that he had made a mistake— "a mistake, in that it was insufficient; insufficient, for the reason that while it was an admirable agent for the inflicting of misery upon the survivor, it allowed the dead person himself to escape from all further persecution in the blessed refuge of the grave" (44). Recognizing that a way must be contrived to pursue the dead beyond the tomb, the Deity pondered this question for four thousand years and then came up with a solution: he invented the concept of hell. "Now here is a curious thing. It is believed by everybody that while he was in heaven he was stern, hard, resentful, jealous, and cruel; but that when he came down to earth and assumed the name Jesus Christ, he became the opposite of what he was before: that is to say, he became sweet, and gentle, merciful, forgiving, and all harshness disappeared from his nature and a deep and yearning love for his poor human children took its place. Whereas it was as Jesus Christ that he devised hell and proclaimed it!" (45).

I had decided to read selections from *Letters from the Earth* last spring, when I began to select the reading list for Love and Loss. I wonder how Raymond would have responded had he remained in the course. I'm glad that he has stopped coming to class, but I'm disappointed that his absence probably means he was suspended or expelled from the university.

～

How did our class discussion of the Book of Job affect my students? The best way to answer this question would be to ask students to write an essay exploring the reader-response implications of the story. I could have done this as an in-class writing assignment, but it would take up an entire class, which I was reluctant to do. We were already falling behind in the reading. And so I decided to ask the students whether they were in favor of allowing me to change the format of the midterm exam. I had told them on the first day of the semester that the midterm exam would be "objective": they would need to identify quotations from the various texts on the syllabus. I knew from many years' experience that some students do well on such short-answer exams but that others do poorly. The main value of this type of exam was that it would require them to read carefully the texts on the syllabus. It would also be easy for me to grade. By contrast, reader-response questions would require far more effort from them and me, but I thought it would have more educational value for everyone. The new format, if the students agreed to the change, would ask them to write on three out of four essay questions. (Everyone had to write on the Book of Job.) It would be a take-home exam, each question being two to three pages long, typed, double-spaced. Since the essay questions I wanted to ask do not have right or wrong answers, I would be grading less on content than on the quality of writing. The idea of reading 360 to 540 pages of midterms was daunting, but I was willing to use this format if they were. Everyone agreed to the change. I gave them the question on the Book of Job as soon as we completed our discussion so that they would remember how the story affected them:

> Discuss three different moments in the Book of Job that challenge your own religious belief (or disbelief). Quote one or two lines (but no more) from each of these three moments in the story and explain how they challenge your own thinking on the subject. To what extent did you find yourself thinking about other biblical chapters that agreed or disagreed with these moments? (It's not a problem if you don't answer this question.) Do you believe that our discussion of Job will permanently influence your religious belief? If so, in what way?

Two students remarked that what they would most remember from the story was not something I had planned. "I do believe that our discussion of the Book of Job will have a permanent influence, if not on my religious beliefs, then on the way in which I view religious texts," wrote Sara, and she then elaborated on how the incident with Raymond affected her thinking:

> It proved to me that many individuals cannot divorce the study of religious texts from their beliefs or acknowledge the benefit of affirming their own biases and working in full knowledge of them. I will be profoundly influenced by having watched a young man hurl insults at his professor out of some benighted inability to welcome new ideas and advances in any text. My own religious belief has a very small part in the Book of Job, and it is due to that ignorant and short-sighted display of emotion in the classroom that I recognize its smallness. Although this text is a useful tool, to some extent, in examining my own religious beliefs, the discussion of the text proved far more useful in affirming one particular disbelief: that religious texts are not whole, immaculate and freed from interpretation. To prevent discussion of a biblical passage out of some misused sense of faith is as detrimental to the study of literature in general, and literature of loss in particular, as it would be to stunt the discussion of any other text. I know that if I study or teach other religious texts in the future, I will engage purposefully in the dual activities of relating the passages to my own beliefs while distancing myself in order to study them as literature.

Anna also commented on this incident, seeing it as an example of growing religious intolerance around the world:

> It is difficult for me to think about our class discussion without thinking about the outburst from a student. I was so struck by what he said, and what other students said after he left, that I wrote much of it down in my notebook. The boy was a proud Christian. He called Jeff a "false prophet." "You haven't read MY Bible," he exclaimed, with a maddened look in his eyes. The other students were silent until he left the classroom. Small bursts of laughter escaped the mouths of nervous students, and one girl responded that he was a "bad example of a Christian." But I wondered if that was true. On one level, he is exactly what I think of when I hear the word "Christian." I imagine the people gathered in front of the Planned Parenthood on Lark Street in Albany, clutching their antiabortion signs and praying for the souls of the women who receive affordable health care. I recall a man I saw in my childhood, walking down a busy street, wearing a board that listed all the people "Jesus hates," including lesbians, gays, and punk rockers. At the time, I was confused because I had learned that Jesus loved, and he did not hate, and that's why everyone wanted to act like him.
>
> On another level, perhaps the student felt like a martyr. In the face of what he presumed to be an adversary, he was vocalizing what he believed in, at the expense of making a scene. If he felt that God was not being taken seriously, I

suppose it is his job to say so, to point it out for all the others. Shouldn't other Christians do the same? Is that what Jesus would have done?

Other students were disturbed by the story itself. Many of those who identified themselves as religious were threatened by a gambling deity who is willing to destroy a man's family as a test of religious faith. "Being a Catholic," writes Jean, "I found a great deal of the Book of Job upsetting and challenging. The image of God that is portrayed in the Old Testament appears to be radically different from the image that I have shaped him to be through religious school and stories told through my church and family. I am confused as to the true 'personality' that God embodies. Is it the gentle and loving God that I have always believed him to be or the dark and unsympathetic God who presents himself to Job?" She was "appalled" when she read about God's wager with Satan. "In this passage, he is taunting Satan into action, wanting to test his own power over his faithful servant Job." Jean adds that she had planned to read the Bible in its entirety, but now she is reluctant to do so, afraid of what she may find. "I would hate to realize the image of a kind and paternal God that I have held in my heart for so long is a false vision." After giving other examples of how the story challenges her beliefs, she implies that a little learning is a dangerous thing. "I found that I prefer my ignorance on biblical texts, rather than reading them and questioning my beliefs. I have never considered the bible to be the 'word of God.' It has been translated and changed over countless centuries, therefore I find it to be from an unknown source. However, I am disturbed to see how God is revealed to the reader of the Old Testament, making him appear almost fearful and almost dangerous. I am certain that this reading will stay with me for a long period of time, although I refuse to allow it to sway my personal vision of God."

Others also wrote that they refused to allow the story to undermine their faith in God. Krystal revealed that only a week earlier she found herself unexpectedly in Job's situation:

> After Job had been cursed with boils and sores from his head to his toes, his wife remarks, "Dost thou still hold fast thine integrity? Renounce God, and die." I am not extremely religious but that does not mean I find the renouncement of my faith in god and death as a solution to misfortune. I believe that god has a greater plan in mind for everyone. It was not until about a week ago that I believed this. My mother had a heart attack that was accompanied with a multitude of other medical problems. I realized despite my tears, confusion, and anger that my mother's sudden illness was not in my hands. I was so angry that something this horrible could happen to my mother; she is the most genuine person I have ever met. I did not think to curse God because she was sick. That is not the answer; instead I put my faith in God and let him show us how things were meant to be.

My mother is now out of the hospital and has been given a second chance. Aside from her living a healthier lifestyle my sister and my father became much closer. A bond that never existed before my mother got sick. My sister held a grudge against my father for something that occurred two years ago. This was the event that shook that distrust and resentment. I know now that my answer was not to reject god and become hostile but to allow him to execute his own plans.

Reading about Job's story also disturbed Cyana. "I am a very devoted believer of God and I have complete faith in what He does and the challenges He makes us face to test our belief in Him. However there were three different moments in the story that challenged my own religious belief." One of these moments was when Job's wife tells him to renounce God and die. "If I was in her position, watching my husband suffer such great losses and then have to suddenly endure such physical harm would have been devastating to me as well. I would be thinking that God is punishing Job for no reason because Job is strongly devoted to Him and fears Him. As I write this paper, I have come to the definite conclusion that Job's wife's reaction could possibly be one of the reactions I would have taken. I believe God does test His believers because He can but to put such an innocent soul through such great misery is not fair. My eyes are becoming watery as I write this because I can only imagine how Job must have felt. It is just a horrible thing to do from God's part and I love my God but it is just plain terrible."

Three other women wrote about past or present crises in which their religious faith has been tested. Each believed she has passed God's test. "Bad things can happen in life," Breanna writes, "but, it is up to us, I believe, how we handle the situation" [see appendix B]. Esther wrote about how Job's wish for God to crush him reminded her of the time she almost abandoned her faith as a result of her boyfriend's near-fatal motorcycle accident. "I was sad when I read that Job had given up and wished for death. Although I can't begin to imagine what kind of anguish he was in, I feel like we are not allowed to give up on God. This passage made me think of a time in my life when I was so mad at God I wished I would die too, even though it was only for a moment I gave up on Him." After visiting her boyfriend at the hospital, she drove home in a driving rain. "I was crying so hard I couldn't see the road through the tears and the windshield wipers but I didn't pull over and I didn't put my seatbelt on. I didn't care whether I made it home or not and I was screaming at God and asking him 'Why?' I don't know how I made it home but I know God guided me there because all along God was planning on restoring my boyfriend's health and healing him into an almost full recovery. But I did lose my faith in a moment of seemingly great loss and this passage struck home for me about that." Carly identified with Job's question, "Why am I always suffering, when I have done nothing wrong":

There is not a day when this question doesn't enter my mind. Dealing with my grandmother's disease is like having it too. My mother is at her apartment six days out of the week. She is there exactly at 4:30 pm and if she is there five minutes late my grandmother will call me on my cell asking where my mom is. Saturday at 4 pm is the day that she gives her a shower. She doesn't get home until 8 pm. Then either my brother or my father goes at 9 pm to put her into bed. My duty is on Sundays, the only day that I have free. Of course it's hard on the four of us but the real person who is suffering is my grandmother. We are not on oxygen 24/7, we do not have a problem going to the bathroom, and we do not have a problem eating our food, she does. Our problem is that we feel like we are constantly being tested by God. The comfort I feel is that someday, God will reward me.

Some students were disturbed less by God's actions than by Job's. "The disquieting part for me," writes Elijah, "is how Job seems unfazed by his family loss toward the end of the story and is totally fine with the new family he gets at the end of the story. I know what it is like to lose a loved one and there is no way I could simply 'replace' them the way Job did. The only rationalization I could come up with was that perhaps Job put his love for God above all things. Maybe in his mind family counted as a worldly attachment and his love and relationship with God comes before that. Unfortunately that conclusion does not match up very well with a man who was ready to throw in the towel as far as God was concerned when he lost all of his things and began to suffer." I must admit that I had never seen this possibility before—that Job's attachment to God was greater than his attachment to his family, a value judgment I could never imagine making for myself. This is why I could never agree with Abraham's willingness to obey God's commandment to slay Isaac in Genesis. Elijah concludes his discussion by conceding he still has difficulty accepting the implications of Job's story. "As a reader it is very difficult to discern what one should learn from the Book of Job. Human lives are likened to a dice game and apparently bad things happen to good people simply because of God's pride. Although this book of the bible is meant to help readers build on their faith, for me it makes me question my beliefs and the intentions of God."

Reading the Book of Job heightened the religious skepticism of those already inclined toward disbelief. "We learn in the epilogue that 'the Lord gave Job twice as much as he had before,'" writes Chad. "This absolutely puzzles me. God only does right toward Job after Job renounces his faith. This, to me, seems like God is apologizing for doing wrong. But how could God, the highest authority, ever do any wrong? This is a contradiction in itself. I cannot put my faith into a God that makes mistakes, as he did with Job. This section of the story also shows that God rewards the people who question his supremacy. I do not believe in God; therefore, is it not possible that I could be rewarded for challenging him in my own way? Even for an atheistic person like me, the Book of Job did affect me. I never had a reason to not believe in God or religion, but this story gives me one. Discussing Job in class opened my eyes to the evils and paradoxes in religion and will influence my beliefs until I have reason to think otherwise. I cannot trust an indifferent God, nor should I. Analyzing the Book of Job has pushed me farther away from a religion that I already did not believe in."

Chad's classmates who shared his religious disbelief seemed to find Job's story less disturbing than those with strong faith. "The contradictions between the Book of Job and the lesson I learned during religion class seem to provide another crack in an already crumbling foundation of religious beliefs," admits Kelly. "I believe our discussion of this text will forever influence me because it addressed the quiet questions that were already popping up in my head. It allowed me to confront my doubts, and while I do not have the answers to my questions, it is comforting to know I am not the only one with doubts." Chuck also felt comforted. "Job was rewarded for being a good man, not for having strong faith. His 'friends,' on the contrary, were punished for having faith in only their religious teachings rather than in Job. If God is kind enough to forgive and reward Job after he had lost faith, then I am hopeful that I will be forgiven my doubt."

I'm glad that I taught the Book of Job, and I intend to have my students read it the next time I teach Love and Loss. I cannot recall another story that raises such age-old questions. Is there a reason for suffering? How do we respond to our own or another person's loss? Is God benevolent, indifferent, malevolent, or nonexistent? Each reader will answer these questions differently. It is naive to assume that we can approach the Bible as literature without being influenced by our religious beliefs. The subtitle of the edition I used, "Designed to Be Read as Living Literature," edited by Ernest Sutherland Bates, underestimates readers' difficulty in suspending their beliefs or disbeliefs. Although a few students predicted the story would permanently affect their religious views, most felt it would not. "I feel that beliefs as strong as religion and faith cannot be altered easily. These beliefs are deeply embedded in us and have probably not changed too much since childhood." I agree.

Nevertheless, a frank and open discussion of a story such as the Book of Job allows readers to test the strength of their convictions. I believe—and this is my credo as a teacher—that intellectual doubt is healthy, reflective of an open mind. This theme may also be found not only in Job's story but also throughout the Jewish tradition, for doubt is necessary for faith. Reading Job's story was reassuring for some students, disillusioning for others, challenging for others, infuriating for still others. Regardless of whether they found it provocative or provoking, nearly everyone found it engaging. For better or worse, Job's story will become increasingly relevant to students as they grow older and find themselves tested in ways they cannot yet imagine.

5

⁓

Writing on Religion and Death

Monday, March 6

I read an article in this week's issue of the *Chronicle of Higher Education* (10 March 2006) that relates directly to our third writing assignment. Amy Rainey observes in "Professors Favor Building Moral Values in Students" that 81 percent of academics consider themselves spiritual while 64 percent call themselves religious. According to a survey conducted by the Higher Education Research Institute at the University of California at Los Angeles, 62 percent of college juniors reported that their professors "never encouraged discussions of spirituality and 56 percent said their professors had never provided the opportunity to discuss the meaning of life." The director of the institute, Alexander Astin, remarked that "this is an area of the student's life that we've been neglecting . . . and where we ought to be putting a lot more attention both in the curriculum and co-curriculum." He also recommended that "faculty members encourage students to become more self-reflective through writing and class discussions." Until this writing assignment, I have rarely asked my students to discuss their religious beliefs. I guess it took Barbara's death to teach me that such assignments are valuable, even for those who like myself lack religious faith. Based on the survey's broad definition of spirituality—"a generic idea involving making sense and meaning out of our lives"—I would include myself with 81 percent of my fellow academics.

Today I summarized the class's response to the religion-and-death essay. The assignment was due last Wednesday:

> Your next writing assignment is on the topic "how your religious beliefs or disbeliefs influence your attitude toward death." Your essay should be, like the first two writing assignments, three pages long. Make sure it is as well written as possible! Try to respond to as many of the following questions as possible. Do you believe in God and a hereafter (such as heaven and hell)? Do you believe that

there is a religious reason for suffering? If so, how do you explain the deaths of innocent people (such as children)? Do you believe that God rewards good people and punishes evil people? How did you acquire your religious beliefs or disbeliefs? Have you ever been in a religious crisis? Is it helpful or harmful to question one's religious beliefs? Finally, is it helpful or harmful to discuss one's religious beliefs with other people?

Since I had expressed my disbelief in God during our discussion of Job, ending the previous class by reading aloud Mark Twain's scathing denunciation of organized religion, I decided to highlight those essays that revealed strong religious faith. In that way I would demonstrate my openness to points of view sharply different from my own. My intention was neither to encourage nor discourage religious belief among my students but to help them clarify their own beliefs. Though I do not believe in the power of prayer, I always expressed gratitude to the people who told us they were praying for Barbara's recovery. That religion offered me no consolation does not mean that I wish to deprive others of whatever comfort they may derive from the belief in God and a hereafter. Near the end of her life, I heard Barbara tell her father that they would be together again, and while I don't know whether she believed that or was telling him what he wanted to hear, I suspect that religious faith would have eased her terror of dying. As Studs Terkel notes, "Invariably, those who have a faith, whether it is called religious or spiritual, have an easier time with loss. They find solace in believing there is something after—that they will in some way, in some form, again meet or even merge with the departed one. Nonbelievers have no such comfort. They go with Gertrude Stein's observation in another context: 'There is no there there.' Nada" (xix).

Two of the essays I read aloud, written by Dean and Jean, reveal "signs from the dead," incidents difficult to describe because the writers know their classmates and teacher may have trouble believing them. Except for the time that the classroom lights went out when I mentioned Barbara's name in my Expository Writing class—a phenomenon that, unhappily, occurred so often during the next few days that it lost its meaning for me—I have never experienced anything that I would consider supernatural. Nevertheless, I'm fascinated when I hear about stories that defy rational explanation. Belle's story of religious conversion intrigues me. I'm struck by the quiet heroism of a young caregiver like Carly, who is forced to make a daily sacrifice that many of her peers cannot fathom. And I'm moved when I hear about people like Sara, who must cope with a life-transforming illness.

The following five students explore the ways in which their religious beliefs influence their attitudes toward death. All five writers describe themselves as religious, and, except for Sara, who was diagnosed with a serious illness that has called into question aspects of her faith, they affirm the existence of God and heaven. They also intimate that the dead are guardian angels who "watch over" the living. My students' religious views are far more representative of most Americans' views than are my own. Sam Harris reports, for example, that a 1996 Gallup poll found that "35 percent of Americans believe that the Bible is the literal and inerrant word of the Creator of the universe. Another 48 percent believe that it is the 'inspired' word of the same—still inerrant, though certain of its passages must be interpreted symbolically before their truth can be brought to life. Only 17 percent of us remain to doubt that a personal God, in his infinite wisdom, is likely to have authored this text—or, for that matter, to have created the earth with its 250,000 species of beetles" (17). [In a poll reported in the 11 September 2006 issue of *Newsweek*, "Americans said they believed in God by a margin of 92 [to] 6—only 2 percent answered 'don't know.'"] I found the five essays poignant and heartfelt, and I read selections from each of them to the class. I offered no commentary afterward, so that the writers' classmates could reach their own conclusions about what they heard. The first essay I read aloud was by Dean, who had written earlier about being a "miracle child":

Dean: "I Know That My Family Is Watching Over Me"

My religious beliefs strongly influence my attitude toward death in a positive way. This is due to the fact that my family is religious, and prayer played a crucial role in me being alive today. On May 15, 1985, my mother was shocked when she went into labor three months premature. I was born weighing only two pounds. After being in the hospital for two and a half weeks, my health continued to deteriorate. The neonatal doctor told my mother that I was bleeding internally due to my intestines shedding.

He said there was nothing he could do to help me, and it was out of his hands. He told my parents to go home and rest up, and prepared them for my inevitable death. My parents fought hard to bring me into this world, and they were going to do everything in their power to make sure that I survived. My mother contacted my religious great-grandmother and informed her of my health. My great-grandmother then proceeded to contact all of her friends and held an all-night vigil praying for my health. My mother likewise did the same, and prayed all night hoping that she would not lose her only son.

At around 7 pm, the phone rang and my mother tiredly answered it. It was the doctor; my mother anticipated that she was receiving the phone call every parent prays they never get. She was prepared to hear the doctor tell her that her only son was dead. Instead, in a cheerful tone the doctor told her that her son was completely healthy and hungry. The doctor himself claimed that I was a miracle, and he did not know how the bleeding stopped. Due to this inauspicious start to my life, I am a very religious person.

Other events have happened in my life since then which reaffirmed to me the fact that there is an afterlife, and I will be reunited with my family and friends once I die. I don't know what the afterlife is exactly, but I know that my family is watching over me. I never met my great-grandmother and have only seen one picture of her. Yet one morning something amazing and inexplicable happened. I awoke and saw a woman standing near my closet. Her back was to me, but she had a long brown robe on and her hair was up in a bun. I was tired so I looked at her, assumed it was my mother, and went back to sleep.

Later on that morning, my mom came in and woke me up for school. Puzzled, I asked why she had returned to my room. I told her that I had seen her in my room earlier in the morning. I then proceeded to describe the person that was standing near my closet. My mother's mouth dropped, and she then told me that when my great-grandma died, she was buried in a long brown Franciscan robe, and her hair was in a bun. My great-grandmother prayed continuously to make sure I stayed alive, and it seems that even in death she is still watching over me. This is comforting, and makes me realize that death is not the end.

A few years ago my cousin's grandmother died. This woman was a saint and it was tough to lose her. I was not related to her but she treated me just like one of her own grandchildren. I attended her funeral but did not attend the wake so I didn't know what she looked like when she was buried. A couple of weeks after the funeral, I woke up early one morning. There was a woman standing by my door with a beautiful red gown on. I couldn't make out the face, I believe it was blurred but at the time I felt a sense of calmness. I didn't think how weird it was to see something like this. I acknowledged it, then went back to sleep.

Later that day, I mentioned the encounter with my mother. Yet again I managed to astonish her. The dress I described was exactly what my cousin's grandmother had worn when she was buried. I have told these stories to many people. Some believe what I have said and others are skeptical. I know what I saw, and am grateful to have family that loves and watches over me even in death.

I do believe that everyone gets tested in life, and in the end good people will be rewarded in heaven. My fear of not making it to heaven is what guides my decisions in life. I try my best to be as good as I can, so I can enjoy a glorious afterlife. This is evident in my mission trips to Cuba and the Dominican Republic and many other church-related events.

One of my favorite topics of conversation is religious beliefs. I could sit and talk for hours about religion and its theories. I am a Catholic, but I consider myself a modified Catholic. I am open minded, and love listening to new opinions. The most recent opinion came from reading *The Da Vinci Code* and hearing all the controversy related to that book. While at school, I have befriended many people who are skeptical about religion. I love sitting them down and having long talks with them. These talks involve mentioning my birth and other unbelievable stories which have occurred during my life time. I'm not trying to convert them to my religion, but I want them to hear firsthand accounts of how religion has affected my life.

Most of these people appreciate my talks and have become more open minded about religion and the thought of an afterlife. I think most people want to believe that there is an afterlife. Who would not want to be reunited with their loved ones whom they thought they have lost forever? Now instead of mourning the loss of loved ones, people can now think of an eternity that they will be spending together with them.

"Wow," I wrote on my copy of Dean's essay; the word describes how I felt about the paper then and now. I believe in medical miracles without invoking the power of the supernatural, but it is difficult for me to believe that the dead *literally* visit the living. Nor do I believe that the dead watch over the living. Yet I tried to suspend my disbelief while reading Dean's essay, embracing what the poet John Keats calls negative capability: "That is when man is capable of being in uncertainties, Mysteries, doubts, without any irritable reaching after fact & reason" (261). Dean knows that people will not easily believe the eerie stories he tells them, yet he is not unduly disturbed by this. Perhaps he would disbelieve these experiences had they not happened to him. He mentions toward the end of the essay that he is "open minded" and loves listening to "new opinions." He asks his readers to be similarly open minded. Regardless of whether one believes in the supernatural, there is little doubt that Dean's faith comforts him. His conviction of an eternal afterlife enables him to see death as a prelude to everlasting life.

Jean: "I Feel That My Religion Has Given Me Guidance in Times of Darkness"

My entire family is Catholic. In each family member's house you will find at least one crucifix on the wall with prayer cards, church donation cards, and the Bible. There is always one religious icon present in a household, and every member of my family wears gold crosses around their necks. My Catholic upbringing is present in every aspect of my life. Even in my college dorm room, I have rosary beads hanging over my bed with several prayer cards.

When I was younger, I did not appreciate religion. Church was a punishment that occurred every Sunday. Being dragged from my warm bed and having to dress up merely to sit in an uncomfortable pew for an hour made Sunday the worst day of the week. I also attended religious schooling until the sixth grade. I received my confirmation, not realizing what it meant. I was thrilled to wear a delicate white dress and walk past everyone in the church, holding a candle. It was not until the death of my Dadzie, my mother's father, that I began to appreciate God.

I was kneeling before my Dadzie's coffin, alone in the room, I asked him if he could hear me. The flower arrangement of a cross which was beside me began to shake. It stopped as suddenly as it began. I asked, aloud, if the person moving the flowers was my Dadzie. It shook again. I walked around the area, believing there was a window open, or an air vent which was causing the movement. There was nothing near the flowers. For several minutes I kneeled before the coffin and thanked God for allowing me to speak with my Dadzie again. I believe with every inch of my soul that I was not alone in that room.

I am unsure whether it is stated in the Bible, but my family believes that when a person dies they walk the earth for forty days. In this time they try to get through to loved ones to tell them what they couldn't while they were alive. In my lifetime, several family members have passed away. Since I have truly accepted God into my life, I have received some sort of "message" from each of them. From my great aunt, there was knocking on my bed post until I spoke her name. When my grandma passed away, every day for months I saw the time 11:11 on the clock, which was the time she always told me to make a wish. The day that my uncle passed away was in the middle of finals, and my parents forbade me to come home for the funeral. Depressed and angry, my suite-mate dragged me out for a few drinks where I met my current boyfriend who I love dearly. I consider him a message from my uncle.

Although I am a Catholic and a true believer of God and spirits, I have brought my own feelings into my religion. I have, what my mother refers to, as "bended the rules." I do not believe the Bible is the true word of God; I believe a woman has a choice for abortion. I support gay marriages and the right to premarital sex. I believe in evolution; all the Bibles in the world cannot destroy the scientific evidence that proves otherwise. I do, however, believe that God was the one who initiated evolution. I don't agree for praying for things I can achieve for myself, such as higher test grades. I also don't believe there is a Hell. If Jesus died on the cross to forgive our sins, then I don't see why God would banish us to a place of fire and suffering for all of eternity. My mother does not agree with my views at all, and does not think that I am a "true believer."

Being a Catholic, along with my own belief that there is no Hell, makes death much easier to bear. I do not consider the person who has passed away as "gone forever." In my religion, we all see each other in Heaven when we die. Our parents, extended family, friends, maybe even pets, all are present to greet you when you arrive. I'm well aware of how juvenile that may sound. It's almost out of a Disney movie, everyone receives their "happily ever after-life." But given the choice between my "happily ever after-life" and knowing that I will never see any of my deceased loved ones, I would always choose the Disney version. I could not imagine myself being able to survive the grieving process of my own parents one day, knowing that there will never be another embrace between us. That would be the ultimate punishment: my own personal Hell. I do realize that there are religions that do not believe that there is a life after death. I cannot help but feel pity for them when they lose a loved one.

There are many ideas of the Catholic religion that I do not agree with. I am almost hesitant to call myself a Catholic. Since I have altered so many of my Catholic beliefs, I feel as if I would be lying to some extent. I am a true believer of God, however, and hold firm to my faith, especially in times of grief. I feel that my religion has given me guidance in times of darkness. Without the idea that when I die I will be able to see my parents and other departed loved ones, my view on life would drastically change. I do not believe I would ever be able to recover from a loss of a family member otherwise.

Jean believes, as does Dean, that the dead are still connected to and protective of the living, a belief that allows them to accept the idea of death. They also believe in reunion with the dead. The loss of religious faith would be unbearable—the "ultimate punishment: my own personal Hell." Given this belief, we can understand why faith is so important to her. Like most of her classmates who define themselves as believers, Jean disagrees with many aspects of her religion, and she appears untroubled by her mother's assertion that she has "bended the rules." For those who, like Jean and Dean, believe that the dead are still in contact with the living, death ceases to be terrifying and final. On the bottom of her paper I wrote, "I enjoyed reading your thoughtful and, at times, eerie essay, Jean." I then circled several grammatical errors, including a comma splice, a misplaced modifier, an incorrect agreement between noun and pronoun, and a "bended" verb.

Belle: "It Is Because of My Religious Beliefs That I Do Not Fear Death"

I will go to heaven when I die. I do not think, hope or believe I will go to Heaven; I know I will go to Heaven. I am saved. I accept Jesus Christ as my Lord and savior. Jesus Christ was crucified for my sins. I will go to heaven because of the grace of God, the blood Jesus shed on the cross for my sins, and my acceptance of him into my heart.

I do not fear death, nor do I worry about the day that it will come. I believe that this is because of my strong Christian faith. It is through my faith that I know what will happen to me when I die. This certainty provides me with an enormous amount of comfort. Without my strong religious convictions, I would fear death, and the uncertainty that is intertwined with death.

I have viewed death from several different standpoints during my life. As a child I was raised Catholic. I was taught in Sunday school that I was not guaranteed a place in heaven. I was told that I had to do good deeds and earn my way into heaven. When I died, I would be judged and sent to heaven, hell or purgatory, based on my actions in life. This left me scared. I never knew if I was going to spend eternity in bliss or would be tortured in the fiery pits of hell. I knew that I had to behave. If I wanted to go to heaven, I had to listen to my parents and the priests. I must confess my sins every week and be forgiven by the priest. As I got older, I began to reject these ideas and practices. I did not like the fact that I did not know what was going to happen when I died. I did not understand how the priests knew what was right and wrong. How did they know how to get into heaven and why could they forgive me for my sins?

As I became a teenager, I wavered between adamantly denying God and not knowing or caring one way or the other about his existence. I could not fathom that if there was a God he would not care if a person went to heaven or hell. My thought was that if there were a God that loved us, he would tell us how to enter his kingdom. If we were the children of God, why wouldn't he love us enough to let us be with him in paradise regardless of our behavior on earth? I had many reservations about a God like that. My reservations made me believe that he did not exist. I thought religion was just something people used to make themselves feel better about their lives. The idea of a God and heaven was just a very creative way to reason away earthly misery. I thought the people that subscribed to a God did so to make themselves feel better about themselves and to provide themselves with a false sense of security.

Then I went away to college. I drank to excess, I dressed provocatively and I stayed out late. I was the stereotypical college kid. Then I went to church. I wish I could say I went to get closer to God, but I did not believe he existed. I went to church because my boyfriend's family wanted me to go. Of course, I wanted to impress them so I put on a skirt and went to church. After service, I found there was something that I liked about it. So the following Sunday I used the excuse of wanting to impress his family to explain my desire to go to church again. Before the service, his grandmother told me how excited she was to see me at church again. As the pastor began to speak, he welcomed everyone. He said he wanted to welcome the new people and to let us know that God loves us and wants a relationship with us. As the service continued, I felt something. I eagerly listened to every word the pastor said. The music was lively, filled my heart and had a purpose. The purpose was to glorify God. Near the end of the service, the pastor told everyone to bow their heads and close their eyes. He then said a prayer. He asked people that wanted a relationship with Jesus to pray the prayer with him. I prayed the prayer with him, and began to cry. He then said that anyone that wanted to kneel before the Lord, to ask for guidance, forgiveness or help to come to the front of the church and kneel. I did.

From that moment on, I began to walk as a Christian. I sat with the pastor and his wife and we discussed all of my problems with God, organized religion and salvation. We spoke for hours. I pummeled them with question after question, trying to wear them down. For every question I asked, they showed me a Bible verse to support what they were saying. Of all the verses we went over that night, one stood apart. Ephesians 2:8–9 says, "For by grace are ye saved through faith; and that not of yourselves: it is the gift of God: Not of works, lest any man should boast." This verse answered my questions on salvation. God did make it easy for us to enter his kingdom. All we have to do is believe in him, and we are saved. We do good works to show God we love him, not so that we can enter heaven. As I read the Bible more, and began my walk as a Christian, more of my questions were answered. Priests do not have the ability to forgive me: they are sinners just like me. God is the only one that can forgive my sins.

  I am a born-again Christian. I am a fundamentalist Baptist. This does not mean that I stand in the street screaming at people, telling them they are going to hell. It does not mean that I cannot mix into the unsaved world. I am an example. I try to live a Godly life and be a light to people, both saved and unsaved. I want to help those that do not believe in Jesus as their savior to see the light. I have unsaved friends and saved friends. Being a fundamentalist Baptist means that the Bible is the untainted word of God. This belief allows me to know that I will go to heaven when I die. It is because of my religious beliefs that I do not fear death. I do not want to die, but I know that when I do I will sit at the right hand of the father (God) for all of eternity.

I can't imagine what it must be like to have the absolute religious faith that Belle describes. That's why I found her opening sentence so astonishing: "I will go to Heaven when I die." What must it be like to have such certitude, to have a belief system untouched by ambiguity? Most people need, even demand, certainty of knowledge. As Tennyson stated, "I would rather know I was to be damned eternally than not to know that I was to live eternally" (R. Martin, *Tennyson* 262). In his book *Meeting Movies*, Norman Holland observes that "all of us who are not fundamentalists have gradually accepted relativism to the point where it dominates the intellectual life of our time. . . . Relativism has been growing for ten decades until it has become the central intellectual paradigm of our century" (141). But there's not a hint of doubt, uncertainty, or ambivalence in Belle's fundamentalist world. As with Dean and Jean, her faith allows her to see death as a transition to eternal life. There is nothing supernatural about the experiences she describes, as there is in her two classmates' essays, and therefore I didn't need to suspend my disbelief in occult phenomena while reading her essay. But I marveled at her conversionary experience.

  Belle had taken several courses with me before enrolling in Love and Loss, and I wonder how she feels about my Jewish atheism/agnosticism. In my Thomas Hardy/D. H. Lawrence course, how did she react to Alec's false conversionary experience in *Tess of the D'Urbervilles?* How did she feel about Hardy's increasingly bleak vision of humankind, in which God either does not exist or mocks human characters' desire for happiness? Given her belief in the Bible as the "untainted word of God," how did she respond to my assertion two weeks earlier that it is impossible to read any text "objectively," especially one as complex and contradictory as Job? I assume that, contrary to Harold

Bloom's statement, she views the New Testament as the fulfillment of the Old Testament. Belle told me that she plans to study at a Bible seminary after college. I hope she stays in touch with me—I'll be curious to see whether her religious faith survives the many challenges of life. I wonder how she feels about her unsaved English professor!

Carly: "My Family and I Are Ready for the Suffering to End"

Ever since my grandmother was diagnosed with fibrosis of the lungs, I believe that I have become more spiritual in mind and body. Every morning before I rush to my 8:45 class, I make sure that I say a little prayer. When evening comes to a close, I sit in my room and reflect on when this pain my grandmother is enduring will come to an end. There is not a night when I don't cry and wish for a miracle that will give back my Mama that I knew for so many years. I have to think realistically because there is no cure for this disease and day-by-day she is getting weaker and every breath she takes is a struggle. I ask myself the same question in my head every night, "When is this going to end?" I used to feel guilty when this question would pop into my mind because it wasn't right for me to wish death upon my grandmother whom I have loved for twenty-two glorious years.

I needed to talk to someone so I went to my father. He told me that it is not guilt that I am feeling, it is sadness. Seeing my grandmother every day at four o'clock struggling just to get out of bed before she wets the bed really depresses me. It takes her thirty minutes in the bathroom. I have to clean her and put the diaper on. I then take her to the dining table, place a stool under her feet, turn on the oxygen, turn on the heating pad, and finally layer her with three blankets. I then go to the bathroom and disinfect it. I then go to the bedroom, check the bed and then make it. I make sure I throw away the soiled garbage as soon as possible because the smell at times is horrendous. I warm up some dinner and make sure that I put chicken broth into whatever food I am giving her. The broth softens it and makes it easier for her to swallow. This process takes about twenty to thirty minutes. After she has finished dinner, it is time to brush her teeth. I bring over an empty basin, a huge cup of water and her toothbrush. She brushes her teeth at the table because she doesn't have the strength to stand up at the sink to do it. I wash the clothes, take her to the bathroom one last time before I leave and then I say goodnight. I usually don't get home until 7 pm and by then my back is killing me and all I want to do is to be left alone. This is what my family goes through every day.

We are allowed to cry and complain about this but no matter what pain we are going through it is nothing compared to what Mama is going through. In this stage of the disease, my family and I are ready for the suffering to end. Our beliefs do not support euthanasia because we believe that God gave us life and God can take away life. We don't believe that Man should take away life but if

God wants to take Mama it just means that it was her time. Her death would not be any easier but at least she would not be suffering. Our beliefs allow us to believe that there is a heaven and she will be reunited with her late siblings. She wouldn't be alone.

There was a professor which I was honored to have who told me that I should never have any regrets about my grandmother. She knew that I was going through this life change and unfortunately she was going through this with her ailing father. Her father was in hospice so she knew that the end was near. She told me that when my grandmother does pass, the worst thing that I could think was, "What if I did this, then maybe she would have lived a day longer." I never want to live with that regret all my life. When Mama is taken from us, I will know that she is in a better place. She will be in a place free from pain and hurt. I will miss her every second of the day and wish she was still with us but my faith will give me comfort. She will be my angel and she will forever be my Mama.

Carly's essay does not directly explore the ways in which her religious views affect her attitude toward death, as I asked her to do, but the essay is bound to move anyone who has been a caregiver. Authenticated by a wealth of details, the essay describes the suffering of both Carly's grandmother and the entire family. These details affirm Carly's loving-kindness toward her grandmother. My wife told me, when she was in irremediable pain, that she thought it must be harder for the caregiver than for the dying person. Anyone in Barbara's situation or in mine must question whether it is harder to suffer or to watch helplessly as a loved one suffers. The answer is that both suffer in different ways. The patient's suffering ends at death, while the caregiver's suffering continues, though for most people the pain diminishes over time. Carly never allows us to forget that as awful as it is for her family, it is worse for her grandmother, for "no matter what pain we are going through it is nothing compared to what Mama is going through." In an earlier section of her essay that I have not included, Carly refers to feeling "empowered" by reading *The Art of Happiness* by the Dalai Lama. She ends the essay by referring to a professor whose empathy, based on a similar experience, has been helpful. So too is Carly's faith helpful, comforting her amid her grandmother's impending death. I hope that my empathy will be as helpful to my students as her professor's empathy was helpful to her.

Sara: "Now I Am the Patient, and Total Acceptance, Like God, Is Always Out of Reach"

I believe that religious systems provide the largest impact on an individual's attitude toward death and dying. When confronted with death, a person of strong religious or spiritual faith may find himself feeling cheated, and a person who has eschewed religion may find herself wishing for the comfort that a system of belief could have provided.

I was raised in an Irish Catholic family, where religious holidays were celebrated as fervently as birthdays and anniversaries. In fact, I did not attend any educational institution that was not Catholic until I entered college at a ridiculously expensive private university. Although the tenets of Rome have been well ingrained throughout my youth, I found myself on entering college questioning and scrutinizing all that I had previously learned by rote and had accepted blindly. Although I purposely distanced myself from the institution of the Church, excepting rare occasions when I could locate a parish community liberal enough in its teachings to suit me, the basic dogma of the Church is something I have nonetheless accepted. The stances of the Church with which I disagree—particularly its positions on homosexuality, women's liberation and participation in the Church, and birth control—have not deterred my belief in Jesus Christ or in the tenets of charity, humility, and peace taught in the Gospels. Although reconciling my beliefs apart from the archaic institution of the Church with my tight-knit, traditional extended family has been difficult, the challenges it has posed have been minute in comparison to the challenges my faith has faced during the last year.

When I was diagnosed with multiple sclerosis in late June (if you read this aloud, Jeff, please feel free to use the name of the disease although you've avoided it in previous readings; anything to promote awareness is a positive act), the role of God or religion from the moment of my diagnosis to, in some senses, this very day has been a void rather than a presence. I have not and do not deny the existence of God; I consider myself long past the laments of "why do bad things happen to good people?" I had seen a great deal of death in my position as a neurological researcher; I had also seen a great deal of death in life, more than I would have chosen to despite any benefit these patients provided to the medical community. Watching elderly men and women struggle to care for partners gripped in the cruel forgetting and regression that the fog of Alzheimer's disease induces and telling young men and women that their MS has become progressive and that they most likely won't be walking again provided periods of deep personal grief for the fate of those around me as well as periods of necessary distancing from my subjects. As is the case for many beautiful or horrible events in life, the confrontation with death or loss of dignity is infinitively more profound when it is made personal.

I never questioned God while working with my patients, although I went to funerals for people who were vibrant and productive individuals and who, in a fully just world, should have had much more time on Earth or should have enjoyed their twilight years with cognition. I did not even question God when my own boss, my fellow researcher, prodded by me to conduct the tests I felt would confirm my suspicions, broke the news of my diagnosis. I was struck by the unbelievable irony of the situation, but I did not ask anything of God.

There are people dying every day who are younger than me, undoubtedly many who are smarter and kinder than I, and multiple sclerosis is certainly no longer the death sentence it was forty years ago, nor is it a direct and immediate route to disability. Keeping that in mind—a difficult task—the very nature of MS necessitates a constant, daily adjustment to the havoc it wreaks. Death is, I hope, still far in the future for me, but its presence dogs me, particularly on my bad days, when I temporarily lose hope. Where, then, is God in this situation? Still there, perhaps more needed than ever, but totally unreachable. My previously unshakeable faith hasn't been shattered; it simply doesn't seem relevant anymore, which is probably worse. Forcing myself to question my faith at this point would force God into the equation of degenerative illness; the inability to question Him indicates an impassable chasm between us.

Elisabeth Kübler-Ross's stages of dying as observed in terminal patients apply aptly to the stages of living in chronically ill patients. Shock, denial, bargaining, and depression—I felt them all. The difficulty in living with an illness as insidious and unstable as mine is that, for many people, acceptance never comes. Patients I worked with had the most challenge in adjusting to the difficulties each day brought, whether it be overwhelming fatigue, motor dysfunction, or cognitive issues, while at the same time valiantly attempting to visualize a future that was so undetermined as to render the attempt ludicrous. Whereas I once counseled and instructed, now I am the patient, and total acceptance, like God, is always out of reach.

I am terrified of the finality of death; at the very least it unquestionably ends one's life as we know it on earth. I have always harbored this fear, which has shown itself in brief, focused spurts throughout my life. Now, however, I am more frightened of the death in life that I have observed in so many of my patients and of the loss of personal dignity and value of life that such an illness can bring. To many patients, death is a blessing. Perhaps, many decades from now, I too will view it as such, as natural and fitting, and I will be able to die peacefully, but in order for that to happen the chasm separating me from God will have to be bridged; acceptance at some point must be obtained. I doubt ever realizing that acceptance instead of doubting God. I do not see Him as malicious or unloving but simply as existing apart from me.

My attitude toward death, dying, and disability has been profoundly and irrevocably affected by my multiple sclerosis. My religious faith no longer seems pertinent; theologians would most likely characterize me as being in despair, for to despair is to turn your back on God. For one who always had a reassuring faith-based view of death and afterlife, I grieve more that I cannot turn around and face Him.

Whereas Carly's faith has helped her to accept her grandmother's imminent death, Sara's diagnosis of multiple sclerosis has created a religious crisis. Sara had been in my Hemingway course the previous summer when she was diagnosed with multiple sclerosis. Struck by the cruel irony that she was a neurological researcher who had suddenly become a neurological patient, she asked me, in her parenthetical comment, not to conceal the name of her disease. I complied with her request. Illness has not resulted in her denial of God but rather the eruption of an "impassable chasm" separating her from Him. She was the only student in class who wrote about suffering from a serious degenerative illness, and for her the urgent question was not the likelihood of premature death but rather the possibility of death with dignity. She asked me on the first day of class, when I spoke about my wife's illness, whether I believed that one can die with dignity. As I wrote in *Dying to Teach*, there was nothing dignified about Barbara's cruel wasting away from pancreatic cancer: such a death is horrific. I wasn't ready, however, to talk about this at the beginning of the course, and so I told Sara that I would answer her question later in the semester.

Time constraints prevented me from reading aloud other noteworthy essays. Two of Belle's classmates wrote about their experiences as born-again Christians. One wrote about how her religious conversion a few years ago allowed her to repudiate a life based on partying, drinking, smoking marijuana, shoplifting, fighting, and running away from home at the age of seventeen. Only when she was in prison and hit rock-bottom was she able to give herself to God and turn her life around. The other wrote about the opposite experience: being raised as a born-again Christian, he is now trying to reject the "many misconceptions that are associated with hundreds of 'crazy religious fundamentalists' that I know." Elijah wrote about being raised by Jehovah's Witnesses after his mother's death and his father's disappearance. He was told as a child that if he believed in God and lived the "right way," he would see his mother again in heaven, but as he grew older he saw "how organized religion did things like fight wars in the name of religion or use religion to do things like genocide or slavery." Now he feels the need to be spiritual but not religious. Other students identified with my estrangement from religion. "In class you mentioned that you had been brought up Jewish. You said that when you were younger, you learned Hebrew prayers that you could repeat without even knowing the meaning behind the words you spoke. In a sense, that is what my religion became to me. I sang and went to church and followed the rules that were given to me in the Bible and the Ten Commandments but I never really understood the meaning behind it all."

Though the religion-and-death essay was not a research assignment, several students included apt quotations. One essay begins with, "Isaac Bashevis Singer once stated, 'Doubt is part of all religion. All the religious thinkers were doubters.'" Another person quoted Thomas Paine: "Infidelity does not consist in believing or disbelieving; it consists in professing to believe what he does not believe." Another cited an observation by Madeleine L'Engle, a prolific contemporary author from whose writings my daughter Jillian and son-in-law Alex quoted during their wedding vows: "Those who believe they believe in God but without passion in their heart, without anguish of mind, without uncertainty, without doubt, and even at times without despair, believe only in the idea of God, and not in God himself." Another quoted a statement by Albert Einstein: "My religion consists of humble admiration of the illimitable superior spirit who reveals himself in the slight details we are able to perceive with our frail and feeble mind." Another quoted Achilles's description of the afterlife to Odysseus: "I'd rather slave on earth for another man . . . than rule down here over all the breathless dead." And another offered quotes from several writers, including Oscar Wilde's observation that "science is the record of dead religions" and Emily Dickinson's aphorism that the "Supernatural is only the Natural disclosed."

Evaluating the Assignment

Based on student responses, this essay generated the most anxiety. "This was the only assignment that frightened me from the very beginning. Although death has been all too prevalent in my life so far, I thought that I was still unsure what my beliefs on death are. This is also the only essay which I did not want you to read aloud." Those who granted me permission to read their essays aloud also found the topic unsettling. They implied that religion is so controversial and explosive—and here some of them referred to Raymond's blowup in class—that they preferred not to write about it. Most students found writing the essay painful but not paralyzing. The topic proved particularly helpful to those who have lost relatives and friends. "I started out apprehensive. I knew writing this essay meant putting myself under a microscope. It was somewhat painful to write because contemplating the influence of religion on my beliefs caused me to recall what role they played in my grieving process in the past. The enlightenment that came with this personal exploration was also uplifting and comforting." Carly, the only student who wrote about taking care of a grandparent, stated: "I didn't find this assignment painful overall. The part when I was describing the process about taking care of my grandmother was hard to write." Those who did not mention losing a relative also found the assignment meaningful. "This assignment made me realize how precious and fragile life is and that having faith can help you cope with deaths of loved ones and even my own death. I didn't find it painful."

The selections I read aloud moved nearly everyone. "I felt a connection with my fellow students as I realized that my own internal battle with religion was not all that different from my peers'." Another felt the essays sounded like entries from *Chicken Soup for the Soul*. Another was "touched" to hear class-mates speak "so lovingly about others." "They were amazing," wrote another. "Although none of the readings agreed with my beliefs, it was great to hear others' beliefs and experiences." Carly observed, "You actually read my piece aloud and I was surprised that you chose mine because I felt like my paper dealt more with my grandmother's illness rather than religious beliefs." There were only a few negative comments, including this complaint: "It seemed like you only read the essays of those who had strong religious conviction. What about those with no conviction?"

Nearly two-thirds of the students believed the assignment heightened their awareness of the extent to which religious beliefs influence their atti-tudes toward death. "Preparing for and writing this essay forced me to put myself under a microscope and figure out exactly what my beliefs are and how I had come to them. I always believed that the religious teachings I had received as a child had little to do with my current beliefs, but I now realize that they influenced my beliefs a great deal." Another observed that "religion develops one's thoughts and feelings about death; everyone should know where they stand." Many felt that the assignment helped them to realize the importance of religion in their lives. "Absolutely because one's religious beliefs can defi-nitely give comfort to those who have lost a loved one." Some students expressed both surprise and envy that their classmates were so religious. "I'm somewhat envious of people who have such strong religious faith. I am sur-prised that so many people in our class are so religious."

The same number of students believed that it was helpful to know how one's teachers and classmates feel about religion. "I find it fascinating to hear stories of faith, and it gives me more hope that maybe my faith someday will be rehealed." Another agreed with this point of view but added a cautionary note: "In some cases yes, but people need to be open-minded about it so that instances such as what occurred two weeks ago are avoided." Another stated that such information is helpful because "if this class is a good representation of the general population's religious beliefs or disbeliefs, I now know some-thing I previously didn't [know] about my classmates' beliefs." Another made an observation with which an increasing number of academics would agree: "Absolutely—to treat religion or death as taboo subjects betrays an ignorance of philosophical dialogue too commonplace in our society." And another wrote, "Yes, I respect you a lot and knowing that you don't believe in God, just as I do not, makes me feel both more confident and less ignorant in my beliefs/disbeliefs."

Regardless of whether I teach Love and Loss again, I will ask future students to write about their religious beliefs, for the topic has the greatest significance to so many people, especially as they grow older and confront their mortality. [Recent evidence suggests that college students tend to be more religious, and more spiritual, than their professors assume. A March 2006 poll conducted by Harvard University's Institute of Politics found that 70 percent of American college students identified themselves as "very" or "fairly" religious; 25 percent of students reported becoming more spiritual upon entering college (*Albany Times-Union*, 19 April 2006).] In light of this importance, the third writing assignment helped students clarify their religious beliefs, reflect on how these beliefs affect their attitudes toward death, and compare their own views with those of their classmates. For many students, the assignment represented an opportunity to put into words what they already know. For others, the assignment reminded them of how much they don't know. "I realize now that I have a lot to discover within myself before I can discover my true religious beliefs." This statement remains meaningful even if we avoid essentialist language. Writing helps us to understand how we construct and modify our belief systems, and for many people, writing is one of the best forms of problem-solving and self-discovery. I suspect a majority of my students would agree with the following statement: "I believe writing the essay influenced my ability to express (and clarify) my thinking on both religion and death." I can't think of any writing topic more conducive to self-reflection than this one, and while most students were apprehensive when I first announced the assignment, nearly all of them recommended I use it again, unmodified. I view this as a tribute to their willingness to write honestly and openly about what may be the most explosive topic in the early twenty-first century.

6

~

Cathy's Letter to Her Deceased Mother in *Wuthering Heights*

Monday, March 6 (continued)

Today we began C. S. Lewis's *A Grief Observed*. I found so many of Lewis's observations intriguing, including those with which I only partly agree. I read this passage in class: "If, as I can't help suspecting, the dead also feel the pains of separation (and this may be one of their purgatorial sufferings), then for both lovers, and for all pairs of lovers without exception, bereavement is a universal and integral part of our experience of love. It follows marriage as normally as marriage follows courtship or as autumn follows summer" (50). I don't believe the dead feel anything or exist in any realm other than within the memory of the living, but I certainly do believe that love always ends in loss. I read another quotation that is for me the most valuable insight of the memoir: "Passionate grief does not link us with the dead but cuts us off from them" (54). I think that's exactly right, and I told my students that whenever I feel sad or lonely I try to remember the joy of our marriage; happy memories help me to feel closer to Barbara.

After class Mandy told me she was surprised that her mother read *A Grief Observed* shortly after Mandy's grandfather's death. She said that both she and her mother found the book helpful. I'm glad that I can help my students with their own grieving. Last week I read aloud a passage from Geoffrey Gorer's book *Death, Grief, and Mourning in Contemporary Britain* that has as much relevance today as when it was published in 1965:

> There is now a very general recognition that human beings do have sexual urges and that, if these are denied outlet, the result will be suffering, either psychological or physical or both. But there is no analogous secular recognition of the fact that human beings mourn in response to grief, and that, if mourning is denied

outlet, the result will be suffering, either psychological or physical or both. At present death and mourning are treated with much the same prudery as sexual impulses were a century ago. . . . It would seem correct to state that a society which denies mourning and gives no ritual support to mourners is thereby producing maladaptive and neurotic impulses in a number of its citizens. And this further suggests the desirability of making social inventions which will provide secular mourning rituals for the bereaved, their kin and their friends and neighbors. . . . Such rituals would have to take into account the need of the mourner for both companionship and privacy; for the fact that it is (almost certainly) desirable for mourners to give expression to their grief without embarrassment or reticence; and the fact that for some weeks after bereavement a mourner is undergoing much the same physical changes as occur during and after a severe illness. (111, 116)

Wednesday, March 8

I am in Texas today for a conference, but I left the class in good hands with Richard. He enjoyed teaching the class, as his diary entry confirms:

Wednesday's class was a joy to teach. Starting with Jeff's material had people paying deep attention. This was perhaps due to the fact that students had a new voice to listen to. I attempted to stay as close to Jeff's format for teaching as possible, though I did say to the class, "I know you'll be disappointed today without Jeff." Still seeing what I hope was a consistency of format legitimated, I think, my conducting of class for them.

Since I do believe in what Jeff's doing with self-disclosure as a foundation upon which individualized learning can happen, I read my own journal entry which, as I said, "will help you frame the way in which I approach *Elegy for Iris* and provide a grounds for comparison with your own reading":

How can we know a disease like Alzheimer's? Especially for a population looking to work with our minds more than our bodies, Alzheimer's is the worst possible of diseases. After the first day of Love and Loss when a student pointed out the terribleness of living life without control over one's faculties, I have to consider how there may be worse things than death. Typically, I've been taught growing up that with age comes wisdom, that what people lose in their bodies and abilities is exchanged for memories and experiences. Alzheimer's with its wrappings of the brain in a thick cloud—an imperfect metaphor at best—results, on the contrary, in forgetfulness. Now I'm afraid I must come to learn how when we grow old we may not be compensated with a rich world of experiences. Inevitably, we all forget certain names, places, and of course algebra, but when people forget loved ones, how to talk and engage in a conversation, when we forget how to breathe, which is usually the last step of this disease unless a respirator intervenes, this is a death more difficult to know than our history can teach us. As our life spans have increased, we have now encountered a new death for which we are supremely unprepared.

Currently, my wife and I have grandmothers [who are] developing Alzheimer's. For each, the disease is different in its effects and in how our grandparents are dealing with it. Perhaps not so strange to understand after reading *Elegy for Iris*, the disease has brought both of our respective grandparents closer to each other. Neither grandfather was ever a caregiver in the domestic sense—one worked as an engineer, the other as a foundry molder—but they have adapted to their new marriages. My wife's grandmother is happy and confused. She likes to move photos and jewelry around the house, randomly placing the items in an attempt at organizing—a flawed organization entirely unsettling for my wife who prides herself on her cataloguing, note taking, and appointment booking. Her grandfather is going to start taking her grandmother to a day program for Alzheimer's patients where she is involved with others who care about whether she is too warm with both a sweater and a winter jacket. Upon their first visit, the patients demanded she take off her knit cap after she shook everyone's hand to say "hi, it's so good to see you" like they are all lost friends.

My own grandmother is happy to see other people, and asks of them every few minutes, "So, how have you been?" She asks this desperate question to fill the empty silences that happen in a conversation almost as if she let silence last too long in the air she would slip away from reality permanently. She would have no attachment to what people are talking about or even who they are, even if at this point she doesn't know her grandchildren's names. When she doesn't ask about how you are doing, she talks about going to an aquatics program at the Y called Rusty Hinges. All her friends attend the program with her, and "they have great fun" she says while flapping her arms like a chicken. Since, in truth, she stopped attending the Y program nearly ten years ago and all her friends are dead, sometimes my grandfather can't help but correct her. Then she is sullen, and says, "Yes, that's right." My grandfather is overwhelmed by the responsibility of caring for her, by her inability to hold a conversation; he can hardly move throughout their flat with a walker and is approaching the limits of his strength. He's eighty-nine years old with a pig valve serving as a replacement in his failing heart. When we've asked him what we can do, he says, "She's my wife, and I'm going to take care of her as long as I am able."

I've never employed this technique, but it did work extremely well, especially considering the midterm question on the memoir asked what kind of caretaker one would be. I think the founding of choices in caring for a loved one worked very well in priming students to think about their own futures. The close readings of passages worked moderately in helping students understand the multiple dimensions of caring in John and Iris's marriage. However, students did a supreme job talking about the ramification of Bayley's water imagery, so I was quite pleased with that—though I must admit I was pleasantly surprised they interpreted it so quickly. This class is an intelligent group.

One snag presented itself when I polled everyone to find that only a third had their books with them; I think this shows that though Jeff said we would be covering *Elegy for Iris* on Wednesday, some thought we would still be spending time on *A Grief Observed*. Again, it's interesting to me that the format can have a stronger effect on student behavior than the syllabus, which is the more binding learning agreement. So in the end, I had to skip my 3 × 5 card activity.

Monday, March 13

Richard came into my office today and told me that he thought his discussion of John Bayley's *Elegy for Iris* had gone well last Wednesday. I wanted to make a few more observations about the memoir, and I read aloud a passage that describes the delicate balance between connection and separation that exists in marriage. "Already we were beginning that strange and beneficent process in marriage by which a couple can, in the words of A. D. Hope, the Australian poet, 'move closer and closer apart.' The apartness is a part of the closeness, perhaps a recognition of it, certainly a pledge of complete understanding." Such "sympathy in apartness takes time to grow," Bayley adds (44). Alzheimer's cruelly shatters this paradoxical apartness-in-closeness, for as his wife, Iris Murdoch, grows increasingly ill, she can no longer remain by herself: she becomes completely dependent upon her husband. He quotes a woman who describes "cheerfully" what it is like to be married to a person who has no memory: "Like being chained to a corpse" (48), a characterization that repels Bayley because of his need to "feel that the unique individuality of one's spouse has not been lost in the common symptoms of a clinical condition" (49).

Toward the end of his memoir Bayley remarks on a disquieting irony: "Life is no longer bringing the pain of us 'closer and closer apart,' in the poet's tenderly ambiguous words. Every day we move closer and closer together. We could not do otherwise" (265). Instead of reciting King Lear's line, "Ripeness is all," the memorist expresses a more distressing insight: "Helplessness is all" (267). Amid such overwhelming pain arising from the loss of a beloved spouse's memory and identity, Bayley reminds us that we are born to live only from day to day—and that we must, repeating an earlier observation, "take short views of human life—never further than dinner or tea." And yet he immediately qualifies this insight by his eloquent elegy, which gives us both short and long views of human existence.

Afterward I briefly discussed Barbara's mother's Alzheimer's and my recent visit to her, when she seemed to remember no one but could still play the piano. There was nothing wrong with her "music memory," which, as Oliver Sacks notes in *The Man Who Mistook His Wife for a Hat*, can remain intact even after nearly everything else is forgotten. Richard records in his diary entry for today that music is also important to his wife's grandmother:

> Jeff said that music memory is the last thing to go. For Christmas, my wife, Jolie, bought a Hallmark piano-playing snowman for her grandmother with Alzheimer's. Even now in March, the snowman sits on the center of her grandmother's counter, and every time Jolie's grandmother walks by, she starts the music. Sometimes she'll say, "Come here, I've got something to show you," and she takes you into the kitchen to play the snowman while moving her shoulders, hips, and arms from side to side like a stiffened but joyful form of the twist. Jolie's grandfather has grown hopeful that the battery will soon give out, but her grandmother appears to tap into a better part of her life every time she hears the Christmas music.

I then read a selection from a memoir written by Cathie Borrie, a Canadian whom I met at the Association of Writers and Writing Programs Conference this past weekend. She describes her relationship to her mother, who died in January after suffering for eight years from Alzheimer's:

> Mum? What's the nicest thing about you?
> *Nothing.*
> What's the second nicest thing about you?
> *My love for music, my love of good music. In fact, it might be the first thing.*

> My mother and I are listening to Bach.
> She's in bed, propped up by pillows. I'm curled up beside her. A tight squeeze.
> Pillows to the north, under her head,
> East and west, under her left and right shoulders and arms,

South, under her knees. Lace circling the neckline of her now loose-fitting
blue nighty.

My mother is beginning to look like a porcelain doll. Delicate. Translucent.

A clean white sheet is canopied over her feet. She hated anything, anyone,
touching her feet. Great fodder for childhood pranks.

She holds her baby-doll against her right shoulder, nestled under her chin.

From time to time—when she remembers he is there—she nuzzles his
forehead with her lips. Eyes closed. Smiling.

It is the most beautiful gesture I have ever seen.

Wednesday, March 15

Today we began our discussion of *Wuthering Heights*, perhaps the most strikingly original of all British novels. Despite having taught the novel several
times, I had to reread it carefully, relearning the complex genealogy of the
story. I'm teaching the novel mainly because of the ways in which the many
characters react to the loss of love. I discovered only a few minutes before class
that the campus bookstore ordered the wrong edition, a highly abridged version that omits three-quarters of the novel. *Wuthering Heights* is hard enough
to teach when students have read it—it's a novel that one cannot understand
on a single reading—but it's infinitely more difficult to teach when one hasn't
read it. I spent most of today's class discussing the first half of the novel,
introducing the main characters, suggesting the major themes, looking at some
of Lockwood's and Catherine's dreams, and hinting at the multiple losses in
the story. What I find so fascinating in the novel, and what I pointed out in
Narcissism and the Novel in 1990, is that *Wuthering Heights* "dramatizes the
dynamics of maternal loss and bereavement. Many of the central conflicts
among Bronte's characters may be attributed to parental loss or discontinuities
in the parent-child relationship" (85). This is strikingly evident in Cathy
Linton, whose mother, Catherine Earnshaw Linton, died while giving birth to
her. In the late 1980s, while reading the vast body of literary criticism on the
novel, I was amazed to discover that not a single scholar noticed that Cathy
never inquires into her mother's life. Indeed, Cathy never refers to her mother
or asks her relatives or friends to describe what her mother was like. I find this
silence so peculiar that I am asking my students to imagine themselves as
young Cathy and to write a letter to the absent mother she has never known:

> As I observe in *Narcissism and the Novel*, "Given Cathy's intense family loyalty,
> it is astonishing that she seems totally uninterested in discovering anything
> about her deceased mother [Catherine Earnshaw Linton]. And it is no less
> astonishing that critics have failed to notice this point, even critics who have

written sensitively on issues of maternal loss, female identity, and orphanhood in *Wuthering Heights*. The fact remains that Cathy—imaginative, inquisitive, and adventurous—not once, neither as a child nor as a young woman, inquires about her mother. In *Frankenstein* Victor usurps the mother's role in the act of creation; in *Wuthering Heights*, another motherless novel, Cathy denies that her mother has ever existed. It is as if Cathy emerges full blown from her father's great coat, like Heathcliff's 'birth' into Wuthering Heights. Cathy knows that her mother has died, of course, but she knows none of the details of Catherine's life or death. The daughter never mentions her mother's name, even when the opportunity arises" (103).

For your fourth writing assignment, imagine you are Cathy and that you are writing a letter to your deceased mother, about whom you know virtually nothing. Write the letter using the first person pronoun. The age of your Cathy should be consistent with the novel's portrayal of what is going on at that time in her life. Discuss in your letter some of the following questions. How would Cathy describe her relationship with her father? How would she describe the other characters in her life? How would Cathy explain the fact that no one has ever spoken to her about her mother? How is Cathy similar to and different from her mother? How has maternal loss affected Cathy? Does she feel guilty about her mother's death (as children sometimes do when their mothers die during childbirth)? How does Cathy feel about the possibility of becoming a mother herself in the future?

Please think about these more general questions as you are writing the letter. How does your letter to Cathy reveal aspects of your own relationship to your mother? How do we console the dying (and communicate with the dead) about all they are losing (or have lost)? Do you think the dead can hear or see the living?

Monday, March 20

Before class I finished Philippe Aries's magisterial book *The Hour of Our Death*, which I had started on the airplane while flying to Texas. I can't imagine a more encyclopedic study of the shifting attitudes toward death, immortality, and the hereafter in Western civilization over the last two thousand years. I've found the book enormously helpful in discussing the fantasy of reunion that Catherine and Heathcliff share in *Wuthering Heights*, a theme that lies at the heart of my interpretation of the novel. I can't help wondering whether Aries's generalization at the end of his book about the "cult of the dead" applies to me:

> We have followed the slow transition from the sleep of the *homo totus* to the glory of the immortal soul. The nineteenth century saw the triumph of another

image of the beyond. The next world becomes the scene of the reunion of those whom death has separated but who have never accepted this separation: a re-creation of the affections of earth, purged of their dross, assured of eternity. It is the practice of Christians or the astral world of spiritualists and psychics. But it is also the world of the memories of nonbelievers and freethinkers who deny the reality of a life after death. In the piety of their love, they preserve the memories of their departed with an intensity equal to the realistic afterlife of Christians or psychics. The difference in doctrine between these two groups may be great, but it becomes negligible in the practice of what may be called the cult of the dead. They have all built the same castle, in the image of earthly homes, where they will be reunited—in dream or in reality, who knows?—with those whom they have never ceased to love. (611)

I don't see myself as a practitioner of the "cult of the dead," and I believe there is a world of difference between devout Christians, spiritualists, and psychics, on the one hand, and nonbelievers, on the other hand. I do not see myself as living with Barbara's memory in a fantasy realm. Nor have I imag-ined, consciously or not, that we will be reunited one day. I find Aries's penchant for sweeping generalizations annoying, yet I can imagine how others might perceive me as unable or unwilling to let go of Barbara. (Sophie Freud told me recently that I am still in denial because I continue to wear my wedding ring.) I dislike "cult" because it is so pejorative. Aries acknowledges that it took him fifteen years to write *The Hour of Our Death*. Would he, then, include himself among the cult of the dead?

I began class today by reading aloud an article that appeared in today's *Albany Times-Union:* "A Good Mourning: Books about Death Become Choice Reading" by Julia Keller. The article focuses on three recent books that have attracted national interest: Joan Didion's memoir *The Year of Magical Thinking,* John Banville's novel *The Sea,* and Sandra Gilbert's literary study *Death's Door: Modern Dying and Ways We Grieve.* I've read the two nonfiction books but not the novel, which I have now ordered. Summarizing Gilbert, Julia Keller observes that "our reluctance to deal with death has forced it to find another way forward, showing up in our literature as opposed to our lunch conversations. We possess a great hunger to confront the reality and inev-itability of death—'Sooner or later, all of us will lose somebody,' Gilbert said—and that hunger must be sated somewhere." After reading the article, I discussed the theme of self-destruction throughout *Wuthering Heights*, focusing on Catherine's refusal to eat (she is one of the earliest anorexics in English fiction); Hindley's collapse and self-ruin after the death of his wife, Frances; and Heathcliff's monomaniacal efforts to destroy Hindley and Edgar Linton, both of whom he perceives as responsible for his separation from Catherine. Mary Jane Moffat has described Heathcliff as "one of literature's least successful mourners. His eighteen-year search for his dead Catherine is a novelistic illumination of the quest of the mourner who has invested too much of his identity in another human being" (216). Unlike Hindley and Heathcliff, who remain obsessed with past loss and who project their rage and depression onto their sons, Hareton and Linton, respectively, Edgar is a loving and devoted father. His attachment to Cathy gives their lives meaning and value.

Wednesday, March 22

Today I began with what must be one of the most astounding statements in *Wuthering Heights:* Ellen Dean's assertion to Cathy, "You never had one shadow of substantial sorrow" (257), a remark that Cathy inexplicably refuses to challenge. I would be dumbfounded if Ellen had said that to me. How odd that the central trauma in a child's life—early maternal loss—remains unspoken throughout the novel. I asked my students to speculate as to why no one comments on maternal loss. I have no explanation apart from the biographical fact that Emily Brontë was only three years old when her mother died. Perhaps the novelist could not imagine what her life would have been like had she grown up with a mother; however, her imagination was surely one of the most powerful among all novelists, so this explanation remains unsatisfying. I then discussed the ways in which both Edgar and Heathcliff die with ecstatic expressions on their faces, anticipating a reunion in death with their beloved Catherine. If I had more time in class, I would have read selections from *The Hour of Our Death,* including Aries's statement that in Edgar's deathbed scene one finds the "two essential elements of the romantic death: happiness and the family reunion. The first is the release, the deliverance, the flight into the immensity of the beyond; the second is the intolerable separation that must be compensated for by a restoration in the beyond of what has been temporarily removed" (436).

Monday, March 27

There was no class today because midterm exams were due. I'm feeling overwhelmed by all the work I've been doing in the course, so I can use the extra time to read the fourth writing assignment, imagining young Cathy's letter to her deceased mother. I didn't realize when I gave seven writing assignments that I would spend so much time commenting on the essays, correcting grammatical and stylistic errors, selecting several to read aloud in class, and then soliciting and analyzing the students' anonymous feelings about the assignment. Yet for me this is the most valuable aspect of the course. I find that I'm more interested in the student writings than in the course readings. I wonder if the students feel the same way.

Wednesday, March 29

I began class today by reading aloud selections from several letters written by "Cathy" to her deceased mother. So many of the essays are beautifully written, capturing the mood and mystery of the novel. Witness the opening paragraphs of Ava's essay:

> With the season bordering upon another bleak year, I find myself desolate and withdrawn. I know this letter shall never reach you and I pen these words in vain but I have no other solace. Melancholy has pervaded me, tears spring easily to my eyes, and my customary activities, which were at one time lively and carefree, are now muted. I have no desire to be out of doors. The once beautiful flowers and sun, the whole of my surroundings, are now pale of life and color, for all my thoughts are bent on forbidden love. Oh, how I wish I had a confidant to whom I could reveal my innermost thoughts! Yet, I feel I am without a friend on this earth and have nowhere to turn to for consolation. I write this letter in hope that it will draw you closer to me in my heart and that maybe, somehow, even in death, you can help me through this troublesome time in my life.
>
> Lately, I cannot help but feel the specters of the past surrounding me. Sometimes when I feel a cold rush of wind pass through the curtains, my heart races and I wonder if it is your ghost coming back to check on me from the beyond. I know I must appear to be a silly girl, with an imagination full of ridiculous thoughts and hopes; yet, maybe I wouldn't imagine the presence of apparitions if I knew of even a few of your experiences. Since I bear your namesake, could it be that we have other similarities? When I was younger, I noticed a faded area on the wall exactly opposite father's portrait. I would spend hours gazing upon that spot, knowing that at one time it held a frame filled with your countenance, and imagining what features we may have shared. Perhaps we had the same blond ringlets and fair skin. I do not understand why father took the portrait down. It must have pained him greatly to look at it, and so, I mention no word of my thoughts aloud. I love father as much as life itself and do not want to cause him any grief. Yet, I wonder, does father dote on me because I remind him of you? Could it be that my voice carries the same tone as your own once did? No one, including my father or Ellen, has talked with me about your life. This avoidance has instilled such a great fear within my being that I have forbidden myself to ask questions concerning your life. Instead, I've created you within my deepest imaginings, never daring to question if what I have conceived is true.

Ava begins her letter by drawing a comparison between the bleakness of nature and her own melancholy, and she then hints at her "forbidden love," whom she identifies later in the letter as Linton, Heathcliff's despised son. But Cathy's deceased mother is also a "forbidden love" since no one in the novel talks about her. It is also a spectral love because there are no longer any portraits of Catherine. Ava's essay is at its best in evoking maternal love—love that is lost for Cathy but not forgotten. Her questions about the mother she has never seen suggest unfulfilled longing, and the most poignant part of the letter for me is when the daughter imagines that she might look like her mother: "Perhaps we had the same blond ringlets and fair skin." Ava realizes that children, especially girls, are closely bonded with their mothers and that this attachment is physical as well as emotional. Cathy feels this connection with her mother. She is also closely attached to her father, and she empathizes with his loss. She can understand why it must have been so painful for him to look at his wife's portrait. She then wonders, as many adolescents in her situation do, whether her father loves her primarily for the person she is or because she is a reminder of her absent mother. The second paragraph of the letter intimates Cathy's guilt simply for thinking about her mother. Cathy's maternal longing will never be fulfilled, her questions never answered, the mystery of her mother's identity never solved. Nor will she know whether the mother of whom she dreams was real or a fantasy created by her own imagination.

Since four-fifths of the students in Love and Loss are female, it is difficult to make gender observations about this writing assignment. Yet many of the essays reveal significant gender differences, beginning with the mother-daughter physical bond seen in many women's essays but in *none* of the men's essays. Like Ava, Mariela vividly portrays this connection:

> I wonder if I am anything like you, Mother. I wonder if I look like you or Papa more. Do I have your eyes, lips, or hair? Are you wild and adventurous like me? I believe you must have been a great deal, so great that no one speaks of you to me. Is this greatness of some odd or evil nature from which I should be protected? Or is this greatness of a love so strong and passionate that [it] would be too painful to remember and relive? Perhaps it is in my face that reflects part of yours, a reflection that is more than enough to bear as a daily reminder. As you can observe from my letter, I like to ask a lot of questions. Were you just as curious as I am? I wonder if you ceased to think about me the day you ceased to live? I do not speak of you because I do not know who you are and have become somewhat fearful of what answers I might find. This is partially due to their silence, a silence which I am not strong enough to question. Although we have not been properly acquainted, I have grown to miss what was taken from me thirteen years ago. I wish there were some memories to recall. Even so little as my entrance into

this world and a glimpse of your face would have been enough. After repeatedly searching my mind and heart for any kind of explanation, I return with vacant images and more unanswered questions than I started with. Perhaps it is better to leave this matter unresolved. I trust my imagination to take its course and grant you gracious qualities. I can only hope to become the woman you would have wanted me to be. After all, you are still my mother, entwined in the wind, rain and wet grass beneath my feet.

Like Ava, Mariela succeeds in demonstrating Cathy's curiosity about her mother, including whatever physical resemblance may exist. There is the same maternal longing, the same wonder about her mother's life, the same desire for guidance and support. Both writers *show* us Cathy's love rather than simply *tell* us about it. Unlike Ava's Cathy, Mariela's speaker wonders whether her mother was a destructive force from which she must be protected, but she prefers to regard her mother as having a strong and passionate nature, just as she does. Note how Cathy yearns to be like her mother in both Ava's and Mariela's letters. Just as Ava's Cathy searches for a confidant to whom she can reveal her innermost thoughts, so does Mariela's Cathy seek a role model to emulate. Both letters convey the daughter's unending questions about her mother, and in both letters the mother remains an absent presence. Both students imagine Cathy as disconnected and incomplete without a mother. The haunting last sentence of Mariela's letter evokes a maternal presence that is both outside and inside the daughter's self, a maternal force that is ethereal but palpable. The special mother-daughter bond also appears in Carly's letter:

Daddy and I are close and you could almost say that I am 'Daddy's little girl,' but I want to be your girl too. God, I miss you so much and I wish that there was some way that I could see you at least once. Daddy tells me every night about how beautiful you were. He tells me about your wedding day and how you wouldn't allow him to see you in your dress because you were afraid that it would bring you bad luck. Whenever a holiday passes, like Christmas, Thanksgiving, our birthdays, and your wedding anniversary, Daddy brings out the wedding album. He points out every moment of the wedding service, every moment that the photographer captured through his lens. Mom, you were radiant that day. Your dress was gorgeous and maybe someday when I meet the man of my dreams, I will wear the same dress. Daddy has kept the dress in the closet in a clear garment bag. It still looks just as white and beautiful as it did when you wore it.

Daddy tells me that you and I are a lot alike. The first and very obvious quality is that we both have dimples on our right cheeks. He says that whenever I smile, he sees you in my eyes. I hope that never goes away. I hope Daddy never forgets you. Daddy also tells me that I am just as bossy as you were. Whenever he walks into the family room with his shoes on, I tell him, "take your shoes off, do you realize how long it took me to vacuum and dust this room!" He says that my cleaning habits are so similar to you that even the way I make my bed in the morning is the same way you did it. How crazy is that? If you think about it, it's not so crazy because I was connected to you for nine whole months, and I would like to believe that those habits and everything else were there before I was brought into the world. I was still your daughter before you laid your eyes on me. There are nights when I wonder if you ever regretted having me?

Carly is not faithful to the plot of *Wuthering Heights:* she describes a Cathy who lives not in early nineteenth-century Yorkshire but in twenty-first century America. Her Edgar is *always* talking about his deceased wife to Cathy. Nevertheless, Carly succeeds in portraying a mother-daughter relationship that seems to be largely unaffected by death. Cathy is both "Daddy's girl" and her mother's loving and faithful daughter. She seems familiar with precisely those aspects of her mother's life that daughters love to imagine, such as her wedding day and her wedding gown, which Cathy knows she will one day inherit. It would be hard to imagine a daughter feeling closer to her mother than Carly's Cathy feels toward Catherine. Moreover, Cathy seems to know intuitively that she has internalized the good mother within her. Cathy hopes that her father will never forget his deceased wife; there is no question in the daughter's mind that she will never forget her mother.

Significantly, many of the letters written by women but *none* of the letters written by men mention the way in which pregnancy affects the mother-child relationship. Carrying a baby for nine months creates a special bond between mother and child that is difficult for a male writer (and a male teacher) to imagine. Gender researchers have theorized that, for a variety of reasons, daughters tend to be closer to their mothers than are sons; it is not surprising, therefore, that the female writers in the class conveyed this closeness better than did the male writers. None of the male writers' daughters wondered how their mothers looked, what they inherited from their mothers, or what their mothers' lives were like before their deaths. Indeed, the male writers' daughters evinced little curiosity about their mothers' lives. Many of these gender differences can be seen in Elijah's letter, which I quote in its entirety:

> I do not know how to begin this letter, nor do I know what to say to you. As you can imagine there is much I would like to know and a plethora of questions I would like to have answered by you. Unfortunately you and I are on different planes and you cannot answer my queries.
>
> Ever since I acquired the ability to speak and my memory has developed, I always questioned myself and how I came about. I have always felt a sense of incompleteness growing up and I think I can attribute that feeling to you not being around. I notice all the other children around me have parents that take

care of them. It has also become apparent that most of the other children have mothers in their lives. Not only do I not have a mother but I ended up with a father who was too focused on revenge and others and his own selfish quarrels to worry about the emotional stability of his daughter. I feel as if I have been very strong about this matter. Most other children would sit and feel sorry for themselves or wallow in their own self pity. Contrary to most children I have always remained strong and never once complained about my unfair situation. Some may misjudge this as me being cold-hearted or not caring, but anybody who thinks that obviously knows little about me. What child would not miss their mother? People make the presumption that "well, if she never knew a mother then she has nothing to miss." Anybody that would say or think something like that probably had a mother and should be reprimanded for making such an absurd and cold comment.

Mother, I have wondered about you since I have had the ability to remember. People wonder why I never inquired about you, but people do not know what it is like for me here. Wuthering Heights and Thrushcross Grange are two places full of deceit and spite. I feel as if I have to watch my every word and walk on eggshells because any one little thing can set off a whole motion of calamitous events. I would love to ask about you and find out what you were like because that information would help me figure out who I am and why I act the way I do. But who shall I ask? It has always been more than evident to me that my father and I do not have much in common with one another. He is more concerned with getting revenge on Heathcliff and maintaining childish grudges. However, I have always been faithful to him and obeyed his wishes. I have always noticed that sometimes he looks at me with a certain gaze and I feel like he is looking past me. The more I dwell on it though the more I realize that he is not looking at me but rather he is looking into me and seeing you. This is when the empty feeling I have becomes the most apparent. I feel so empty inside and the idea that everyone else has a memory of you and sees you when they look at me almost seems so ironic. There is another reason I do not ask a lot of questions about you. I know how you passed away and I see how everyone here misses you. I have always felt some measure of responsibility for your death because you died giving birth to me. I do not ask questions about you because I do not want people to bring up the memory of me being the death of you. It tears me up inside every time I think about it, and I would have rather not been born than to have taken your life.

There is much you have missed here amongst these miserable people at Wuthering Heights and Thrushcross Grange. As you know ever since Heathcliff has come back to Wuthering Heights he has used all of his energy on making everyone else miserable. He has gone as far as locking me in his son's chambers and forcing my hand in marriage to his weak and sickly son. He never really cared about his son's feelings but was only concerned with setting himself up to own Thrushcross Grange. I understand that you not only had a relationship with my father but also with Heathcliff. He makes it his business to dwell on your memory. This is where I feel you and I perhaps have something in common. We differ on our feelings about Heathcliff but we both did things to defy the tyrannical authority around here. I know you had a marriage with my father that Heathcliff did not approve of and you defied his wishes by marrying father. I know it caused a lot of pain for all three of you and made everything difficult and uncomfortable. You and I are very much alike because I too defy Heathcliff with my relationship with Hareton.

I bet you and I would have been very close and I am certain that if you were around, everyone in Wuthering Heights and Thrushcross Grange would be much happier. I miss you, Mother, and I would give the world to have you back.

One never senses in the women's letters that they have trouble writing to their mother: their prose is spontaneous, warm, engaging, intimate. But Elijah's letter reveals a distance and formality that may be explained as much by gender as by personal history or prose style. One suspects that for a son, unlike a daughter, the deceased mother is on a "different plane." There are gender implications behind this different plane. "Mothers tend to experience their daughters as more like, and continuous with, themselves," asserts Nancy Chodorow. "Correspondingly, girls tend to remain part of the dyadic primary mother-child relationship itself. This means that a girl continues to experience herself as involved in issues of merging and separation" (166). It's not that Elijah's Cathy loves her mother less than his female classmates' fictional daughters love their mothers. Nor does his Cathy have less need for a mother than they do. Rather, as a male, Elijah has been brought up to believe that sons must break from their mothers, a cultural and psychological separation that is more radical for sons than for daughters. The reader detects yearning and loneliness in Elijah's Cathy, but he feels the need to be "strong," a word he mentions twice in his letter. Significantly, the word does not appear in *any* of the letters turned in by his female classmates. The female students' fictional daughters hunger for their mother's love, imagining endless questions they would ask Catherine if she were alive. By contrast, Elijah's Cathy will not allow herself to "wallow" in self-pity. Maternal closeness appears too threatening to her.

Elijah's Cathy strikes us as more of a son than a daughter and recalls Carol Gilligan's influential observation that men and women have different relational bonds to their mothers. "For boys and men, separation and individuation are critically tied to gender identity since separation from the mother is essential for the development of masculinity. For girls and women, issues of femininity or feminine identity do not depend on the achievement of separation from the mother or on the process of individuation. Since masculinity is defined through separation while femininity is defined through attachment, male gender identity is threatened by intimacy while female gender identity is threatened by separation. Thus males tend to have difficulty with relationships, while females tend to have problems with individuation" (8).

Elijah's Cathy is right when she says that she is not cold-hearted or uncaring, but she has been taught by the culture in which Elijah himself has grown up to be independent and autonomous. Ava, Mariela, and Carly imagined daughters who would give anything to learn more about their mothers. Such knowledge seems crucial for their intergenerational continuity as well as for their identity. But maternal knowledge is dangerous to Elijah's Cathy, partly because it reminds her of unmanly dependency. It's true that his Cathy is curious about her mother, but her curiosity does not arise because she is interested in learning about the kind of person Catherine was. Nor does she seem interested in becoming closer to her deceased mother or in becoming like her. Rather, Elijah's Cathy desires maternal knowledge because it will tell her more about *herself*.

Ava, Mariela, and Carly imagine Cathy as having a loving relationship with her father. Elijah does not: his Cathy will obey Edgar but will not love him. His Cathy feels more guilt for her mother's death than do the other fictional daughters, and she expresses the wish never to have been born, something implied by none of the other daughters. Although Elijah's Cathy ends her letter with the statement that she and her mother would have been "very close" had Catherine lived, the style and tone of the letter suggest otherwise. The letter focuses more on revenge and defiance than on intimacy.

In Elijah's earlier essays he reveals his sadness over the early death of his mother and the loss of his father. The grievous loss of both his parents may help explain his need to be strong. Of the four students from whose "Cathy" letters I have quoted in this chapter, he was the only one who has lost a parent—*both* parents. In all of Elijah's writings to date, I see the profound effects—and affects—of mourning. But I don't think that the gender differences between his letter and those of his female classmates can be explained entirely by biographical factors, for his male classmates' letters reveal many of the same gender characteristics. Dean, the "miracle child," also imagines a Cathy who never inquires into her mother's life. "It has been tough growing up without a mother. Dad tried his best, and Nelly is always there for me. However, I know if you were still alive I would be much closer to you. Nelly has been a mother figure for me, but since she is not my mother, there will always be a distance between us." Despite her desire for closeness, Dean's Cathy spends the rest of the letter describing her relationships with Linton and Hareton. There is none of the daughter's wonder about her mother's life that we see in the female students' letters, none of the hunger for a mother, none of the need to be like her mother. What we do see, however, is Dean's strong religious faith, which he projects onto Cathy, who ends her letter by thanking her mother for "watching" over her. "I will be eternally thankful that you gave your life for me. Thanks, Mom. I love you and wish that I could have met you. I hope that one day we will meet for the first time." This religious faith, which he has revealed in his earlier essays, is as much a part of Dean's identity as is his characteristically masculine way of relating to others.

I read aloud selections from Ava's, Mariela's, and Carly's letters. I did not comment on the gender differences, but I remarked that all the letters I read aloud from were written by women. I ended with Gladys's letter, which describes Cathy's marriage to her first cousin Hareton and their two young children, named after Cathy's deceased father, uncle, and two aunts. I could feel my eyes well up with tears as I finished reading Gladys's letter:

> My life at Thrushcross Grange had seemed so removed from my solitude at Wuthering Heights. But now it seems there is a balance, for I have brought a measure of Thrushcross Grange into Hareton, and he has brought Wuthering Heights into me. We've returned to the Grange, but there will always be Wuthering Heights here with us. On our last ride to the abandoned place we could have sworn . . . but no. It had been days since I'd had a good night's sleep and surely I was seeing things. [This is a reference to the possibility that the ghostly spirits of the deceased Catherine and Heathcliff may still be seen.]
>
> I see myself in Hareton, and our eyes are yours I know. Now, those eyes have found two new lives. Life has come full circle and Earnshaw will once again merit its engravement; little Edgar Hindley and Frances Isabella are quite a pair, Edgar with his blond hair and Frances a portrait brought to life. Having them has made me think more of you. It seems all past issues have come to a resolution through my marriage to Hareton and the birth of our children this fall, quite a conclusion indeed.
>
> Your daughter,
>
> Catherine Linton (Heathcliff) Earnshaw

The reason I became so emotional, I told my students, is that as I was reading about Cathy's two children, both of whom remind her of her deceased mother, I thought about how I now look at my young grandchildren for signs of their resemblance to Barbara. I'm sure that my children also look for traces of their mother's appearance in their own children. I ended class by reading two passages from Hope Edelman's book *Motherless Daughters*, the first indicating the "bad news" about maternal loss, the second the "good news":

> More than three-quarters of the motherless daughters interviewed said they're afraid they'll repeat their mothers' fates, even when the cause of death has no

proven relationship to heredity or genes. Ninety-two percent of the women whose mothers died of cancer said they feared the same demise either "somewhat" or "a lot." The same was true for 90 percent of those whose mothers suicided, 87 percent whose mothers died of heart-related illnesses, 86 percent whose mothers died of cerebral hemorrhages, and 50 percent who lost mothers to accidental death. . . . (219)

Throughout history, early mother loss has acted as an impetus for a daughter's later success. Just as tuberculosis was the artist's disease, mother loss was her early tragedy. Dozens of eminent women throughout history lost their mothers during childhood or adolescence, including Dorothy Wordsworth [and Mary Shelley] (at birth); Harriet Beecher Stowe (age 5); Charlotte, Emily, and Anne Brontë (5, 3, and 1); George Eliot (age 16); Jane Addams (2); Marie Curie (11); Gertrude Stein (14); Eleanor Roosevelt (8); Dorothy Parker (5); and Margaret Mitchell (19).

History books are also filled with men who lost their mothers young, including statesmen (Thomas Jefferson, Abraham Lincoln), artists (Michelangelo, Ludwig van Beethoven), thinkers (Charles Darwin, Georg Hegel, Immanuel Kant), and writers (Joseph Conrad, John Keats, Edgar Allan Poe). When the psychologist Marvin Eisenstadt conducted a historical study of 573 famous individuals from Homer to John F. Kennedy, he found that the rate of mother loss among "eminent" or "historical geniuses" in the arts, the humanities, the sciences, and the military is as much as *three times* that of the general population, even after the mortality rates of earlier centuries are taken into account. (260; emphasis in the original)

Evaluating the Assignment

Thirty of the forty-four students who turned in anonymous responses believed the *Wuthering Heights* assignment did not encourage them to think about their relationship to a deceased relative or friend. Most wrote "not at all" or "not applicable" in their responses. Many of them would probably agree with their classmate who wrote, "No deceased relatives or friends to think about. Knock on wood!" The remaining fourteen stated that the assignment did encourage them to think about a relative's or friend's death. "I thought of my aunt who died five years ago after giving birth to my cousin. I didn't know her very well because she wasn't exactly my aunt but more of a family friend. I wish I had the chance to get to know her. I am now very close to my cousin. It's a joy to watch him grow. I can see my aunt in his eyes. It's a beautiful thing." Another wrote: "I have in the past considered writing a letter to my father and grandfather to express the things I will never get to say. This assignment caused me to think a little about what I might have written." And another wrote: "It made me think of my deceased grandfather that I never met. I began to wonder what it would have been like to meet him." As with the other assignments, students expressed gratitude that their parents were still alive. "It increased my thoughts about my own mother and how fortunate I am to have her around."

The class was equally divided over whether maternal loss is more difficult for a child (of any age) to come to terms with than paternal loss. Half the students believed the answer to this question depends on the child's age and relationship to the deceased parent. These students believed that a father's death could be as devastating as a mother's death.

> I don't wish to think about losing either [of my parents], but I have an incredible bond with my father and believe [his death] would crush me completely.
>
> I could never say that because my father passed away and I am now going through therapy even though I have my mom still.
>
> My best friend, female, lost her mother when she was fourteen and it has affected many aspects of her personality. She is changed. The first boy I loved lost his father when he was thirteen and the same can be said of him. Neither one has recovered.

The other half of the class believed that the mother-child relationship is unique and that maternal loss is more difficult than paternal loss.

> I do—biologically, sociologically, and psychologically, the tie to the mother is singular and [maternal death] creates a greater and darker void.
>
> In general, yes, because the mother usually takes a more involved, nurturing role than the father.
>
> Yes, because a child is carried by the mother for 9 months. They are connected literally to the mother before they come into the world.

Two-thirds of the students found the *Wuthering Heights* assignment valuable:

> Yes, it was because it allowed me to think of my own relationship with my mom and how I would be affected by loss.
>
> I enjoyed being creative.
>
> Yes, it was interesting because it made me appreciate my parents more because I am lucky to have them.
>
> Yes, because it really made me think of the day I will lose my own mother someday. I thought about all the things I still want to do with her.

Richard also found the assignment valuable, as he suggests in his diary entry:

What I find interesting about the *Wuthering Heights* assignment where students write a letter to Catherine from her daughter, Cathy, is that it's considered a creative writing assignment. I don't really view it this way at all, although I do understand why students have difficulty approaching this text. The assignment defines a rhetorical situation in a genre where one must imagine the writer, the receiver, and the life content. Yes, on the surface this appears to be a creative writing assignment. To add to this feeling, literary figures are involved, and writers we call "creative" produce the literary. The complex genius/writing of Emily Brontë impedes the reading for some of the students. How many? It's difficult to say, but there's no doubt that in order to understand and write from Cathy's perspective, one must first follow the story details and character interactions that define her. Cathy is a product of the previous generation's love-war. Second, once one can reasonably understand Cathy's context, one must try to speculate why it is that she never engages in talk about her mother. Is it simply because Heathcliff makes it taboo/other worldly? Is it because Cathy is in denial of how the loss of her mother has affected her?

This assignment investigates an informational hole in the novel that is not directly addressed by Brontë, and so it is, I think, the better readers who may better construct what is necessary to understand "the Catherines" and complete the assignment. Students who are bothered by the assignment or by the process of uncovering a case where a mother/daughter did not get a chance to build or finalize their relationship must empathize with Cathy's situation throughout. This is where students face another impediment to this "creative writing" assignment, for to do this, a writer must appreciate Cathy's situation in addition to knowing the novel's content. Once removed from one's own life situation, one must work to imagine another's situation. This is where I think literary representation can best help writers in getting the assignment to work for them on a level that is at least one or more degrees separate from them. Thus, the assignment allows for a different approach to the writing cure than most of the other papers.

In the end, I'd argue that all writing requires imagining; the challenges here rest with reading for subtleties in the novel and empathizing with people writers can only imagine.

The "Paradox of Grief"

Like Richard, I found the *Wuthering Heights* essays intriguing, and I will use the assignment again the next time I teach the novel, regardless of whether the course is Love and Loss or the British Novel. Maternal loss is not only central to the novel's vision but also perhaps the *central* loss in life. In the epilogue to *Motherless Daughters*, Edelman quotes Adrienne Rich's observation in *Of Woman Born:* "The loss of the daughter to the mother, the mother to the daughter, is the essential female tragedy." Edelman points out that early maternal loss results in lifelong mourning for most daughters. "Of the 154 mother-less women surveyed for this book, more than 80 percent said they were still mourning their mothers, even though their losses occurred an average of twenty-four years ago" (23). Later in the book she quotes an even more disturbing research finding. "When Mary Ainsworth and her associates at the University of Virginia studied infant-mother attachment behaviors among thirty mothers who'd lost an attachment figure during childhood or adoles-cence, they found that *100 percent* of the mothers whose mourning was judged as 'unresolved' had children who seemed anxious and disorganized. Instead of seeking comfort from their mothers, these children acted as if the mothers were a source of distress" (241; emphasis in original).

We do not choose when death will come to others or ourselves, nor do we know how we will respond when we lose a relative or friend. Sometimes years, even decades may pass without a major loss, and then death strikes with a vengeance. The midterm exam question on *Wuthering Heights* asked students to speculate on their responses to the loss of a loved one. The most compelling observation came from Sara, who illuminated a central paradox of grief:

> I have not yet lost a loved one to death, and I can only imagine that the grief it would trigger would vary intensely with the degree of closeness which I felt to the individual. I believe that the longer I remain unshadowed by death in my circle of friends and family the more crippling the loss will be when it occurs. In the way of such things, I am willing to wait a lifetime before facing the loss of a loved one, no matter how compounded the pain becomes, and I dread the day that mortality proves itself to someone I love. Still, the longer I am untouched by personal loss the more vulnerable I become to it. When I do finally lose someone through death, I fear that my response will be not all healthy but tinged with the inexplicable and hopeless mourning that is begat from negative grief. Such is one paradox of grief: to prolong it is to worsen it, to experience it young brings pain to a life that much sooner.

Barbara and I were also willing to wait a lifetime, and given her many long-lived relatives, and the complete absence of cancer in her family, I assumed that I would predecease her by decades. Death waited, and waited, and then stormed into our life full force. Our daughters, Arielle and Jillian, were thirty-one and twenty-nine, respectively, when Barbara died, and unlike Cathy Linton, they have thousands of memories of their mother. Photos of their mother can be seen throughout our homes. But Barbara's death was so devastating to them that they have been unable to finish reading *Dying to Teach*. The book is too painful for them. As close as they are to me, they were closer to their mother. Barbara not only spent far more time with them but was also their "confidant," to use the word that Ava's Cathy calls her deceased mother. Both my daughters were so grief-stricken by their mother's death that they could not understand why I needed to write a book about her. For several months their mother's death was literally an unspeakable story. Now, however, we are all adjusting to the loss. Married to loving and understanding men, they are now mothers themselves and experiencing the joy of raising children, as Barbara and I did. Gladys's Cathy, a new wife and young mother, makes an observation to her deceased mother that aptly characterizes what Arielle and Jillian, new wives and young mothers, might make to their own mother: "Life has come full circle."

7

~

A Problem with Another Student, and Evaluating the Evaluator

Monday, April 3

Today we began A *Farewell to Arms*. The class did not want me to give away the ending, but I nevertheless suggested that the novel is about Frederic Henry's farewell to the arms of war and to the arms of his lover, Catherine Barkley. I read to them the passage in the beginning of the story in which Frederic and Catherine meet for the first time. She is carrying a "thin rattan stick like a toy riding-crop, bound in leather" that had belonged to her fiancé, who was killed the preceding year in the Somne. The stick has symbolic suggestiveness ranging from a memento mori, on the one hand, to a fetishized sexual object, on the other.

Zoe, a student in my Expository Writing course, gave me permission today to read aloud anonymously in Love and Loss her poignant essay about her younger brother, who four months ago was diagnosed with a rare and virulent cancer. The essay, which was on the topic of love, moves me deeply because I can understand the family's devastation and also because it evokes memories of Barbara's pancreatic cancer. The essay is beautifully written, as are so many personal narratives on illness and death. I paused several times while reading it to comment on the nearly flawless language:

> When I was ten years old, my brother fell into a doorframe and cracked his head open. We were home alone playing Ghostbusters, and I was attempting to capture him in my trap. His four-year-old feet slipped on the hard wood floor and I watched in slow motion as he tilted into the metal door catch and it tore through his thick head of hair. There was a moment of electric silence, right before he began to scream. Rushing over to his side, I remember touching his head and pulling my hand away covered in blood. Digging through his hair, I

tried to find the source of the incessantly flowing liquid, eventually locating an incredibly deep and long gash on the side; I really thought his brain was going to fall out. Panicking, I grabbed a roll of paper towels and began wrapping my brother's wound in a mummy-like fashion, covering his entire head and eyes. I then repeatedly called my grandparents who arrived a half hour later, only to find us both surrounded by layers of bloody paper towels and eating Popsicles. My brother had stopped crying and had his entire head and face wrapped up in a cocoon; I had made a hole for the Popsicle stick. After recovering from this image, they took him to the hospital as my father came to claim me at home; only then do I remember crying. I distinctly recall the wave of concern and love that suffocated my body at that moment, and I was overtaken with sobs.

Perhaps this was an odd way to begin a paper on love, or the falling in and out of love. When this assignment was given, I had immediate thoughts of discussing a boyfriend from my past or present. Watching the hands of my female classmates shoot up at an unusually quick rate, I could only assume that they too had this idea and were jumping on the opportunity to discuss a wonderful or painful romance in their lives. However, as I sat down and began to write about a current relationship struggle, I received a call from my mother. My brother had just been hospitalized.

My brother Joshua was diagnosed with a rhabdosarcoma one week after his seventeenth birthday, which was almost four months ago. This is a type of cancer that occurs in the muscles, and spreads quickly and aggressively. He had waited over a month to tell anyone about the enormous lump he had found, and as a result, once the sickness had been discovered, everything had to be carried out quickly and expertly. In a flash Josh's life became filled with surgeries, tests, hospital visits and stays, depression, anger, frustration, missed school, delayed applications and graduation, tears from family and friends, gifts from people he had never seen or spoken to, pity from strangers, and weakness in his once infallible body. This shy young man now had to show his most precious of manly organs to every doctor who wanted a peek, and had to rely on my mother to feed and clothe him on the days he felt too weak to move.

My brother is quiet and secretive, and extremely hard to read. It is rare to see him laugh or even smile, and he is known as a mystery to most of my family; however, Josh and I have always been close. When we were young my mother would ask me to translate his infant noises into coherent words; call me crazy, but I remember being right most of the time. Josh was always as introverted as I was extroverted, but we share the same cynicism and sarcasm that allows us to spend family vacations clinging to one another for escape. I was assigned to baby-sit from an extremely young age; we spent hours outside with water guns or upstairs sneaking up on my grandmother, and we shared a room for years. As he got older, I began to include him in my own activities, and we became friends as well as siblings. However, as I went away to school and he stayed away from home as much as possible we spent less and less time together.

When I found out that my brother had cancer, I was on the train to meet friends from Australia and then head back up to school. I was alone, and my mother broke the news via cell phone as the train dipped into a tunnel, and I lost service. Immediately transferring to a Brooklyn bound train, I decided to stay home from school, and to lecture my mother on the beauty of inappropriate timing. I spent nearly every hour of every day in Mt. Sinai pediatric ward, waiting around with Josh as he went through tests, results, surgery, and then began chemotherapy. Not since we were children had we spent so much time together with nothing to do but talk. I asked and Josh answered. It was as if he were back to being the infant no one could understand; my mother would ask me how he was feeling, if he needed something, or wanted someone. At the moments where I felt most helpless I clung to the idea that I was there for my brother to speak to and through, that my hours spent by his sleeping side weren't empty. I bought him books, clothes, magazines, and a Saint Peregrine necklace, because although we are not religious, I wanted him to have something or someone watching over him when I couldn't be there.

I am now trapped at school while my brother is sick at home. On Friday his white blood cell count went down and they rushed him to the hospital. When I called, he said he couldn't feel his legs and he thought he was paralyzed, one of the very few complaints I have heard him make throughout the ordeal. There are no words to describe how helpless I feel, how far away from where I feel I should be, and how much love I wanted to send over the wires of the phone.

It is amazing how sickness, weakness, or pain seem to intensify those feelings of love. Josh recently lost all of his hair, and on the right side of his head there is a large and somewhat forgotten scar. I can't help but wish it were as simple as wrapping some paper towels around his head and giving him some dessert. I suppose some day I will be grateful that this experience brought us so much closer; however, I can't help but be bitter at a world that allows us to feel so much love for someone without being able to help.

Despite telling us that there are "no words" to describe her helplessness, Zoe conveys her helplessness as well as heartache. The essay demonstrates that her brother does indeed speak to and through her. She not only depicts his quietness and secretiveness but also writes about his illness with unusual sensitivity. No one can read the essay without feeling her love for him. The description in the last paragraph of her brother's "large and somewhat forgotten scar" returns us to the opening paragraph, recalling an incident a decade earlier when, attempting to flee from his sister's effort to capture him, he cracked his head open while crashing into a metal doorframe. We feel at the end that both brother and sister are entrapped in a situation beyond their understanding and control, and we can only hope that he will recover from the present crisis as he recovered from the past one.

Wednesday, April 5

Today is the second anniversary of Barbara's death, and Judith Harris emailed me a poem she had written to mark the event:

On the Anniversary of Her Death
(in memory of Barbara Berman)

You expected she would
have been gone by March,
but instead, dying was tenacious,
and hung on, making
Her belly distend, as if it was
suddenly ripe, again
with daughters.

Today, two years later,
a cruel April wind
roars and carries off the seared
blossoms that now
flood my yard,
like heaves of snow, glinting
with atomistic hooves of gold—

The earth was not ready for them, either.
It would rather toss,
and give away,
but on this day, let's think of her
not in pain, or horror,
but as this flight of ivory petals,
ferrying fro heartbeats
swift as beaming wings.

Yes, let's think she has flown away
somewhere, like them, indelibly,
where the flesh of trees no longer bleeds
and nothing left is visible,
to disappear.

I would admire Judith's poem even if it were not about Barbara, but knowing that it is about her makes it special to me. The poem reveals her struggle to hold onto life despite unbearable suffering. It also brilliantly juxtaposes birth and death: Barbara's swollen stomach filled not with new life but with metastatic cancer along with the ever-increasing fluids that her kidneys could no longer eliminate. I can recall the maternity clothes she wore during the last months of her life; she was horrified by the murderous growth in her body. Judith lives in Washington, D.C., and the "seared blossoms" hint at the once-beautiful cherry blossoms that now symbolize loss. Portraying nature as both our creator and destroyer, the poem never allows us to forget Barbara's horrific ending, but Judith concludes affirmatively, with both the dead blossoms and Barbara's spirit flying away to a place where they are free from agony.

Judith had met Barbara several times and felt kinship with her. In an email sent to me several months ago, she described Barbara as a "worrier-warrior," a term so accurate and compelling that I used it in the last sentence of *Dying to Teach:* "Wherever I am, she is, my beloved wife, friend, soul mate, and worrier-warrior" (236). I couldn't stop thinking about Judith's poem the entire day, and I intend to use it as the epigraph to *Dying to Teach.* Coincidentally, I received a letter today from Dana Foote, the production editor at SUNY Press, informing me that the manuscript is now ready to go to the copy editor. I wouldn't be teaching Love and Loss were it not for Barbara's death. Nor would I be writing *Death in the Classroom* had I not completed *Dying to Teach.*

Today we continued our discussion of *A Farewell to Arms.* I raised the question whether we find Frederic and Catherine's torrid love affair convincing. I read aloud Hemingway's two-page "A Very Short Story," which he later developed into *A Farewell to Arms.* The unnamed male narrator in "A Very Short Story" is betrayed by a beautiful nurse named "Luz," an early version of Catherine. Luz apparently breaks the narrator's heart when she decides not to marry him, referring to their love as merely a "boy and girl affair." I don't want to destroy the ending of the novel by revealing too soon that Hemingway conveniently ends his heroine's life during childbirth; as Leslie Fiedler famously remarked, had Catherine lived, she would have "turned into a bitch." Hemingway also kills off the infant at birth, absolving Frederic from any parental responsibility. In class I limited myself to the observation that she is a fantasy woman, as when she tells Frederic, "I'll say just what you wish and I'll do what you wish and then you will never want any other girls, will you? . . . I'll do what you want and say what you want and then I'll be a great success, won't I?"

After class ended, a student gave me a card with "Jeff" written on the envelope. I assumed it was either a request to write a letter of reference or a "thank you" for having written one. I opened it when I returned to the office and discovered that it was a condolence card signed by everyone in the class.

How did they know that it was the second anniversary of Barbara's death? A student later told me that on the first day of the semester I remarked that my wife had died on April 5, 2004; another student reminded me that I had written the date of Barbara's death on the syllabus. I was too busy teaching to notice the card being passed from student to student. I was deeply touched by the comments written on the card:

> Thank you for sharing your experiences with us. I hope we help the healing process.
> With another anniversary comes wonderful memories.
> Thank you for teaching both life and academic lessons—you are a wonderful professor.
> Thank you for teaching such a wonderful class. I'm sure your wife would be proud and honored.
> Thank you for being so understanding when my mom was so sick.
> Your class has touched all, and helped many. Thank you.
> Thank you so much for sharing your story. It has helped me cope with things.
> Thank you for being so dedicated to all of your students.
> Thanks for forcing me to become a better writer.

The last comment surprised me, for it was written by a student with whom I had had a difficult conversation during my office hours before today's class. Esther had walked out of Monday's class immediately after I returned the midterm exams, and in the evening I left a message on her answering machine indicating that I wanted to speak with her in my office about her abrupt departure. I told her today that I thought walking out of class was rude. She said she was stunned that I felt that way. She believed I had insulted her when I remarked in class that students who had received a grade of below B minus had turned in "terribly written" exams. She was so distraught, she added, that she would have burst into tears had she not immediately left the room. We then had a long discussion over why she received a C. In my written comments I had pointed out all of the comma splices, sentence fragments, dangling modifiers, split infinitives, and run-on sentences—precisely the grammatical mistakes that I have spoken about after returning every writing assignment. Esther said that she has received an A as a final grade in nearly all of her college courses but was now afraid that she would fail Love and Loss. She was angry, hurt, confused, and demoralized. Implying that I was a hard and unfair grader, she said that before this class she wanted to become a writer but now was considering abandoning English as a major because she no longer had confidence in her ability to do well.

Throughout our conversation Esther struggled to avoid crying, and it was painful for me to see her so upset. I tried to be as sensitive as possible, reminding her that she has a solid B average in her four writing assignments and that the midterm exam accounts for only 25 percent of the final grade. I told her I was hopeful that her writing would improve significantly once she mastered the fundamentals of grammar. I hadn't recalled using the words "terribly written" on Monday to characterize the ten midterms that received grades of below B minus, but I don't doubt I made the statement. I was more temperate in my comments on her exam, noting that she shouldn't allow "mediocre writing skills to sabotage excellent ideas." At the end of our conversation I decided to allow her and her nine classmates to revise and resubmit their midterm exams so that they could improve their grades, and I made this announcement at the beginning of today's class.

How could I have avoided shaming Esther? It's ironic that one student regarded my behavior as "christ-like" while Raymond was denouncing me, but only a few weeks later Esther regarded me as punitive. What could I have done differently? Was she too sensitive, or was I insensitive? I don't think I was unreasonable for criticizing her early departure from class. Leaving class during a discussion is distracting, and leaving at the beginning of class, after receiving an exam, is disrespectful. And yet I do give students permission to leave class if they are upset—though I hadn't anticipated that a C would be traumatic. In the future I will try to avoid using words like "terribly written" to explain why exams and papers received disappointing grades. I'm determined, however, to point out my students' grammatical and stylistic errors. Like nearly all college (and probably high school) teachers, I've noticed that most students need to improve the quality of their writing. Many students receive no instruction in high school or college on how to avoid basic grammatical errors such as dangling or misplaced modifiers, comma splices, colloquialisms, split infinitives, and wordiness. Some university writing centers, including my own, are ideologically opposed to teaching grammar, which in my view exacerbates the problem.

Did I make the right decision to grade mainly on form rather than content? Should I have emphasized both equally, as I do in my other literature courses? Is it counterproductive to spend extensive time on grammar in a course that is emotionally charged? When I explained my grading policy at the beginning of the semester, part of my reasoning was that I didn't want students to feel pressured into self-disclosure. Nor did I want them to believe that I favored certain religious beliefs or disbeliefs over others. I remember thinking that it was precisely because the course is so intense that I wanted students not to worry about the content of their writings. I have seen an improvement in their writing. Forty-seven percent of the class received a plus on the fourth assignment, as opposed to 36 percent on the first assignment. (The figures were lower, though, on the second and third assignments, 22 percent and 26 percent, respectively. The number of students receiving a minus has ranged from

5 to 10 percent.) I'll ask them when we return from spring break to indicate in an anonymous in-class paragraph whether they believe I am grading them fairly. If they believe I have been grading harshly, I can emphasize content in the last writing assignments and on the final exam. Until then, I wonder whether Esther was being sincere or sarcastic when she thanked me for "forcing" her to become a better writer. In any event, despite my troubling discussion with her, today was a good day for me, and I'm grateful for Judith's poem and my students' condolence card. I didn't feel as sad today as I did a year ago, which marked the first anniversary of Barbara's death.

Monday, April 17

Esther came into my office today with her revised midterm exam. The quality of the writing was significantly better, and I raised her grade to a B. I asked her if she would provide me with a written description of how she felt last Wednesday during our discussion. She agreed. It will be useful for both of us to understand each other's point of view. At the beginning of class I asked the students to describe in a brief, anonymous in-class assignment how they felt about the way I have been grading their writing assignments and midterm exams. I'll summarize the results during next class. I then handed out copies of a "My Turn" column appearing in last week's issue of *Newsweek* titled "We Had the Love, but I Long for the Letters," in which William Shaw, happily married for forty-six years, laments the fact that he and his deceased wife had not written letters to each other:

> There is not much that is more personal than a letter, particularly a love letter. No card, no poem, no gift is as intimate as a letter. I'm sorry now that I never wrote to her, even if it would have been in my nearly indecipherable handwriting. I probably shouldn't feel this way—there never really was a need, and who thinks ahead to what might happen? I know that what I'm sorry about is that I don't have a letter from her, in her bold, beautiful script, to read and reread. . . .
>
> That thought brings me back to my original realization: that no matter how close my wife and I were, no matter how much we loved each other, and no matter how many heartwarming memories I have of our togetherness, I don't have any tangible record of her heart speaking to mine. And how I wish I did. (17 April 2006)

This is, after all, one of the reasons I'm teaching Love and Loss: to remind my students of the importance of writing about our loves and inevitable losses, to leave a written record—in poems, novels, plays, memoirs, and diaries—of our heartfelt thoughts. I am so fortunate that I have Barbara's writings, which convey an intimacy that no photograph, tape recording, or video can capture. Nothing can bring her back to life, but I feel close to her when I write and speak about her—and when I read her own words. And writing a book about her gives me the illusion that she will live for as long as copies of the book exist. I believe in what David Blacker calls educational immortality: "When one educates or is educated, one does so outside of time; in teaching and learning one is immortal" (83). Blacker realizes, as I do, that one has only an illusion of immortality, not immortality itself. Moreover, memory is treacherously unreliable and short-lived. I've just finished reading John Banville's new novel *The Sea*, in which the narrator mordantly observes, "We carry the dead with us only until we die too, and then it is we who are borne along for a little while, and then our bearers in their turn drop, and so on into the unimaginable generations" (87). I can't disagree with the narrator here, though I find him disagreeable in many other ways. Throughout the story he meditates on his wife's recent death, but he is so self-conscious and cerebral, so mistrustful of emotions, that one senses his failure to love anyone.

Wednesday, April 19

Today I summarized the results of the anonymous "Evaluating the Evaluator" assignment, which my students had filled out during the preceding class. All but three students endorsed my emphasis on writing. "I think it's excellent. It helps to keep me on my toes and not get lazy about my grammar. You're the only English prof I've ever had that actually tries to teach his students how to write." Nearly everyone admitted to having problems with grammar and punctuation. Other problems included not having the time to proofread, wordiness, and the need to strengthen one's writing voice. One person answered the question with the word "grammar" misspelled, so obviously spelling is also a problem. All but five students believed that their writing has improved as a result of my comments, which they found helpful. One wrote, "Very helpful," then underlined the word "very" and wrote "useless modifier"—a comment I make on nearly every essay. The students were split on whether I should place more emphasis on content and less on form. Eighteen people said they would like a balance between content and form; the remaining twenty-two wanted me to emphasize only writing. Based on these responses, I told the class that I would grade the remaining two essays on writing alone but that I would grade the take-home final exam on both content and form. They seemed pleased with the decision. After class Esther gave me a page-long essay titled "A Summary of My Feelings after Having a Discussion with Professor Berman":

The meeting was not going to be the highlight of my day, I thought to myself before I began the long hike up the three flights of stairs where English professors perch. I thought over my paper and the reason for going to the office. I thought about how the previous class I was so upset I felt the need to leave class, lest I cry the whole time. I thought about the comments that were made in class about papers that received my grade range. I thought about how I was a failure in this class. But I was hopeful that this teacher cared enough to call me out of concern the night before, although I didn't speak with him, I could only assume he was worried about me.

When I sat down in his office chair, that reminded me of a psychiatrist's couch, with it's long ottoman and cushioned rocking chair, I was very upset to hear the first words from Professor Berman's mouth. He told me he was offended I left his class the other day. I was reeling with disbelief as I tried to make sense of why he would be offended. I remember what he had said the first day of class about being perfectly OK when someone needed to leave if they were emotionally overwhelmed. I didn't know that this statement carried stipulations. I was emotionally overwhelmed. I was putting my best efforts into writing these papers but because of my lack of practice with grammatical and other stylistic things I was doing worse than I ever had in an English class before. I always got A's and so I ignorantly assumed that my papers were close to flawless. My ideas were good and my papers were interestingly written.

As Professor Berman and I began our argument, which softened into a conversation, I began to realize that his criticisms of my papers were out of purely what he calls a "quality" problem. I strongly disagree [with] this word because quality seems to describe the overall paper. My papers are not overall bad. They are simply full of grammatical mistakes. As we hashed out these definitions I dimly began to understand what he was saying and there emerged a light at the end of the tunnel.

I was upset about being graded a C for a paper that would have received an A in any other class. Most other teachers skim over grammatical problems and see the paper as a whole unit of ideas which are expressed well. I came to understand that these teachers were not doing me as many favors, as I thought they were. Professor Berman, through his ever entertaining analogies, told me I need to stop speeding through papers. If the speed limit was 65 then I feel the need to go 80. I wouldn't get in trouble for going 60. But if I was going 80, with my lack of driving or writing skills, surely I would get a ticket. I do know I am seriously deficient in the grammar department. Even though I have done well to date on these papers, it doesn't mean I am qualified to have a writer's license. Professor Berman helped me to see that I need to focus on the technical stuff to make the other stuff good, so that my papers can eventually be great.

I did disagree with the comment made in class about a paper being terrible. I think it the teacher's responsibility to be as honest as Jeffrey Berman can no doubt be otherwise. But it is also the responsibility of the teacher to be sensitive to the student's feelings. Even though I was thoroughly upset during the majority of the conversation with Professor Berman, I am grateful that I have a teacher who is willing to deal with an upset student to make a better student out of them.

Esther was certainly correct when she reminded me of my announcement on the first day of the semester that students could leave the classroom whenever they felt they were becoming emotionally overwhelmed. I hadn't anticipated that students would be overwhelmed by an unsatisfactory grade or that they might feel like a "failure" simply because they did not have an A average in the course. Two of Esther's four essays were in the A range, and the other two were in the B range, and she had a solid B average even with a C on her midterm exam. In light of her essay, I now believe that I was insensitive to the ways in which she experienced my class comments as a blow to her self-esteem as a student. Esther graciously accepted my apology for the distress I caused her, and I believe that each of us has greater respect for the other. The teacher's challenge is to motivate students to do their best work without making them feel like a "failure" when they fall short of the teacher's or their own expectations. I failed the test in Esther's case, but it is not too late to improve my relationship with her—and to help her improve her writing. In the future, I will continue to call students who walk out of class after receiving an essay or exam, but I've learned that it's better to express concern rather than anger to those who may be distraught over a grade. [Postscript: The quality of Esther's writing dramatically improved in the second half of the course, and she earned an A– as a final grade.]

8

~

Ten Things to Do before I Die

Wednesday, April 19 (continued)

Two weeks ago I gave instructions for the fifth writing assignment, "Ten Things to Do before I Die." The assignment was due on Monday:

> Imagine that you have just learned you have a terminal illness. You are still feeling well, but you do not have much time left. What are the top ten things you wish to do before you die? (Rank them in order of decreasing importance.) For each wish, write a brief paragraph explaining why it is important to you. How would you attempt to justify an action that may be immoral, unethical, or illegal? Would you tell your relatives and friends that you are dying or conceal this information from them? Your ten paragraphs should be about three pages long, typed, double-spaced. (This assignment is based on the film *My Life without Me*.)

This is the most unusual writing assignment I have given in any literature or writing course. The assignment arose from the 2003 film *My Life without Me*, directed by Isabel Coixet and adapted from a short story by Nanci Kincaid. Ann, played by Sarah Polley, is a twenty-three-year-old mother of two young daughters who learns that she has metastatic ovarian cancer and has only two or three months to live. I knew as soon as I saw the film that writing a list of "ten things to do before I die" would make an intriguing assignment for my Love and Loss class. What would my students do in Ann's situation? Would they pursue activities they deemed self-centered or selfless? Would they wish mainly to say goodbye to relatives and friends, get their affairs in order, experience as much pleasure as possible, pursue religious or spiritual truths, or search out new activities? Would they act in ways that are consistent or inconsistent with their lives before their diagnosis? Would they act immorally, unethically, or illegally to fulfil their final desires?

Ann decides to tell no one about her impending death, including her husband, Don, played by Scott Speadman. She informs him in a tape-recorded message he will hear only after her death that she concealed the illness from her family, especially her children, so that they will not feel unhappy. "Don't let them be sad when they remember me. . . . I love you, Don." Nor does she consider a second medical opinion or treatment options, fearing that chemotherapy will prevent her from enjoying the little time she has left. Instead, she creates a list of "things to do before I die," and then she proceeds to do them systematically:

1. Tell my daughters I love them several times a day.
2. Find Don a new wife whom the girls like.
3. Record birthday messages for the girls for every year until they're eighteen.
4. Go to Whalebay beach together and have a big picnic.
5. Smoke and drink as much as I want.
6. Say what I'm thinking.
7. Make love with other men and see what it is like.
8. Make someone fall in love with me.
9. Go and see Dad in jail.
10. Get some nails (and do something with my hair).

Ann's list contains both admirable and questionable desires. Number 1 on her list, telling her children several times a day that she loves them, strikes me as a great idea. Her intention to record birthday wishes to her children is also excellent, along with her concern for Don's happiness after her death. Some wives in her situation might want their husbands to remarry, if only to find women who will mother their children, but Ann actually finds a woman for Don. This proves unexpectedly easy because the future replacement wife, coincidentally also named Ann (Leonor Watling), lives next door and is single. Ann's decision to reunite with her father, whom she has not seen for ten years, is also commendable. Some of the small pleasures in which she indulges are harmless, such as going to the beach and having her nails done. (It will not be easy for her to drink alcohol with a cancerous liver.) Nor can one fault her for saying what she is thinking—though she says nothing that is hurtful to another person.

What Ann does not say proves problematic. Even if we can assume that her death will be mercifully easy and quick, which is not true for most ovarian cancer patients, how will her relatives and friends feel when they discover she has concealed her illness? Will they be grateful or, more likely, angry and hurt that she has not disclosed the truth to them? Will recorded birthday messages make her children feel better that they did not say goodbye to their mother? Will Ann's husband feel relieved or deceived that she did not trust his ability to cope with the truth? And how will Lee (Mark Ruffalo), whom she has shamelessly manipulated into falling in love with her, react when he discovers that the woman who has rekindled his passion for life refused to tell him about her impending death?

My Life without Me never raises any of these disturbing questions, and for this reason the film is disappointing. No one can dispute the truth of Ann's recorded message to her children—"Dying is not as easy as it looks"—but the film only *tells* rather than *shows* us that she is dying. Additionally, the film would be more honest if it explored Ann's ambivalence in pursuing desires that she must know will hurt others. My Life without Me is not as sentimental as Erich Segal's Love Story, but we never see the darker side of metastatic cancer: the irremediable suffering, wasting away, and loss of will to live. Nor does the film depict how death affects loved ones. "The dead don't feel anything, not even regret," she says, but the living do feel regret, and she is naive to assume that events do not have unanticipated consequences. It may be unreasonable to expect My Life without Me to probe the moral and ethical implications of a dying woman's actions. Nevertheless, Lee is reading a copy of Middlemarch when he meets her, and if he is sympathetic to George Eliot's ethically nuanced vision, he will surely question Ann's motivation in beginning a dead-end relationship. Ann knows how to bend the truth, and when she tells Lee in a tape that "I just want you to know I fell in love with you," adding that she didn't realize she had so little time, she conveniently ignores what the doctor told her at the beginning of the film. She also conceals the fact that Lee allows her to fulfill items seven and eight on her list of ten things to do before she dies.

My Life without Me would be a more satisfying film if it acknowledged the selfish nature of many of Ann's wishes. Few of us could avoid being self-absorbed in Ann's situation, but her lack of self-awareness is exasperating. Even some of her selfless decisions, such as her tape recordings intended to be played on her children's birthdays, become problematic in light of her refusal to tell them about her illness. "If I were one of those daughters and had grown old enough to have a vote on the matter," Roger Ebert asserts caustically, "I would burn the goddamn tapes and weep and pound the pillow and ask my dead mother why she was so wrapped up in her stupid, selfish fantasies that she never gave me the chance to say goodbye." My Life without Me does not hold up to critical scrutiny, but its central thesis remains provocative. What will college students include on their own lists? Will their lists be similar to or different from Ann's? To judge from their initial reactions when I gave them the assignment, my students seemed enthusiastic about it. The smiles on their faces suggested they would have fun while writing their lists and that they would be interested in hearing their classmates' lists as well. The assignment is an opportunity to engage in wish fulfillment, albeit short-lived. When I told them that I will read aloud some of the wishes on my own list, Elijah exclaimed challengingly, "Why don't you read all ten to us?" I agreed to his request but said that I would read them only after they wrote their own lists. What will I include on my own list of ten things to do before I die? Good question.

Love, Marriage, Children

Getting married received more first place votes than any other wish. Twelve out of fifty-five students chose it as their top wish, and another ten included it on their lists. The total number of students who desired to marry is probably higher, however, for several implied that "falling in love" led quickly to marriage. Some students had a specific betrothed in mind, while others did not. Marriage followed by immediate death did not appeal to most students, but the majority remained undeterred. "The most important thing in my life at this moment is the love I have for my girlfriend. It fills me with warmth, confidence, purpose, and joy. For about a year now I have dreamt about our wedding day. The immense happiness and bliss we would share throughout the ceremony and the after-party invades my thoughts constantly. Of course my partner would have to agree to marry me first, which may prove to be no easy task given the situation. I am not sure how I would react if the woman I loved asked me to marry her, a breath after she told me she was dying. Nevertheless, I understand the marriage day to be a monumental occasion for the two lovers involved, packed tight with pleasure, merrymaking, humor, and cheer, and I would like to experience this before I die."

A cynic might argue that marriage followed immediately by death would certainly lower the divorce rate. No one expressed this view—perhaps because no one wished to debunk the idea of marriage. I was surprised that marriage occupies the first spot for so many students, including those who do not have a specific person in mind. Several women implied that the wedding may be more important than marriage itself. Is this because they know they will soon die or because our culture emphasizes the ceremonial rituals of weddings? Having a wedding ceremony is important to men too, though not all are constrained by monogamous marriage. "I want to get married. I do not know if I would marry my present girlfriend. Maybe I like her too much to put her through that pain. But then again, much of what I will do before I die is selfish. I want that ceremony. I would like to have a plural marriage, which is polygamy."

Thirty-seven students included "falling in love" on their lists. This category received the greatest total number of votes, though only four selected it as their top choice. Several people indicated that they wanted a tempestuous, larger-than-life love, preferring intensity to duration. After all, they knew they would soon be dead, so they did not have to worry about permanence or constancy of love. Quoting a passage by D. H. Lawrence—"Love is the flower of life, and blossoms unexpectedly and without law, and must be plucked where it is found, and enjoyed for the brief hour of its duration"—Gladys elaborated on the wish: "I want a great passion, a flame (maybe 2 or 3; I'm very greedy). I have had this kind of love in my life, but it went too fast. Ironically, Lawrence claimed that 'Death is the only pure, beautiful conclusion of a great passion.'"

Beginning with Horace's ancient and much-borrowed theme of "carpe diem," there is a long literary tradition urging people to enjoy life before it is too late. The theme of *ubi sunt*, "where are [those who were before us?]," found throughout medieval Latin poetry, highlights life's transitoriness. I don't know how many of my students have read Robert Herrick's seventeenth-century poem "To the Virgins, to Make Much of Time," in which readers are urged to "Gather ye rosebuds while ye may, / Old time is still a-flying." Nor do I know how many of them have listened to Richard Wagner's ravishingly beautiful opera *Tristan und Isolde*, in which forbidden love culminates in a swan song, "Liebestod," followed by a double death. Nevertheless, the idea of a passionate love relationship appealed to many students, even if it resulted in rejection or disappointment. "[I want to] fall for a 'bad boy' even though I know he will ultimately break my heart. I've had a crush on the guy that was off limits before but I never did anything about it. I would take this opportunity to go wherever the wind took me including into the arms of the wrong guy. If my family and friends knew I was dying they would probably be more sympathetic to my need for adventure. Although I'm positive they would try to suggest several less hurtful/destructive ways to live on the edge. Falling for a 'bad boy' wouldn't be so painful when he broke my heart because I wouldn't have long to hold it against him."

Nineteen students included having one or more children on their lists. Many of these people did not mention falling in love or getting married. Two of the three who selected this as their top choice are men, and both wished to have sons to carry on the family name. (None of the women expressed this wish, perhaps because they've decided to give up their family name.) Elijah wanted to have a son to whom he would be a role model. "Although it will be very far down the road, I would like to have a son after I am financially established and settled down. I am not saying if I had a daughter I would be mad, but it would be really nice to have a son to teach how to play basketball and football. I think not having a father had a lot to do with wanting to raise a son but a lot of things would have to be in order. I would have to be married and financially sound in order to be in a situation to have children. I would like a son to show all of the things that I missed or never got as a child." Elijah's desire for fatherhood is so strong that he apparently has forgotten he has only a few months to live. Some of his classmates also ignored this crucial detail, for they desired having several children and inculcating them with moral values. Sara begins her list by assuming that, for the purpose of the assignment, she has eighteen months to live, but her desire to have the same close relationship with her daughter that her own mother has with her requires more time than she is allotted:

> For many years now, I have had a recurring dream of my own motherhood; in each, I am giving birth to a daughter whose face I can see so clearly that it is as if I could touch her. Only this dream daughter, if borne into flesh and blood one day, could ever be as entwined with my soul and marrow as my mother. She has been my rock throughout illness and tragedy, and she knows me better than I give her credit for. I can only imagine that this relationship will be mirrored with the one that will develop with my own daughter; it is a phenomenon completely of my mind and instinct, and I do not question either that a daughter will be born to me or that this metaphysical sympathy will be repeated. Whether I am a mother at the time of this [terminal] diagnosis or simply a daughter, I will need to spend some solitary time with both of these women. I do not doubt my relationship with my mother, and although she is not yet born, I do not doubt my relationship with my daughter. I know that I will need long windy nights of talk with them, by water. More even than the sky, I have always believed that I draw strength from the ocean. I will need all the strength of the tides to do this most difficult of tasks: to say all of the things that were never said to both of them.

Sara's dream depicts strikingly the special mother-daughter bond we discussed in the *Wuthering Heights* assignment. Words like "entwined" and "mirrored" suggest the symbiotic closeness of the intergenerational mother-daughter-granddaughter relationship. Everything about the dream is female, including the feeling of mystical oneness between mother and child and the mythic water imagery from which Sara draws strength. [In her later essay on euthanasia and physician-assisted suicide, Sara made an observation that highlights the mother-daughter bond: "There is a mystery within the workings of the relationship between a mother and a daughter; the death of one causes an unspeakable loss to the other. It is a loss different from others and more, perhaps, a loss of self. To be the individual who severs the tie between her mother and life is perhaps fitting in that sense, for it speaks to that mystery and symbiotic understanding, but it remains the most difficult of tasks."]

"Words of Comfort and Love"

Six people wanted to repair broken relationships. Many of these paragraphs are written to a parent and are among the most poignant on the list:

> First and foremost I would like to sit down and meet with my father, who I haven't seen or heard from in over sixteen years. In our conversation I would not

ask him the obvious and expected questions such as why he really left or whether or not he even loves me, because I know the answer to them. Deep down I know that my life is better off without him being a part of it. He was a self-destructive man dealing with drug and alcohol issues, and his behaviors could only have hurt our family. I want to let him know that my mother did an amazing job raising my brother and I singlehandedly and that we both could not have turned out better. Although I constantly deal with abandonment and trust issues because of his absence, which I would tell him about during our conversation, I think that I was raised into being a mature, independent woman with a good head on her shoulders. I am proud of the person that I have become and I want him to know that. I want him to know how amazing my mother is and that he should regret ever putting her through the pain that he did when he couldn't take care of himself and had to leave. Finally I want him to feel confident that neither my brother or myself will take the same path in life that he did. If he contributed to our lives at all, he made us more motivated to succeed.

Nine students listed religious or spiritual activities on their lists—a surprisingly small number in light of the overwhelming majority who wrote in earlier essays about their belief in God and in an afterlife. Some students wrote about seeking forgiveness from others. "I have to reconcile with those I may have wronged and those who have wronged me. I do not want to bring grudges to the grave. I also need to find that elusive, though lasting, spiritual peace. I am not referring to some new-age touchy-feely 'all dogs go to heaven' theology; I think I am going back to the faith of my youth. I wonder if God will take me back. I wonder if this 'eleventh hour' or deathbed conversion even counts for anything. Maybe I should forget everything else [on my list] and just concentrate on seeking forgiveness. After all, I am facing eternity." A woman intended to go to confession after a ten-year absence. "I am not sure what waits for me after this life, if anything at all, but I want to experience the ritual again. I will also like to feel safe with death, if there is such a feeling. I want to imagine that the things I have done wrong, the problems I have had or have created, will be left behind." Another woman listed baptism as her seventh wish. "I was never baptized as a baby, and now it doesn't really bother me. However, if I didn't have much time left, I don't think it would hurt to have some holy water sprinkled on my head." Another woman desired to make peace with God. "I tend to blame him for everything bad that ever happened to me or to anyone. I was infuriated at God when I lost my boyfriend to a terrible death, and I never made peace with him. In the end, I do believe in God, and I want to ask for forgiveness. Not just because I am dying, but because it is necessary at this point even if I lived." A man also vowed to be reconciled with God. "Religiousness has been something that I have long questioned. I was raised in a Catholic family; however, I have also seen how hypocritical a follower of that faith can be. I have a sense of feeling that there is something bigger than all of us beyond this life; however, again, I feel as though I am left with a sense of uncertainty and it is something I would like resolved before parting this life."

Saying goodbye to relatives and friends was a top wish for nine students, most of whom would do so through a letter. "Writing letters to the people who have had an impact on my life would be therapeutic for both myself and the receiver of the letter. It would allow me to reflect on my relationships with others, as well as my life experiences. Also, through writing I can better articulate my emotions. I think my friends and family would be comforted with the knowledge of their effect on my life. A letter is something that my family and friends can keep as a reminder of my love for them." Elijah vowed to say goodbye to his mother by visiting her grave:

> I was only four years old when my mother was taken away from me. I lived in a really dysfunctional family situation and I was not even aware she was dead until about three months after she passed. I was totally removed from the situation that I was in and taken away from the most important [person] in the world to me. I had to live with a family that I didn't know and I didn't get to go to my mother's funeral. It wasn't until I started college here at SUNY Albany and I had to get my mother's death certificate for school records that I saw where she was buried. Her grave is in Long Island, but I never had the opportunity to visit it. I don't know if it is because I don't have the strength to go or what it is, but I feel there is a void that needs to be filled before I can go on, and visiting her would bring me a lot of peace of mind. Out of all the things on my list, I feel that this is the most important thing.

Unlike Ann in My Life without Me, all but two of my students imagined they would tell their family and friends that they were dying. "I would meet with each person in my life that has held an important place, and tell him or her exactly how I feel. It would be a great comfort to me to leave this earth knowing that those who have meant something to me know how much they have influenced and touched my life. This is an important step that would allow me to die without regrets." One of the advantages of saying goodbye through a letter, another woman suggested, is the ability to maintain composure while expressing emotionally charged sentiments. "I have always been of the mind set that as long as my family is safe and secure, then I am at peace. Knowing that my death would greatly upset my family, it is important to me that I leave them words of comfort and love. I would be able to tell them everything that I could never manage to verbalize while I am alive. How much I appreciated every moment spent with them, and the laughter and love that they brought to my life."

Some students imagined having large, extravagant parties to say good-bye to relatives and friends. "My family is the most important aspect of my life, and this is my chance to show them how important they truly are to me. Each guest will receive a gift, a quote that says, ' 'Tis better to have loved and lost than never to have loved at all'—Alfred Lord Tennyson." One woman would attempt to reunite her family that has been riven for years by bitter hostilities. "Ever since I can remember, my family has had issues with each other. One aunt felt betrayed by another aunt, and therefore uncles do not talk. It is a complete mess, which leads to not seeing the ones I love. I chose to reunite my family before I die because I would love to have the remaining members of my family all together as we always used to be. I think I would die happy knowing that my family was whole again." Another person would meet an illegitimate sibling for the first time. "Without getting too personal, I have a half brother that was born out of wedlock. My father had an affair when I was young. The boy is much younger than I am. Right now he is not old enough to understand who I am, and I would prefer waiting until he is older. No one in my family would appreciate or want me to see him because of personal feelings. I have been told he looks like me when I was young, but the only difference is he has brown eyes rather than the deep green eyes that radiate from mine and my mother's faces. I want to meet this boy despite the circumstances simply because *he is my brother.*"

"I'd Keep My Passport in My Back Pocket"

Forty-eight students listed the desire to travel to another part of the world. Of the fifteen who would visit the country or continent of their family's origins, five would go to Italy, five to Ireland, two to the Dominican Republic, one to France, one to Israel, one to Sweden, one to Scotland, and one to Africa. (Some students have a dual heritage.) Several people believed that visiting their countries of origin would cast light on their families' histories and strengthen their connection to ancestors. This was especially true for Elijah, who promised to visit Africa to learn about his family's history:

> Many black people growing up in America feel disenfranchised their whole lives. We do not relate to people who are born in Africa today nor do we fit in well in white America. Dubois's theory on "Double Consciousness" is one of the most fitting and relevant pieces of writing I have ever had the opportunity to read. Black people in America have no real place to call home. Every type of people in America has somewhere they can call "home." White people can trace their heritage to whatever country their family came here from. Latinos, Asians, Native Americans all have that privilege to trace their lineage from somewhere. Even black people from the Caribbean have somewhere to relate to and have

pride for. But because African Americans are products of slaves who were brought here by force from a handful of west African countries, it is hard to pinpoint where you are from. And when people cannot be in tune with their roots, it makes them feel like something is missing. Fortunately, there are saliva and hair follicle tests that can be done to match up any person of African descent's DNA in order to find out what country they originate from. I would like to take the test, find the results, and visit that country before I die.

Apart from visiting their countries of origin, students wished to travel both to experience the beauty of other parts of the world and to expand their understanding of life. "If I had only one more year to live," one woman wrote, "I'd keep my passport in my back pocket and hit the road." Europe was the overwhelming top choice followed by the mainland United States, Hawaii, Canada, Egypt (especially the pyramids), the Caribbean, Australia, Mexico, Africa, and Asia. The leading sites within the United States were New York City, Las Vegas, California, and Disney World. Some of these students stated that they would feel ready to die after visiting other parts of the world.

Skydiving, Eating, Shopping, Fighting

Many people included daredevil activities on their lists: danger wasn't a problem if they were going to die soon. By far the most popular of these activities was skydiving, which eleven students mentioned. "I have not exactly been an extreme sports kind of girl, but I believe everyone needs a little excitement in their life. Skydiving is something that I have always had an interest in. It has got to be one of the most incredible feelings. Just the thought of being weightless in the air with only the clouds and sky around you would be amazing. I honestly do not think that there could be another experience quite like that. As scary as it may be, I feel that it would bring an overwhelming sense of clarity to life, especially when faced with the idea of death." Other adventurous activities included white water rafting, bungee jumping, hot air ballooning, race car or motorcycle driving, airplane piloting, and hang gliding. One woman was determined to break 100 miles per hour on the highway. "I drive an Audi A4 and the speedometer goes to 160. I think the highest I have ever gotten is to 90. I have always dreamed of breaking 100 mph on a safe road where I know no one will be hurt. There is something about driving with the wind in your hair, and the vroom of that German engine that is just indescribable (or so I imagine)."

Two men spoke less affectionately about their automobiles. "The sensation of putting a .45 Magnum to the grill of my 1997 VW Jetta would bring more gratification to me than I can express and help me rest at peace. Knowing that no poor soul will ever have to have this financially draining piece of shit in their possession by putting a bullet (or many) through it would make me feel as though I have settled a huge debt to society." His classmate imagined a different form of mercy killing. "For the past five years, my 1997 Mercury Sable has been nothing but trouble for me. Every time that I save a reasonable sum of hard-earned money, a problem arises that I must fix. I worked as a technician for three years, and have become quite handy with car maintenance services. However, I am rarely able to fix the problems with my car, and must spend my savings to keep it on the road. I believe it is understandable why, as I approach the end of my life, I would choose to set my car on fire. I would have no use for it when I'm dead, and it would not be worth much money if my family sold it. It would make a great bonfire!"

Five women—but no men—listed food cravings, including the wish to indulge a voracious appetite. "I am a bottomless pit. However, no one believes how much I can really shovel down in one sitting. I am pretty positive if given a whole day I can eat an entire Thanksgiving dinner all by myself—turkey and all. It would be a pretty amazing story for people to tell their friends in the future. I'd love to be the girl who took a whole Thanksgiving dinner to the face." Another woman savored the thought of sushi. "Since I am going to die, no one is allowed to comment on the health risks of eating raw fish." Another relished eating as much food as possible. "Delicious salty and fatty food would be preferable, and as I will be dying, I don't have to worry about my health." Another salivated over the thought of spending two weeks gratifying food cravings. "I spend so much time watching everything that I put into my mouth. I love food. I love food that tastes great, and it would feel great to eat whatever I'd like for awhile." And another dreamed of a food-tasting tour. "I would travel all over the country to experience the authenticity of flavors, taste, and ingredients. I would not want to die on an empty stomach." She added that she is so "completely and utterly serious" about her passion for food that she would steal boxes of chocolate pudding at a local supermarket even if it meant getting caught. "I believe getting arrested for stealing chocolate pudding would make me the greatest thief of all because it is so ridiculous and unheard of. This is better than stealing money; you can't eat money." As with food cravings, many women wished to alter their physical appearance. Two women planned to dye their hair blonde. "My hair color is naturally dark, and although I enjoy being brunette I've always wondered what I would look like blonde. As the saying goes, they do have more fun, and I figured if my time was limited, why not experience life as a blonde? Of course when I die I would ask that my hair be dyed back to my original color. I'm not sure if there's an afterlife, but I don't think that I would want to spend all of eternity with bleached blonde locks."

Women were just as interested in daredevil activities as men, but the latter seemed more inclined to resort to violence to avenge perceived historical or personal wrongs. Thus Alen, presumably a diehard New York Yankees fan, dreamed of setting fire to Fenway Park. "I despise Boston, the Red Sox, and anything related to either. It would please me a great deal to see the century-old green monster engulfed in red flames; the look on the faces of Red Sox faithful would be priceless." Not all the violent fantasies came from the men in the class, however. Three women listed the wish to get into a physical fight with another person. "I am not an advocate for violence," one wrote, "but I have always wondered what it would be like to get worked up to the point where I would punch someone. Before I die, I would like to get into one solid fistfight that people will remember." "This is a weird one," a second woman admitted, "but I think it's something I have to do before I die. Haven't you ever just wanted to smack the living daylights out of someone, but held yourself back because of the consequences? Well, if I'm dying, and I want to whack someone, I'm not going to hold back. I'm not saying I want to go around punching every person who cuts me off or takes the last blueberry scone at Starbucks, but if you deserve a good smackin', I'm going to give it to you." "I know this sounds terrible," wrote a third woman, who had defined herself in an earlier essay as a born-again Christian, "however, I have always wanted to hit my mother. She was a terrible parent. She is a perfect example of someone that should never have had children. She was cruel and hurtful. I want her to feel at least a fraction of the pain she has caused me throughout my life. I want to stand over her and watch her cry. As she is crying, I want to tell her that I am glad I mad her cry, the same phrase she has uttered to me on many occasions." The presumed Freudian slip—"mad" for "made"—confirms the depth of her anger.

Sex, Lies, and Videotape

Two women wanted to spend a night in jail before the arrival of the grim reaper. "I want to commit one comical, yet mildly serious crime so that I land myself in the slammer for one night. Possibly after a night of consuming significant amounts of alcohol so that I would not be acting my particular sober self. I want them to handcuff me, read me my rights, and then take me down to the station. I do not want it to be anything too serious, just a one-night experience. It would be completely unexpected of me, but I feel as though it would be something people would be talking about for years to come." Her classmate had the same fantasy. "As strange as it might sound, I would like to get arrested before I die. I want to experience the feeling of being in jail, almost as a thrill. Even though it would mean I had to do something illegal, I am having my life taken away from me; this is justification enough."

Four students imagined illegal or unethical ways to obtain money. One saw herself taking out a loan of $100,000 under the name of her mother's former friend (a woman who had "backstabbed" her mother a few years earlier) to buy herself a new Mercedes Benz. After acquiring additional revenue from selling drugs, she would then give the money to her mother. A second would take out as many loans as possible to fund the other nine activities on her wish list, including renting a beach house in the Bahamas. A third would exhaust the limits of her credit cards. The fourth would rob a bank. "It wouldn't be just a put your hands in the air and give me all your money type of robbery. I would plan it out and steal the money without bringing attention to myself. Instead of putting people in harm, I would try to figure out a way where I could steal the money at night. After months of planning I would commit the act and leave untouched with bags of money. From there I would drive to Las Vegas and I would gamble and drink until it was all gone." Five students would experiment with illegal drugs, such as cocaine, ecstasy, and mushrooms. One of these students longed to go on a "drug spree" while having a friend videotape her. "I want to see how I acted while I was under the influence of drugs. I would also enjoy seeing what I would say. This video footage will turn into a documentary for adolescents and adults. The video will focus on the dangers but also the funny moments of dabbling in illicit drugs."

Only eight students included sex on their wish list, a smaller number than those who wished to go skydiving. Does this imply that skydiving is now sexier than carnal pleasure or that few of my students' sexual lives need improvement? Three women identified themselves as virgins but pledged to have sex before they died. "I am a virgin by choice," wrote one, "but I am not waiting for marriage specifically. I was debating putting this on my list but I think it is important. I put this on my list only with the intention of being with someone I love. I think it's an experience you must have before you die." A second classmate agreed. "One of the few regrets of my life is that I did not yield to this temptation when I had the chance. Since this mistake I've yet to be tempted. I am a very sensual person and sex is something that is very important to me. While I am a virgin, I suffer no mild libido; I'm simply waiting for the temptation to present himself." A third classmate felt so strongly about losing her virginity before death that she was prepared to incur her mother's disapproval. "I can hear my mother right now saying to me, 'you're not married and you [know] what the Bible says about having sex before you're married.' My response to her would be, 'Mom, I love you, but I'm going to die in two months, so Jesus should understand.' I would then explain to her that I've always been a 'good girl' and I want to be naughty for once." The most unusual sexual fantasy came from a bibliophile. "Everybody has sexual fantasies. One of mine is to commit fornication in a library. Libraries are quiet areas of study and learning, which is precisely why I find them particularly challenging to commit such an act in. I am adventurous and seek thrills; libraries are no exception. The difficulty is achieving this goal without getting caught in the act. Successfully completing this task would require quickness, alertness, and bravery, qualities I hope to master."

Richard's Responses to the Students' Wish Lists

The following are interesting "to do's" from the essays Jeff read today in class. My comments are in italics:

1. With my father gone, I'd like to hug my mother while sleeping. *The willingness to be unashamed at touching another family member because of genuine caring is remarkable.*

2. Get married. *This seeking of connection is here; is there also connection in repeating of the past, dream weddings, and completion through another?*

3. Go to Africa (feeling the effects of diaspora, as a person of one race is forced to lose his place of origin, hopes such a trip using genetic testing will reveal much about himself). *This origin-seeking act was very powerful. The unwilling migration of Africans to this country is in need of healing. I wonder if this would do it. There is a Visa commercial in which a daughter travels to Ireland with her mother claiming that the original environment explains the mother to her. People have settled the U.S. without real interest in staying; America is a land of opportunity, not necessarily life. Immigrants send money back home; people from India and Latin America are most known for this today. Going home to one's native land seems like a beautiful completion narrative. I wonder how it would work. If one got genetic testing done and discovered one was from Ghana, Nigeria, and France, what would this say? Are the tests likely to show further divergence than these three places? Origin seeking would then be complicated, to say the least.*

4. Get in a fight. "Haven't you ever wanted to smack someone?" *Even with all our technology, language, and psychology, this points to our inability to solve problems. Fighting is probably our oldest destructive urge, and we have yet to be able to deal with it fully. Of course, if this urge is so primary, the denial of it can't be healthy, can it? I'm glad people spoke of these physical urges that are considered unspeakable in public. Still, how we deal with it is unknown for me. What steps in talking about this will lead to a cure? Does the urge need a cure?*

5. Fornicate in a library, which would require quickness, alertness, and bravery. *The physicality of this surrounded by the cerebral as represented by books is fun and shows how body and mind are important in some combination.*

6. Beat up my mom—stand over her and watch her cry and mutter the same phrases she has over me. *We expect so much of our parents. In this case, abuse seems to be present in that the parent put a burden on the child. However, even without violence, this power struggle with parents, generation to generation, seems unavoidable.*

7. Spend one night in jail. *Was this taken from* One True Thing? *I often wanted to be in a psychiatric hospital when I was younger. Now I take this childhood desire as my continued ability to miscommunicate with other people. Truly, I never wanted to be in jail or in a psychiatric hospital. I think there wouldn't be much gained except perhaps empathy for the underprivileged—a close look at what can happen to those who don't make it in the country.*

8. Set my car on fire! It would make a great bonfire. *I would like to be brave enough to do this now and start taking the bus. It's terrible that we'd need to be dying before we could get rid of some of the things that actually bring us little joy. I love this person for putting this in his top ten.*

9. Fake my death and attend my own funeral to see what people say and how they care about me. *This would be very interesting. I also think it has been part of a few stories—for example, the movie* We're No Angels. *For me, I'd hate to trick anyone this way. Perhaps I'm living a fiction, but I get enough understanding of what people think of me when I'm alive. It's something that literature teaches us. Information can be gathered by what people say, how people talk about third parties, and eventually when gossip returns to my ears. I think I have enough information to make fair conclusions about how people care and feel. Still, it is an interesting proposition that someone would know only through being absent.*

10. Talk to a priest and feel safe in the ritual of it again. *I feel this way about sports. I mistrust sports because I think they're rituals that blind people to important issues in life. This is especially true for people who love watching sports. Watching is a poor replacement for real life, yet as a child playing dodge ball, kick ball, or soccer there was such purity in the game. Everything made sense if you played your hardest. I do think this is the benefit of roles, even if I still don't trust anything ritual.*

11. Dye my hair blonde. *This was funny for the class. Personally, I've always found it unusual that before my wife, I ONLY dated blondes. I never consciously did this on purpose, but I wonder about what catches our eyes. The TV show* 20/20 *has done several tests on "the blonde effect," most recently showing blondes are better able to sell door-to-*

door merchandise and get attention. Dyeing one's hair blonde or not, I think seeking attention before one died would be a possibility for many (most?) people.

My Own List

My own list seems ordinary compared with my students' imaginative lists. But that's partly because I'm three times older than most of my students, and I have no interest in skydiving, fast cars, illicit drugs, expensive clothes, body tattoos, shopping, fighting, or endless eating. Unlike Ann in *My Life without Me*, I would not include on my wish list smoking, drinking, or doing something with my hair (other than preserving the little that I have). Nor do I need to wait until death to say what I think. Getting out of bed each morning and running two miles with my dogs fulfills my need for adventure. I've never dreamed of robbing a bank or getting arrested or spending a night in jail. Like most people, I have less need for money as I grow old. Since Barbara's death, my life has become more introspective, more inner directed, and I spend most days and nights reading and writing, activities that require solitude. Not surprisingly, most of the items on my list revolve around reading, writing, teaching, and grandparenting, activities that affirm education, continuity, and generativity:

1. Tell My Children and Grandchildren Every Day That I Love Them. From the moment of her diagnosis until her death, I told Barbara every day that I loved her. Indeed, I said this to her nearly every day of our married life. I will make the same statement to my children and grandchildren every time I speak with them. This was also number one on Ann's list in *My Life without Me*, but I thought of it first. Long before her illness, Barbara and I ended every telephone conversation with each other and with our children in this way. Admittedly, "I love you" can become trite and mechanical, but when heartfelt, they remain the three most beautiful words in the English language.

2. Write Letters to My Children and Grandchildren. I will write letters to my children and grandchildren, telling them how much I love them, how proud I am of them, and how they are the joy of my and Barbara's life. In all of these letters I will recall my favorite memories of each person and leave something special to him or her. I hope I can write enough new books to dedicate each one to a different grandchild. And I will make each grandchild promise to read the entire book carefully.

3. Write Letters to My Closest Friends. I have been fortunate to have so many dear and trusted friends, and I will write a letter to each

one, recalling our favorite times together and expressing my gratitude for his or her friendship. I will remember those friends who have predeceased me and will ask those who survive me to remember how important they were to me.

4.   Finish the Book or Article I Am Writing. It will be important for me to finish whatever writing project on which I'm working. I suspect that my last writings will have something to do with Barbara, for both in life and death she has been my muse. Writing has long been one of the sources of great pleasure and satisfaction in my life, but this is even more true now that she is no longer here. Writing has not completely filled up the void left by her absence, but it has helped me through a time of intense sadness and loneliness. Writing has also allowed me to focus my life on other people, especially my students, who have been at the center of my life since I began teaching. My early books were psychoanalytic studies of literature, but beginning with my 1994 book *Diaries to an English Professor*, I have taken special interest in writing about my teaching. Both my teaching and scholarship have become student-oriented, and my pedagogy demonstrates how they respond intellectually and emotionally to class readings and writings. Many of my students have written about traumatic experiences, and nearly all of them have concluded, in signed and anonymous evaluations, that they felt better as a result of writing. So too did I feel better as I was writing *Dying to Teach*.

Writing about Barbara has been a form of communion with her, a way of keeping her close to me. Writing creates or re-creates an absent presence, reminding us that remembering the dead brings them back to life again in our hearts. If "dying is simple," as Jane Kenyon suggests near the end of her life, "what's worst is . . . the *separation* (Donald Hall, *Without* 42). Writing helps to overcome that separation by creating a verbal portrait of the deceased and by allowing author and reader to enter into an imagined dialogue with the dead. This helps to explain the popularity of memoirs that celebrate the lives of deceased spouses, such as C. S. Lewis's *A Grief Observed*, John Bayley's *Elegy for Iris* and *Iris and Her Friends*, Donald Hall's *The Best Day the Worst Day*, Sandra Gilbert's *Wrongful Death*, Joan Didion's *The Year of Magical Thinking*, and Calvin Trillin's *About Alice*. These memoirs are all life affirming, enabling us to grasp, to quote Trillin, "what Ernest Becker meant when he said something like 'To live fully is to live with an awareness of the rumble of terror that underlies everything,' or to begin to understand the line in *King Lear*—'Ripeness is all'" (9). These memoirs offer us a glimpse of beloved spouses and enlarge our understanding of the possibility of love, passion, kindness, intimacy, and dignity. Barbara also embodied these qualities, which I have tried to convey first to my students and then to my readers. I hope that my books will be read by many students, particularly those who have generously allowed me to use their diaries and essays in my research. I also hope that these students will recall with pleasure the classes they took with me that inspired their writings.

5. Finish the Semester. I hope that I will be teaching to the end of my life and that I will finish the term before I expire. I don't want my students to be saddened by my death. I have loved every class I have taught and regard my teaching career as the best part of my life. And I hope that my students remember me with the same great affection with which I remember them. They have made a difference in my life just as I have tried to make a difference in theirs.

6. Update My Self-Eulogy. I intend to end this book with the chapter "A Teacher's Self-Eulogy." I intend to update the self-eulogy, and I will ask someone to read it at the memorial service I would like to have at the university. This memorial service will replace a funeral service. I hope that the eulogies delivered at my memorial service will be as deeply felt as my self-eulogy. Remember, I will be watching you.

7. Get My Affairs in Order. I already have a New York State Health Care Proxy, allowing my children to make medical decisions for me if I am incapacitated; a New York Living Will, directing my attending physician to withhold or withdraw treatment that merely prolongs my dying; a Durable General Power of Attorney, allowing my children to handle my property during my lifetime; and a Last Will and Testament, leaving all my assets to my children. I have already opened 529 College Savings Accounts so that I can help to fund my grandchildren's higher education. I have also signed the back of my driver's license so I may donate organs or body parts to those who might need them. I will endow an annual prize at my university for the best undergraduate and graduate essays on literature as a healing art.

8. Visit Israel and Greece. Barbara and I loved to travel together, and we journeyed throughout the United States, Canada, and Europe. I traveled little on my own for the first two years after her death. During the summer of 2006, when I started writing this book, I attended a weeklong psychoanalytic conference in Helsinki, Finland, and when it ended, I flew to Russia, where I traveled for another week. Now that I am emotionally able to travel alone, I

intend to visit places I have not yet seen. While visiting an Albany museum, I saw a book called *1,000 Places to See before You Die*, by Patricia Schultz. The opening paragraph captivated me: "The urge to travel—to open our minds and move beyond the familiar—is as old as man himself. It's what drove the ancient Romans to visit Athens's Acropolis and Verona's Amphitheater. It's what sent Marco Polo off on his momentous journey east, and what moved Saint Augustine of Hippo to write, 'The world is a book, and those who do not travel, read only one page'" (xi). I agree that travel is a "classroom without walls," and before I die I will visit Israel and Greece. I could easily visit them now, and I suspect I will in the next few years. Both countries hold special interest to a dying person: Israel is the cradle of the world's three major religions, and Greece is the birthplace of Western literature, art, and philosophy. Visiting Delphi, the site of the fabled oracle in ancient Greece, will reaffirm my belief that knowledge is power.

9. Spend Three Weeks in New York City, London, and Paris. Barbara and I loved visiting these great cities, visiting museums, literary sites, architectural wonders, and concert halls. If possible, I will take my children and grandchildren with me.

10. Attend a Performance of Beethoven's Ninth Symphony at Tanglewood. I will attend as many classical music concerts as possible. Beethoven is my favorite composer, and although he was a difficult and at times overbearing person, he remains an inspirational figure for me. Music helped him to endure perhaps the cruelest irony that can beset a musician—deafness. "When I am playing and composing," he told a friend, "my affliction . . . hampers me least" (Solomon, *Beethoven* 124). The only time in my life that I have experienced something akin to transcendence is when I listen to Beethoven. I love all his symphonies, but my favorites are the Third (the Eroica); the Fifth, containing the most famous four notes in music; the Sixth, called the Pastoral because of its idyllic depiction of the countryside; the Seventh, with its Bacchic dance rhythms that drive the listener to a state of delirium; and the incomparable Ninth, which ends with Schiller's "Ode to Joy." As Beethoven's biographer Maynard Solomon observes about the ending of the Ninth Symphony, "Elysium can be gained only by overcoming terrifying obstacles: the road to immortality leads through death" (*Late Beethoven* 218). Barbara and I heard the Ninth Symphony performed many times at Tanglewood, and after hearing this work in a live performance, I will be ready to die.

"Live like You Were Dying"

This was my students' favorite assignment to date, and they found it challeng-ing and fun. Nearly everyone felt that it was more about life than about death. "As proclaimed in the lyrics of a song by Tim McGraw," one person wrote, "everyone should 'Live like You Were Dying.'" The assignment helped them to order their goals and values. "It made me think of all the wonderful things I haven't yet experienced and might not be able to." Remarked another, "It made me think about just what I want to do in my life, and I made a promise to myself that I would try to do everything on my list."

The students felt they had learned a great deal from the assignment:

I learned that I'm lucky to be alive.
I learned that life is full of opportunities and most of them are worth doing before the end. I learned not to waste my time. Life doesn't wait.
I learned how sad and scary it will be to know that your time is limited.
I learned that my parents are even more important to me than I thought.
I learned that I love my father, and I miss him.
I learned that I really want to travel and go on adventures.
I learned that I am a lot closer to my mother than I originally thought and over spring break we really bonded because of this.

Nearly everyone enjoyed the selections I read aloud:

I wish I had thought of some of them.
I think that making peace is important. Although it is not part of my list, I would like to make peace with my own mother.
They were funny and heartfelt. I was saddened by the series of tumultuous relationships many students have with their parents.

The overwhelming majority of students believed they would do more than half of the items on their lists. Money and time would be limiting factors. "I would attempt to do most but due to monetary restraints, I'm not sure how many would be possible." Twenty-two believed they would do all ten. One person wrote, "As many as I could. For Christ sake, I'm dying. It's not that easy."

What did my students' lists reveal about how they imagined spending their last months alive? I asked each of them to rank the following statements in order of importance. Twenty-eight students selected as their first choice the statement, "I was mostly interested in saying goodbye to relatives and friends (including expressing my love for them, asking for forgiveness from them, etc.)." Eleven students selected as their top choice the statement, "I was mostly

interested in experiencing as much pleasure as possible." Seven students selected as their top choice the statement, "I was mostly interested in doing
things I've never done before." Only two students selected as their top choice
the statement, "I was mostly interested in pursuing spiritual or religious
truths." No one selected as a top choice the statement, "I was mostly interested
in getting my affairs in order (such as in writing a will, giving away my
possessions, finding a cemetery, etc.)." Like the overwhelming majority of my
students, my own top choice would be to say goodbye to relatives and friends:
three items on my list are about leave-taking, and another four are about
getting my affairs in order. The fourth and fifth items on my list—finishing a
writing project and completing the semester—indicate the importance of
work in my life—far more important than pleasure. Expressed differently, my
work is my pleasure.

Nearly everyone recommended that I use the assignment again. Most
preceded "Yes" with words like "definitely" or "absolutely." One person wrote,
in capital letters, "YES, OH GOD YES" with eight exclamation points. This
was also my favorite assignment, and I started thinking about my own list as
soon as I saw My Life without Me. Like some of my students, I found this
assignment more challenging than I anticipated. What I did not include on
my list—I don't think I was ready to read this to my students—is the desire to
fall in love again. Barbara told me twice shortly before her death that she
hoped I would find another woman—not a "replacement wife," as Ann finds
her husband in My Life without Me—but a companion so that I would not feel
sad and lonely for the rest of my life. This was her gift to me—one of the many
gifts she bequeathed me. But unlike Ann in the film, I would want to fall in
love again *before* a diagnosis of terminal illness. Whether this will happen is
anyone's guess. Love is always risky and unpredictable, like life itself, and the
best we can do, as Dickens reminds us, is to accept happiness as a gift and
delight in it when it comes.

9

~

Writing about Euthanasia and Physician-Assisted Suicide

Monday, April 24

I wasn't sure whether I would tell my students how distressing it has been to reread Anna Quindlen's novel *One True Thing*, but I decided to do so, especially after discovering a Freudian slip I made yesterday while writing my notes for today's class. In the prologue to the novel, Ellen Gulden recalls telling her mother, Kate, who is racked by unending pain from metastatic ovarian cancer, that "I am dying with you." She then admits, "The truth is that I did not kill my mother. I only wished I had" (12–13). In my notes for this page, I intended to write, "Ellen denies killing her mother," but instead I wrote, "Ellen dies killing her mother." I stared at the sentence for several seconds before realizing what I had written. However melodramatic it sounds, sometimes I feel that my life has ended with Barbara's death. I know there are still many reasons to live and enjoy life to the fullest, but I can't deny the fact that the best part of my world is gone. While driving to school, I saw another meaning to my verbal slip: if I were in Ellen's situation, I would have felt so guilty honoring Kate's request that it would have been like killing both her and myself.

I could hear my voice tremble when I read Kate's desperate plea to her daughter for morphine. "'Help me, Ellen,' she whispered. 'I don't want to live like this anymore. . . . Please,' she said. 'You must know what to do. Please. Help me. No more'" (229). I then pointed out how, in real life, Ellen never would have been charged with homicide, since physicians can prescribe as much morphine as is necessary to alleviate a terminally ill patient's suffering— even a fatal dose. I learned about the "double effect" only after Barbara's death, when I began researching end-of-life care. As the bioethicist Margaret Pabst Battin states in her book *The Least Worst Death*, the double effect implies that "one may perform an action with a bad effect—for instance, the death of a person—provided one foresees but does not intend that bad effect; one must be doing the act to achieve a different good effect (hence the name, 'double' effect)" (17). Four conditions must be met to justify the double effect: "the action must not be intrinsically wrong"; "the agent must intend only the good effect, not the bad one"; "the bad effect must not be the means of achieving the good effect"; and "the good effect must be 'proportional' to the bad one, that is, outweigh it" (17). Battin cites the example commonly used in Roman Catholic moral theology: "A surgeon may remove a cancerous uterus in order to save the life of the mother, though this will also bring about the death of a fetus developing there, provided the surgeon's intention is to save the mother: the surgeon foresees, but does not intend, that the procedure will also kill the fetus" (17). An even more common example is a physician prescribing a massive dose of morphine to allay a terminally ill patient's unendurable pain, knowing that it will lead to death.

Finally, I described the agonizing moral, legal, and psychological dilemma in which I found myself when Barbara asked me, shortly before lapsing into a semicoma, if I could give her "all her medication." As I acknowledge in *Dying to Teach*, it was for me the most distressing moment of Barbara's illness.

> She asked the question in a weak, barely audible voice, and I had to strain to hear her. Troubled by the question, and not exactly sure what she meant by it, I told her that I couldn't do that. She seemed to accept my answer, to which she offered no response, but a day or two later she made the same request over the telephone to our children, who responded in the same way that I did. Arielle then asked me if I should hide the morphine pills from her mother. The question compelled me, almost against my will, to ask Barbara what she meant by it. "Did you mean that you wanted me to give you a fatal overdose of morphine?" I asked, chilled by my own words, to which she responded, in a whispering voice, "yes." "I can't do that, sweetie; it would be too upsetting to me." After a pause, I added, "Do I need to hide the morphine from you?" "No," she responded, faintly, and we never discussed the subject again. (87)

Barbara's question and my response are fraught with so many painful ironies. Since Len's death by his own hand in 1968, I have spent my life studying, writing, teaching, and talking about suicide, yet not for a moment had I anticipated Barbara's request. How could I have been so unprepared for it? I would have gladly sacrificed my life for hers, and I did everything I could to ease her suffering, yet I rejected her plea because it would have been too upsetting for *me*. How could I have ignored what was in *Barbara's* best interest? Nor can I invoke religious belief, as many would in my situation, to justify rejecting a beloved spouse's request to die mercifully. Throughout my life I have believed in the value of talking and in the Socratic injunction that knowledge is power, but I did not want to hear Barbara's question nor did I want to understand what she meant by it. Fear overwhelmed me, as it may have overwhelmed her, and I will never know whether she was in her "right mind" when she asked the question—she was already taking a massive amount of morphine, which resulted in confusion and disorientation. Nor do I know what she would have wanted me to do had I answered her question affirmatively. Such requests, I discovered later, are not uncommon, as Ira Byock explains: "It is a rare person dying of a terminal illness who does not think about suicide. Most often, I have found, persistent thoughts of suicide are really a response to unbearable pain" (44). Eric Cassell makes a similar observation, arguing that the major reason for such requests is the desire to end pain, even if it means ending life: "Sometimes patients with terminal illness will ask for help in dying. It is important to understand that such requests do not arise because someone wants to die. Rather, the patients would rather die than live as they are" (289).

Barbara's question to me is the same question Kate asks Ellen—the most excruciating question imaginable. The question is so appalling that neither Kate nor Barbara used the word "suicide" in their pleas for help. One can only imagine how horrifying this question must be for the dying person, who is forced to speak indirectly, euphemistically. This is precisely the question that I asked my students to write about in the sixth assignment, which is due on Wednesday:

> Perhaps the most wrenching question raised in *One True Thing* is whether Ellen will honor her mother's wish to end her life—a life that is tortured by unbearable suffering. Kate's request, however, places Ellen in a legal, moral, and psychological dilemma, since euthanasia is illegal, contrary to the Judeo-Christian tradition, and likely to produce intense guilt.
>
> What would you have done in Ellen's situation? To what extent do your religious beliefs influence your thinking on euthanasia and physician-assisted suicide? If you decide to honor Kate's request, would you inform your relatives of what you intend to do? Do you believe there is value in discussing in class the topic of euthanasia and physician-assisted suicide? Please explain.

Unlike Kate, Barbara did not take her own life, and I was not arrested and investigated by a grand jury, as Ellen is after her mother's death, but I identify with Ellen's feelings of horror and helplessness as she watches her mother die. "Death is so strange, so mysterious, so sad, that we want to blame someone for it. And it was easy to blame me. Besides, when people wonder how I survived being accused of killing my mother, none of them realizes that watching her die was many, many times worse. And knowing I could have killed her was nothing compared to knowing I could not save her" (370).

I was not trying to change my students' minds about euthanasia and physician-assisted suicide by having them write on this question, but I was attempting to open their minds to this complex and controversial subject. Before Barbara's illness I was opposed to helping a person die, fearing that it might lead to relatives pressuring loved ones to die. After Barbara's death, when I began to study the growing body of research on end-of-life care, I discovered that the opposite scenario is much more likely. On 5 October 2004, exactly six months after Barbara's death, I attended a lecture at Union College by Gerrit Kimsma, a Dutch expert on physician-assisted suicide. He told me that caregivers are generally unable to let their loved ones die, contrary to the patients' wishes. He indicated that 90 percent of the Dutch public favor physician-assisted suicide, and that there is the same high support from the medical and nursing professions. Our hospice aides told us that it is helpful for a family to give a relative "permission" to die: such consent seems to hasten merciful death. I now believe that the system of physician-assisted suicide as practiced in the Netherlands and in Oregon, the only state in our country where it is legal, is both wise and humane. Nevertheless, even if I knew then what I know now, I doubt that I would have been emotionally able to give Barbara a fatal dose of morphine, if only because I would not be able to withhold this information from my daughters, with whom I consulted on every important medical decision concerning their mother. I would not have wanted to make my children unintentional accomplices of my illegal act. I don't believe there is a simple right-or-wrong answer to the question of whether Ellen should have honored her mother's request to die, but I do believe that much will be gained by an honest and forthright discussion.

Talking about the parallels between Kate's and Barbara's requests to die was by far the most torturous discussion of the semester for me, and for that reason I was interested in Richard's perception of the class, which he offered in his diary:

> Jeff has said that *One True Thing* is going to be a very difficult book for him to teach, and though he shares that rereading it brought him to tears—a tearful state he was fearful of showing to a colleague who saw him in the hall—he appears to be holding it together for the sake of his students quite well. The questions of why Kate stayed with George, despite his infidelity, centered much of the discussion in class. I sensed that students had trouble with this faithful, loving act on the part of Kate, something that Ellen surely does not appreciate. "Love what you've got" is a difficult concept for many students. It may seem like settling. I feel very sad for George. I'm angry at him too, but mostly sad that he cannot overcome his fear enough to actually connect with his wife. At least it's

positive that Ellen does learn to appreciate her mother, wants to take her lessons over those she always valued as characteristics from her father.

Most interesting Jeff quote: "As a primary caregiver, one will feel guilt no matter what one does or doesn't do for the loved one." This is a Catch-22 situation that many would avoid. As a matter of psychological survival, we would like to avoid this double-edged sword of choice where we cut ourselves no matter what.

Wednesday, April 26

Today my students turned in their essays, which I began to read immediately. They were divided over the issue of whether they would honor Kate's request to die. Of the fifty-five students who turned in essays, twenty-four (almost 44 percent) indicated they would honor Kate's request, eighteen (33 percent) would not, and twelve (22 percent) were not sure. (One person did not respond to the question.) Thirty-three students (60 percent) wrote that they would feel guilt regardless of their decision. Interestingly, those who would not honor Kate's request were more likely to feel guilt than those who would help her die. I did not expect this finding, but I can understand it. Many students would agree with the following observation: "Guilt would play a big role in my decision. I'd feel guilty if I did and guilty if I didn't. If I killed her and got away with it, I would have to live forever with the fact that I ended my mom's life. If I didn't get away with it, I'd not only be torturing myself mentally but I'd physically be suffering in jail. On the other hand, if I didn't end her pain, I'd have to live with the fact that she suffered until she died, and I could have saved her from all that." Not surprisingly, religion played a much stronger role in influencing those who would not help Kate die. Some people said they would feel guilt not from honoring Kate's request to die but from being unable to tell anyone what they did.

Over the years I have given hundreds of writing assignments, and one of the most emotionally charged topics has been writing about suicide. But writing about euthanasia or physician-assisted suicide is more gut wrenching, for it involves the decision to end—or *not* to end—a beloved relative or friend's unbearable agony. The assignment posed difficulties for those who have confronted end-of-life care and for those who have not. Most students were in the latter group, and many of them said that regardless of their position on euthanasia, they could not predict whether they would be able to end another person's suffering. As one remarks, "we are tongue-tied when we are asked the highly emotional question, 'Would you help your mother commit suicide?'"

Several female students in this group observed that assisting in their mothers' deaths was the most horrifying thought imaginable. "I, like Ellen, could not deal with the guilt of knowing I am the reason my mother is dead. The guilt alone would kill me. I do not think I could live with a secret like that." The guilt is stronger for those who grew up without a father. "I have had no contact with my father since my parents' divorce when I was four years old. Because of this, being asked to assist my mother in death would be like asking me to kill both my parents." The closer the daughter is to her mother, the more painful it is to contemplate her death. "Unlike Ellen and her mother early in the story, my mother and I are incredibly close. I don't know what I would do if I were faced with the idea of losing her; she is essentially all that I have left. Ironically, the last time that I was home from school, my mother insisted that she and I go over the living will that she had begun creating; the very thought of it made me ill." Some students believed that they would lose their sanity if they honored their mother's request to die. "How could I live with myself if I helped my mother end her life? For the rest of my life I would live with an immense guilt over what I did. My thoughts would not let me go through with normal daily activities. I would develop a psychological disorder and would seriously go insane." Even those students who responded humorously to the question could not imagine themselves ending a mother's life. "I strongly believe that my mother is completely indestructible and in the event of worldwide nuclear destruction, the remaining inhabitants of the earth would be her, Cher, and the cockroaches. However (and knock on wood), if I was ever in the situation where my mother requested of me, from her death bed, to kill her, I could not. Unintentionally, I'm sure I've whittled a few years off her life but so have my sisters, and such is the case with any mother and child. Even taking into serious consideration that those were her wishes, I could not physically take action that would in any way lead to my mother's death."

The assignment was stressful for several students in the "hypothetical" group—those without personal experience. "[While] writing this essay I had called up my boyfriend a number of times just to tell him I love him, because I really do not want to take my life, or anyone else's whom I love, for granted." Another begins her essay by stating, "After reading the novel, and crying in the bathroom of the school library for what seemed like hours, I knew I had to call my mom. When she answered, I simply stated, 'Mom, I love you.' She asked me what was wrong, and I told her about One True Thing; she told me to bring it home with me after finals, so she could read it." She ends her essay by declaring that only those who have been in the situation can know how they would respond to a request to end a loved one's life. "I had a friend who was against abortion until she got pregnant by a married man. Suddenly abortion was her only way out, and her views have changed ever since. This is why I cannot fully say that I would or wouldn't euthanize someone I care about if asked. I may say no now, knowing that it would take their life away from mine sooner than letting them die naturally, but Kate wasn't dying naturally. She was in pain: she lost her dignity and respect for herself, and couldn't bear to live another day. If I heard these words come out of my mother's mouth, my heart would break in two. Maybe I would euthanize her, so she wouldn't have to die in pain and be heartbroken."

If the euthanasia assignment was distressing for several students who have not yet confronted this question personally, what word should we use to describe how their classmates felt when writing about their own family experiences? "Painful" is too weak and "traumatic" may be too strong. Consider how Chad felt when writing about his grandfather's death:

Chad: "My Mouth Opened, but All That Came Out Was an Empty Sigh"

January 14, 2001, was the most excruciating laundry day of my life. I realized one of my white shirts would have a red stain on its sleeve forever, and I found a small hole in the backside of my faded blue jeans. I spilled laundry detergent on the floor, which took forever to clean up. Luckily, I found a note a female classmate had written me before a pair of pants dropped into the washing machine; I smirked with embarrassment as my stepfather made a joke about it. Then, the phone rang; this phone call would eventually be the most important phone conversation of my short life.

My mother had flown down to Florida to visit my sick grandfather. After she arrived, every time the phone rang a chill traveled through my spine; this one was no exception. My stepfather answered the phone, spoke a few words, and then immediately handed me the phone. My lips were trembling as I muttered a "hello" in a "tell me everything as quickly as possible" tone. My mother sniffled as she responded with a "hi." She was obviously crying, and I asked her how things were with a full expectation of the absolute worst. She then asked me a question that I cannot and will not ever be able to burn from the bowels of my mind.

"Would you be mad at me forever if we pulled the plug on Papa Tom?" she asked through her sputtered speech caused by emotional crying. I froze, and my usual olive complexion turned pale. The only color on my face was the blood-shot red in my eyes, which was concentrated in the center and stretched out to the edges of my eyes, like the rays of the sun in a child's drawing. I could not respond for a few minutes; I did not know how to answer. My mouth opened, but all that came out was an empty sigh. My mother spoke before I could muster out a word. From the other end of the phone I heard, "They can save him, but he will be a vegetable."

I closed my eyes and immediately imagined my pale skinned grandfather strapped to a wheelchair with drool dripping down his chin onto a half-finished plate of mushy food. I saw the helpless look in his eyes; his stare burnt a hole through my dilapidated heart. Through his gaze, I could tell he was asking for my help. There were so many words he wanted to say, but could not. I never would have wanted to see my grandfather in that condition, and he never would want to be seen in this scenario.

"Do what's best," I finally answered as my mother and I started to cry in unison. My tears would have been enough to fill up the washing machine as they dripped down my chin and into the abyss of water under me. We hung up with each other knowing we had made the most painfully correct decision that either of us would have to make.

It was not a simple task to make this decision three hundred miles away over the phone; I could only imagine how I would have reacted if I was actually in the hospital that day, which would be similar to Ellen's situation. I do not know if my heart is too small or too large to answer a request of this magnitude. I have no religious affiliations at all, so that would not have influenced my thought process. As I type this paper, I am telling myself I would have assisted Ellen's mother's and my grandfather's death. Metaphorically speaking, just because you put the gun in my hand does not mean I have the ability to pull the trigger.

We recall Chad's touching eulogy of Papa Tom, the larger than life grandfather who could be simultaneously menacing and endearing. The eulogy masterfully describes Chad's complex relationship to the man who has made a lasting impact on his grandson. But now we see a different portrait of grandfather and grandson, one darkened by unspeakable suffering and grief. Chad literally could not speak when his mother called with the news of his grandfather's impending death—and what makes Chad's speechlessness more remarkable is that he was rarely at a loss for words during class. In light of his muteness during the phone call five years earlier, the essay's eloquence becomes more striking. He opens by referring wryly to the "most excruciating laundry day" of his life, and after setting up the reader for one kind of story, he then tells a different one. The "red stain" on the sleeve of his white shirt foreshadows the color of his face upon hearing his mother's heart-rending words: "The only color on my face was the bloodshot red in my eyes, which was concentrated in the center and stretched out to the edges of my eyes, like the rays of the sun in a child's drawing." The simile is particularly apt, since Papa Tom had been such a radiant figure in Chad's childhood. The aesthetic power of this sentence is palpable, as is the sentence one paragraph later about his grandfather's eyes: "I saw the helpless look in his eyes; his stare burnt a hole through my dilapidated heart." Chad then returns to the image of laundry on which his first paragraph opens: "My tears would have been enough to fill up the washing machine as they dripped down my chin and into the abyss of water under me."

Strictly speaking, the decision to "pull the plug" on Papa Tom implies taking him off life support, which is not the same as euthanasia or physician-assisted suicide, which are *active* interventions ending in death. Chad doesn't question his mother's decision, but he realizes that ending his grandfather's life by giving him a fatal dose of morphine would be different and more difficult than taking him off life support. He ends by wondering whether he would have agreed or disagreed with Ellen's decision not to end her mother's life—a question that remains unresolved.

Anyone who can write so movingly about the most excruciating experience in life is able to transmute sorrow into eloquence, speaking the grief that might otherwise break the heart. To write artistically about a horrifying experience, as Chad does, is a gift; to share that experience with one's teacher and other students is another gift. Jean also writes affectingly about a horrific experience:

Jean: "As I Write This Paper, I Am Listening to Those Screams Echoing in My Ears Again"

When I was younger, I watched a movie where a woman crushed up pain killers and fed them to her dying mother to help her to her death. I was appalled, and I couldn't understand why anyone would help another die. It seemed cruel and sadistic. Euthanasia, as I know now to be its proper name, was always set under the "could never ever possibly do" category until I watched the slow death of my grandmother Bopzie.

Whenever I hear the word "pain" a very clear and horrifying memory flashes through me. I am running down the stairs of my grandparents' house, hearing screaming and yelling. Rushing into the once-upon-a-time living room that was now turned into a bedroom by hospice, I see my Bopzie writhing on the sheets of the hospital bed screaming out incoherent sounds. My mother and her sister are gently trying to wrestle her back down on to the bed as they are trying to sponge her body while she continues to scream what sounds like "a-sipa-a-sipa-a-sipa-a-sipa" over and over again, eyes wide open like a terrified child. Cancer had torn apart the woman I once recognized as the strongest woman in my life. She could no longer speak real words, and any sound she made was one of utter anguish. I have tried for years in vain to try to scratch the sound of her screams from my memory and hearing the soft sounds of my mother's voice cooing to her, "Mommy, Mommy, I'm here." As young as I was, I knew that if I had a gun I would have shot her right then and there to set her free.

As I write this paper, I am listening to those screams echoing in my ears again. While reading One True Thing, I could not help but feel complete sympathy for Ellen. Although I was not the primary caregiver as she was, I saw my mother play the role and it broke my heart. As a Catholic, it has been preached to me that murder and suicide are punished by going to hell after death. However, once again my own views are mixed into the beliefs of my religion. Once again I feel that I am betraying my religion as I admit that in Ellen's situation, I would have carried through with the euthanasia. I see it as a torture to be able to release someone you love from suffering, but just standing to the side for legality reasons. We are allowed to euthanize pets to ease them from pain, yet we do not deem humans worthy enough for the same blessing. I use the word "blessing" in contrast to having seen numerous loved ones die slowly with only cries of pain as their last sounds on earth. If I am fated to have the same slow death of cancer like the rest of my family, I would hope that someone would help me end my life.

Jean had written in an earlier essay about her beloved maternal grandfather's death, but now she writes about her maternal grandmother, whom she associates with the word "pain." She re-creates for her readers the awful sounds and sights of her grandmother's intractable suffering. She uses active verbs throughout the essay: "running" down the stairs, "hearing screaming and yelling," "rushing" into the makeshift bedroom, seeing her grandmother "writhing on the sheets," "screaming out" incoherent and blood-chilling sounds. She uses an oxymoron, "gently wrestling," to describe her family's efforts to subdue Bopzie, whose image—"eyes wide open like a terrified child"—will not soon be forgotten. The image may also characterize Jean's appearance at the time. Indeed, she succeeds in sketching a double portrait of horror: the horror of a dying grandmother who is reduced to infantile screams and the horror of a young child watching helplessly, unable to exorcise this image from memory. Jean uses excellent diction throughout the essay, and she ends the paragraph with a jarring and unexpected sentence: "As young as I was, I knew that if I had a gun I would have shot her right then and there to set her free."

I suggested earlier that the word "traumatic" may be too strong to describe students' experiences with grandparents' deaths, but the word is appropriate in Jean's case. It is easy for teachers to become inured to students who tell them that a grandparent has recently died: recall the email Richard received on a composition listserv describing students' "well intentioned but trite narratives about how grandpa's death broke their hearts." Jean's essay reminds us how terrifying this experience may be to a young person—or to an older person. Nor does the "naturalness" of a grandparent's death make it easier to accept.

Ava: "The Pain That It Caused Both Her and My Family Was Unbearable"

One True Thing was a brutal reminder of the recent death of my grandmother. The cruelty of cancer was all too familiar: watching the slow deterioration, the rages, and the eerie reversion to a state of infancy. Kate went through the same humiliation that my grandmother had experienced; she was ashamed that she had become incontinent and that my sister and grandfather had to help change her diapers. The main difference is that, throughout everything, my grandmother never asked for anyone to end her life, although we all wished we could help ease her suffering, one way or another. We felt the same as Ellen's father, George: "No one should ever have to live like that. No one." She was terrified of death and fought until the bitter end. She was suffering so immensely that if she had asked for one of her sons to help end the pain, I wonder if anyone would have been able to do it.

There were a few times early on during her illness that we weren't sure if she was going to make it, and the pain that it caused both her and my family was unbearable. She had been taken to the emergency room because the radiation treatments lowered her immune system and allowed an infection not fully treated from an earlier surgery to enter her bloodstream. She was frenzied and wailing ungodly cries of pain. As I walked into the emergency room, I found her crying and screaming, saying to my grandfather, "Please, Zip, don't let me die. I don't want to diiiie." The sound of the "I" was drawn out as she writhed on the hospital bed. Her eyes were dilated and glazed over with what can only be described as a primal, animalistic awareness and fear. I wish I could forget the look in her eyes but I never will. Those eyes passed me by as she searched for someone to help her. She didn't know who I was. She turned to my father, who was also by her bedside. "Tom, I don't want to diiiiiiie." My father stood in utter helplessness, trying to console her, desperately trying to find the right words to soothe her fears. I was heartbroken and terrified. I couldn't bear to see her anymore, so I left. I sat in the waiting room, listening to her cries. I did not know what to feel but that didn't matter because it seemed as if I couldn't feel anymore. It was a surreal nightmare; this couldn't really be happening. I walked over to the vending machine and I got some candy. I waited. I remember sitting in the room, populated with a half dozen sick people who were waiting to be seen by a doctor. I watched a baby cry, suffering from a high fever. Maybe the same doctor who wasn't helping my grandmother would soon be able to help this poor baby, I thought. I was shocked, and still am, by my ability to distance myself from it all, both spatially and emotionally.

A few weeks later, this nightmare recurred. The doctors claimed it was triggered by the poison they had pumped into her frail system. This poison, the chemical radiation that was supposed to make her better, was apparently making her suffer from hallucinations. Still, they couldn't guarantee that she wasn't in actual pain. You could hear her screaming and crying the minute you stepped off the elevator. This was not my grandmother. My demure, introverted, southern belle grandmother would have been mortified to know that she was overheard by the whole sixth floor of the hospital. This time, I did not enter the room. No one in my family could stand to be in there. It was unbearable to see her like this, to have her ask you for help and not to be able to do anything. But if she wasn't fully aware of the situation as the doctors said, we didn't want her to regain consciousness and wake up alone. So, my father and each of my uncles took turns; they sat with her for fifteen-minute clips because they couldn't bear any more than that without a break.

When she died, I couldn't cry. We had been on a "death watch" and my sister called me at work to tell me that they thought she wasn't going to make it through the day. Come home, she said. By the time I got there, she was already gone. As I walked in the house, my sisters sat along with my mother at the table, all in tears. I walked over and took my place beside them. But unlike them, I couldn't cry. They looked at me as if I was cold. My mother kept saying, "Ava, you need to let it out." I'm still not quite sure if it has "come out" yet, whatever that means. If they wanted my tears, they got them at the funeral. My grandfather had asked me to read a passage of scripture. All my family was there, but I was alone. I was in awe of how alone I felt around so many people. I wore the standard black death uniform, the outward sign that you are grieving properly. At the wake, she looked like a different person; I didn't know the woman in that casket. My grandmother was given a black wig since she had lost most of her hair during the radiation treatments. She was made up to look alive and at peace by a stranger who hadn't known her. Her skin was made dull by the excessive makeup except for the too-red lipstick and the hints of blush that had been carefully dusted across her cheeks. I kept trying not to look at that woman. Who is she? This isn't the woman who I spent my childhood with every summer. *That* woman is going into the ground, not *my* grandmother.

I stood up from the pew in the church, shaking a little as I walked up the podium. I felt I had to do this right. If I could read this scripture with conviction, and keep it together for my family, then I will have done right by her. I stood at that podium and I tried to act. I would play the role of the suffering granddaughter. If I am playing a role, then it really isn't me. It was a reading from the Book of Wisdom. One line stood out from the rest: *But the souls of the just are in the hand of God, and no torment shall touch them*. It was true, I guess. She was no longer in pain, and death brought her peace. But there is something cruel and unjust about having to perceive the ending of life as a welcome event; it was almost a "look at the bright side" kind of argument, as if the fact that she wasn't in pain anymore was supposed to bring solace to the fact that she was no longer alive. Maybe it does.

As I walked back to the pew and sat down, I cried out. Within seconds, I was ashamed that I had allowed any noise to escape. I didn't deserve to cry. How dare I cry? I didn't make enough time to see her. I let my academic pressures come between us. My last chance to spend time with her was encroached upon by my desire to succeed at school. It was my sister and my father who had cared for her daily. My father warned me that I would regret not seeing her more. How dare I cry? My poor grandfather sat there and was able to keep it together; why couldn't I?

Regardless of my own experiences, if I had been in Ellen's situation I still don't think I could have done it. I would have always wondered whether she meant it. Maybe she was just so depressed and in so much pain at that moment that she would have said and done anything to make it stop. The doubts would always have haunted me. All I could have done was exactly what I was forced to do with my own grandmother: sit idly by and watch her suffer immensely and slowly wait for her to die.

Parts of Ava's essay could appear, with little revision, in a novel like *One True Thing* or D. H. Lawrence's *Sons and Lovers*, which ends with the bildungs-roman hero giving his mother a fatal dose of morphine. Ava makes her grand-mother's death scene come alive through description and dialogue. So too can we feel her inability to feel. Her sentence—"She was frenzied and wailing ungodly cries of pain"—captures in a few words so much of the horror of uncontrollable suffering. And it is suffering that Ava depicts here, not simply pain. As Eric Cassell points out, suffering and pain are not identical. "Suffering is an affliction of the *person*, not the body" (xii; emphasis in original). Like Chad and Jean, she focuses on the dying person's eyes, which seem to be a reflection of inner horror. Unlike her classmates, she describes herself as both spectator and participant. She depicts the paradoxical state of feeling alone in a crowd of people and the sense of lingering derealization in the presence of death. The portrayal of numbness arising from tragedy recalls Septimus War-ren Smith's state of shell shock in Virginia Woolf's *Mrs. Dalloway*, in which the line "He could not feel" functions as a leitmotif throughout the novel. Ava's self-consciousness compels her to admit she is "playing the role" of a "suffering granddaughter," yet she cannot imagine any other way to act. The most poignant moment of the essay for me occurs toward the end, when, unable to stifle an involuntary cry, she nevertheless feels too guilty to experi-ence grief, fearing that she has become a bad granddaughter by remaining a good student. Such guilt can only heighten grief and shame. Her conclusion—that all she could do was to "sit idly by and watch her suffer immensely and slowly wait for her to die"—recalls the statement that Barbara made to me twice near the end of her life: it is harder for the caregiver than for the dying person, an observation that can remain unchallenged only when it comes from the dying person.

We do not generally regard death and dying as "scenes of shame"—to quote the title of a volume of essays edited by Joseph Adamson and Hilary Clark that explores the significance of shame as a central emotion—but students often feel burdened by the decision (made by them or their parents) not to attend a relative's funeral or by their inability to mourn in a way they deem appropriate. [After the semester ended, Ava showed me a diary she had kept throughout Love and Loss in which she wrote, in an early entry, "Yours is the first class where we are made to feel that it is okay to discuss literature in relation to our emotions. Why is this taboo in other classes? This seems to be a crucial element that is missing in education; we are not allowed to explore our emotions." She analyses her feelings in her entries, revealing the fear of being with her dying grandmother and a related fear that her grandmother might be disappointed in her. She also records a conversation with her sister in which they both disclosed to each other for the first time their struggle to come to terms with loss. "It was sad that she is having the same difficulties I am, but we also admitted that it made us feel better to know that we weren't crazy."]

Guilt and shame always complicate the grieving process, heightening feelings of regret. So too does anger exacerbate grief. Recall Brooke's feelings about not being allowed to attend her great-aunt's funeral: "I felt angry because my parents had not told me she died; my parents knew I would have driven home, immediately. The woman who had been my second mother was gone. I did not get to say goodbye. I wanted to attend her funeral, but my parents refused and sternly advised me not to come home. I cried for two days straight."

Sylvia Plath expresses similar anger in her largely autobiographical novel *The Bell Jar* in which she reveals that her mother prevented her from attending her father's funeral when she was eight years old. "I thought it odd," Esther Greenwood admits, "that in all the time my father had been buried in this graveyard, none of us had ever visited him" (146). Plath observes in her *Journals* that during her psychoanalysis in 1959 she visited her father's grave, presumably for the first time, and felt tempted to "dig him up. To prove he existed and really was dead" (299). Although she demonized her mother, blaming Mrs. Plath for her own inability to mourn her father's death and her self-destructive perfectionism, it is more difficult to mourn when one feels frozen emotion. As Ann Kaiser Stearns writes, "Water, as it freezes and the molecules expand, has the power to burst steel pipes wide open. Likewise, frozen emotion assumes a power out of proportion to its original nature. In the middle of a very harsh winter it's wise to see to it that the water flows fairly regularly through your home plumbing system. Similarly, during the harsh seasons of grief, it is best to keep the channels open so that hurtful feelings are freely expressed. Frozen emotion, like a frozen pipe, has the potential for causing unexpected problems" (60–61).

I routinely ask my students for medical documentation when they tell me they have missed a class because of illness, but I do not ask for "proof" of a missed class because of a relative's illness or death. Such evidence may be difficult for them to obtain, and I don't want to add to their anguish. I realize that some students may not tell me the truth about such absences, but I am prepared to take the risk. I would not have wanted my daughters to be required by their employers to document the days of work they missed while attending to their dying mother. Even before Barbara's death I can recall many students telling me that they felt guilty for not being with their dying relatives, and I don't believe that the "desire to succeed at school" should prevent students from being with loved ones at the end of life.

Monday, May 1

Before reading selections from several essays aloud in class today, I reminded my students that they could leave the classroom if they found themselves becoming emotionally overwhelmed. No one left. I had practiced reading the essays in advance to make sure that my voice would not break while reading them in class. During the reading I had no problem maintaining my composure. Afterward, I returned the essays, and, following my usual procedure, I asked everyone to respond anonymously to several questions about the writing assignment. I also asked them to comment on whether they thought it was appropriate for me to share with them Barbara's request for all her morphine. I'll summarize their responses at the beginning of Wednesday's class.

After collecting their responses, I spent a few minutes talking about how Barbara's request for her pain medication was so traumatic to me that after her death I forgot I had immediately shared this information with her doctors and hospice nurses. How could I have forgotten this crucial detail of Barbara's illness when I remembered without difficulty thousands of less important ones? The best explanation is that the question was so horrifying to me that I repressed it. As I write in *Dying to Teach*, by forgetting that I had shared Barbara's suicide question with her doctors and nurses, "I unconsciously made it into a terrible secret, one that caused me unspeakable guilt and self-blame. My only explanation is that the dark shadow of Len's suicide had cast itself over Barbara's suicide request, causing me to conflate the two events. For years neither Barbara nor I spoke about Len's suicide; now memory played a trick on me, forcing me to conclude that, contrary to reality, I withheld knowledge about Barbara's suicide question from the people who were helping us to take care of her" (95).

I also finally answered the question Sara had asked during the first class of the semester: whether I believe one can die with dignity. I related how I began reading books about dying and death soon after Barbara's diagnosis. The most disturbing was *How We Die*, by Sherwin Nuland, a surgeon with encyclopedic knowledge about the subject. At the time I did not want to accept his thesis that death with dignity rarely occurs: "The belief in the probability of death with dignity is our, and society's, attempt to deal with the reality of what is all too frequently a series of destructive events that involve by their very nature the disintegration of the dying person's humanity. I have not often seen much dignity in the process by which we die" (xvii). I then read to my students the following passage in *Dying to Teach:*

> I reread Nuland's book shortly after her death and found myself agreeing not only with his descriptions of the final state of terminal cancer but also with his many wise statements about how we can prepare for death, including learning as much as possible: "Better to know what dying is like, and better to make choices that are most likely to avert the worst of it. What cannot be averted can usually at least be mitigated" (143). Nuland argues, on the one hand, that patients and their caregivers should pursue every opportunity for cure or effective treatment—"It behooves every patient to study his or her own disease" (260)—and, on the other hand, that "heroic" measures for cure may interfere with a patient's wish to die. I began to understand and accept his paradoxical statement that "hope can still exist even when rescue is impossible" (241). Most of all, I agree with his conclusion that dignity arises not from the process of death but from the way in which we have lived. "The greatest dignity to be found in death is the dignity of the life that preceded it. This is a form of hope we can all achieve, and it is the most abiding of all. Hope resides in the meaning of what our lives have been" (242). (110–11)

The essays I read aloud today made a strong impression on Richard, who titled his diary entry "How Do We Begin Talking about What We Can't Talk About?"

> In today's class Jeff began by reading three essays. The themes of loneliness and loss pervaded. These themes assumed love, but unlike much of the course, they focused on the more difficult side, namely, the withdrawal, removal, or change in a love. One image that struck me in the reading was how a loved one's living room was turned into a bedroom by hospice. Cancer was the cause for this change. The contrast between a deathbed and living space was especially powerful as I've seen these transformations unfold in my own grandparents. For years they took the stairs to their bedroom, separately. When we learned they needed to take the stairs together—my grandfather in his late eighties clutching the handrail and leaning into his wife in case she fell so that they might both fall together, hopefully forward and not backward down the steep and winding staircase—my parents changed their living room into their bedroom. Though the family doesn't talk a great deal about it, we know what is to come. It's obvious while it is still unknown and undisclosed.
>
>   The class readings, as always, were powerful. In listening to the final essay, I could feel the blood drawing back from the skin in my hands. The writing was personally significant but also significant to the rest of us as I looked up to

observe the class in a near frozen state. It was as if we moved, our ability to comprehend would fail and we would lose a chance at finding answers to the difficult questions we all know are associated with euthanasia. In her conclusion, the final essayist indicated that a discussion of physician-assisted suicide would be impossible for her. She felt she would attack anyone who believed it wrong.

Jeff continues the class by affirming that "literally, the suicide question is an impossible one to ask," that the nature of hope changes as we near the end of life, that death with dignity can happen only for the caregiver who allows the process to be dignified. And so death itself cannot be dignified; people cannot even hold on to their dignity. Even this last shred of "humanity" we cannot control in ourselves, but for others, there is possibility. Impossibilities in life and love result in many kinds of loss, but foremost in these losses is the realization that we cannot be God and cure a person. We don't have the power; we can't win in certain ambitions or arguments. Apparently, then, one coping mechanism in dealing with loss is traumatic memory. We forget in order not to realize we cannot maintain control. Thus the trauma robs us of knowledge in addition to the control. In reflecting on this, I wonder how we can then begin talking about what is currently impossible to talk about. How can we know something if we can't even possibly form the questions that might lead us in the direction of knowledge, if not answers? I believe that empathy is at least a partial answer to this.

Wednesday, May 3

I began class today by summarizing the students' anonymous responses to the *One True Thing* writing assignment and to my discussion during the preceding week of Barbara's illness. All but two students felt positively about my self-disclosures. "I was happy to see a teacher open up to his students," remarked one student. "[I was] honored that you trusted us enough to tell us about your wife's illness and death," commented another. Those students who had lost relatives to cancer identified with my experience. "When you spoke about Barbara, I could feel myself tearing up. Most of the deaths in my family (and there have been many) were due to cancer, so I know exactly what it's like." One person emphasized the reciprocity of self-disclosure: "I think it is a good thing that you share with us as much as we share with you." Another felt that my discussion would be helpful to others. "I was deeply moved, to the point where I actually got emotional. Thank you for sharing such a painful story in order to benefit the class." There were only two statements that might be interpreted as negative: One person felt that my discussion was "relevant to the topic" but a "little too real," and the other person could not "relate" to what I said.

Forty-five of forty-eight students felt it was appropriate for me to talk about Barbara's death in the context of *One True Thing*. My self-disclosure was appropriate because "it directly related to the subject we were discussing" and because our class was "about love and loss." Forty people felt that my discussion of the caregiver's dilemma whether to honor a loved one's request to end life would help them if and when they find themselves in my situation. (The remaining eight did not respond to the question.)

> Yes, your lecture on the "double effect" was very powerful and vital to both the course and our lives.
> Yes, it made me understand how my mother and grandmother must have felt.
> Definitely. After your story I thought about this dilemma even more than I did while reading the novel.
> Yes, it was a perspective which I had never heard before.
> Your dilemma is another example of the real life reality people face every day with a dying loved one.
> Yes, because reading it in a book is one thing, but reading the expression on your face adds a completely different element.

Most of the students knew this would be a formidable essay to write when I announced the topic in class. "I was scared. It had touched me personally," wrote one person. "I was excited and afterward discussed with my parents what my decision would be if they became sick," wrote another. The topic was emotionally intense for several students. "Writing this essay brought thoughts and feelings to the surface that I had not touched in quite a while. Thinking of my mother at the end of her life scared me the most." The assignment triggered a painful memory for another student. "I was replaying the day when I heard my parents talking about hospice care. I was in a state of shock. My whole body was numb." The assignment evoked not only recent memories but also distant ones. "[I felt] a mix between happy and sad. It made me remember the amazing times I shared with my grandfather and the wonderful man he was; however, this also caused me to vividly remember his death, which made me burst out in tears. It's been over a decade since his death and I still cry about it when I think of it."

The students believed that they learned a great deal from the assignment. "I had never really thought in detail about what I'd do if I was in the position of Ellen Gulden. This assignment helped me to put my thoughts into words." Another learned to listen carefully to a dying person's words. "I pray I will never have to make such a decision, but if I do, I know to keep the terminally ill person's desire in mind at all times and not be selfish." Others discovered that they have not yet come to terms with loved ones' deaths. "I learned that I still haven't dealt with my grandmother's death."

Others reminded themselves to appreciate their inner resources. "I learned that life throws you hard and difficult choices, but if you get through them, it makes you stronger." Others resolved to look at difficult questions from as many points of view as possible. "I learned that it's hard for me to land distinctly on one side of this issue. I can see the points of both sides. I'm truly torn."

The selections I read aloud affected both proponents and opponents of euthanasia and physician-assisted suicide. "I was happy to know that even some very religious people do not let these beliefs interfere with ending the suffering of loved ones." That comment presumably came from a student sympathetic to "mercy killing," but a classmate presumably unsympathetic was also impressed with the readings: "There was a common theme in the essays—people will hold the gun but will not pull the trigger." Many could empathize and sympathize while being grateful they were not in their classmates' situations. "I felt sympathy for those who have been in similar situations and thankful that I have not had to deal with that (knock on wood)." For some, the selections I read aloud triggered painful memories, though none so painful as to be incapacitating. "It brought back memories from my childhood when my grandparents both died within months of each other. Things that I'd been trying to forget once again plagued me." Others were impressed with the quality of their classmates' essays. "They were amazing. I become more and more impressed with the amount of talent in our class every day." One of the most interesting responses came from a person whose essay I read aloud. "I almost cried when I heard mine being read, but I was nowhere close to tears when I wrote it."

Many felt that this assignment was the most demanding of the six essays written to date. "I think it was more difficult, in the sense that it brought up a lot of emotions I have not been able to deal with and have tried to bury for many years." The assignment was timely for others. "It required more thought of losing someone else by a slow death, which is a more sensitive issue to me now." Others felt it was more "emotional" than the preceding assignments because they made a moral choice that clashed with their religious beliefs.

The overwhelming majority of students believed that the writing assignment would encourage them to discuss euthanasia and physician-assisted suicide with relatives and friends. All but two recommended that I use the assignment again. My last question was one I had never before asked: what was their "tear-to-smile" ratio in the course? Twenty-six people said there were more smiles; six said there were more tears; five called it a tie; and ten people ignored the question. I suspect that had I asked this question about the previous assignment, "Ten Things to Do before I Die," most students would have said there were far more smiles than tears.

The anonymous responses confirmed students' conclusions about the value of careful discussions of controversial issues like euthanasia and physician-assisted suicide. I emphasize "careful" because we never publicly debated these issues. I did not force students to defend one ideological position over another, nor did I demand that they take sides. Chad was one of only two students who believed that a discussion of these issues was too risky, and his argument is worth quoting. "Even though I agree with euthanizing an individual, I do not think a discussion in class is necessary, or even possible. The topic of physician-assisted suicide is usually based on a foundation of beliefs. Whenever deep and personal beliefs are the focus in a discussion, tempers and emotions are bound to rise. I, for example, have been in a similar situation, which tested my morals, and I would be quick to attack someone who strongly believes that euthanasia is wrong. The people who feel euthanasia is wrong have obviously not been in the situation to make the choice between the mental retardation of a loved one or a peaceful death." The other dissenter makes a similar point. "I've seen situations where a student's religious beliefs are so strong that it [allows] no room for discussion. Their mind is made up [so] that their way is the only way. The result is students rising up and calling their professor a false prophet and storming out. Now who wants that??"

I certainly don't want that. I am sorry that controversial discussions sometimes erupt into angry, even violent, confrontations, but I don't believe debates should be avoided merely because of the possibility of uncivil discourse. And I believe that an empathic classroom minimizes the possibility of hostile exchanges. I encourage empathy by reminding students that we are not to challenge another person's feelings, that we will reach our own conclusions about the essays I read aloud, and that we need to listen carefully and respectfully if we are to understand another person's point of view. Talking and writing honestly and openly about an issue like euthanasia or physician-assisted death is fraught with peril, but I believe that it is more dangerous *not* to talk about these contentious subjects. True, it is impossible not to feel ambivalent about certain kinds of knowledge. As the speaker in Ecclesiastes observes, "For in much wisdom is much vexation / and those who increase knowledge increase sorrow" (*New Oxford Annotated Bible* 1.18). The central ambiguity in Robert Penn Warren's novel *All the Kings Men*—"the end of man is knowledge" (9)—can be read in antithetical ways: knowledge is the goal of life but certain types of knowledge may be fatal. Or as the speaker in T. S. Eliot's poem "Gerontion" asks, "After such knowledge, what forgiveness?" Knowledge about the end of life may be the most wrenching to discover and accept, which contributes to our reluctance to discuss end-of-life issues. Nevertheless, however understandable it is to turn away from dark knowledge, those who confront it may be better able to prepare for their loved ones' deaths as well as their own. The knowledge that others share our fears and doubts about euthanasia and physician-assisted suicide can be reassuring. [Postscript: After the semester ended I received a letter from Kelly, who said that Love and Loss was "relieving, not because I was given some divine answer regarding my faith or the afterlife, but because I learned that many people are unsure. To learn that I was not the only one with questions or worries gave me a comfort that I had not experienced in a long time. Thank you for creating a course that was so honest; it made a difference in my life."]

10

~

Writing about Jeff's Former Students
in *Empathic Teaching*

After I finished summarizing the students' anonymous responses to the *One True Thing* assignment, Richard took over for the rest of the class. He began by offering his impressions of the essays that I read aloud on Monday, and he spoke about his own experience with love and loss as he watched his grandparents suffer the ravages of old age and Alzheimer's disease. The students listened to him with rapt attention. It's clear that they respect him a great deal, as I do. I'm glad they are on a first-name basis with him, as they are with me, because that helps to establish a close bond between all of us in the classroom. With about fifteen minutes left, he divided the class into groups of two, and he then walked to each group and gave each person a small piece of paper on which he had written instructions. I couldn't tell what he was doing, but almost instantly the classroom was buzzing with noise. He reconvened the class a few minutes later and explained the results of his unusual psychological experiment. He had instructed one person in each group to speak about the events of his or her week while the other person in the group was told not to make eye contact with the speaker and to ignore what was being said. The classroom erupted into laughter when Richard discussed his findings. His diary entry reveals how much he enjoyed teaching the class:

> I gave my talk on the values of empathy today for Jeff's class on love and loss. It went well and I accomplished much. The gist of my talk was that logic/current argumentation in language takes us only so far. The roadblocks occur when difference is involved, and difference between people is always involved. Thus greater mutual empathy might be a partial solution. In addition to Jeff's book, what really began my thoughts on empathy as an alternative was how Solvay—

my home now for three years—was a place of nonunionized collaboration in the mid-twentieth century when the rest of the country faced labor strikes and failed productivity. The federal government actually went so far as to send researchers to Solvay's soda ash manufacturing plants to see how it was that labor and management didn't break down. The conclusions made about how management and labor were part of the same northern Italian immigrant tradition, and therefore, were from the same cultural materials were too easy in my thinking. The feds added that since management worked on the production alongside the workers, trust was possible. But it occurs to me that much more than labor practices and a cultural foundation were in play. I theorize that empathy was readily possible for these residents of the same small community and cultural heritage. Empathy occurred fluidly and naturally—if we are to consider that the "natural" can even exist. The one could more easily see what the other needed, so feelings were less hurt and less daily trauma happened. The pedagogical implication of this is that classrooms need to work very hard in attending to empathy levels. Something we know but may not be doing in ways that achieve heightened learning performances.

Of course, what was most interesting about class was my exercise at the end, in which students were paired and given a different set of instructions. Student 1 was to tell a partner about his/her week thus far, not the most important events but the ordinary. Student 2 was told, "Don't listen; don't give too much eye contact, etc." The results were striking. Many Student 2's were unable to follow the directions, implying that Jeff's course provided the grounds for students' empathy. One student, Elijah, noted, "Well, that's the way she normally acts when I tell her things," implying that this couple's less than empathic listening promoted a disconnection in their friendship. Incidentally, the wall around Elijah was something I noticed in him throughout the semester. While perhaps not damaged, there was perpetual resistance in his demeanor. If this resistance was unproductive, I'm not able to say. He is still meeting the goals of the course.

Part 2 of this activity is that Student 1 is to talk about his/her plans for after the semester ends, and Student 2 is to listen and respond by encouraging further disclosure through phrases like "So you're saying that. . . ." My point was that in much discourse we are not actually able to consider what others are saying. We think we know what they say, but, in fact, we are falsely inferring on a continual basis. And though it is impossible to know fully the other, reconstituting another's words back to the speaker allows both the listener to acknowledge the other and to take some of the speaker into him/herself.

Richard's experiment demonstrates our need to be heard and affirmed by others: we become frustrated, even angered, when we discover that others are indifferent to what we say. His experiment reminded me of Carl Rogers's observation in *A Way of Being* that I used as the epigraph to *Empathic Teaching:*

> Almost always, when a person realizes he has been deeply heard, his eyes moisten. I think in some real sense he is weeping for joy. It is as though he were saying, "Thank God, somebody heard me. Someone knows what it's like to be me." In such moments I have had the fantasy of a prisoner in a dungeon, tapping out day after day a Morse code message, "Does anybody hear me? Is anybody there?" And finally one day he hears some faint tappings which spell out "Yes." By that one simple response he is released from his loneliness; he has become a human being again. There are many, many people living in private dungeons today, people who give no evidence of it whatsoever on the outside, where you have to listen very sharply to hear the faint messages from the dungeon. (Rogers, 10)

Carl Rogers's affirmation of empathy reveals the crucial importance of our connection with other people, an emotional attunement that conveys warmth, understanding, and support. New research into neuroscience has provided stunning confirmation of the degree to which we are hard-wired for social connection. In an article titled "Cells that Read Minds" published in the 10 January 2006 issue of the *New York Times,* Sandra Blakeslee reports on the discovery of "mirror neurons" that "specialize in carrying out and understanding not just the actions of others but their intentions, the social meaning of their behavior and their emotions." These mirror neurons, also found in animals such as monkeys, demonstrate that both animals and humans are hard-wired for empathy and imitation. "We are exquisitely social creatures," explains Giacomo Rizzolatti, a University of Parma neuroscientist whom Blakeslee cites. "Our survival depends on understanding the actions, intentions and emotions of others." Mirror neurons, he adds, "allow us to grasp the minds of others not through conceptual reasoning but through direct simulation. By feeling, not thinking." Blakeslee also cites the research of UCLA neuroscientist Marco Iacoboni, who believes that mirror neurons allow us to feel the emotions of others, especially when they are anxious or sad. "If you see me choke up, in emotional distress from striking out at home plate, mirror neurons in your brain simulate my distress. You automatically have empathy for me. You know how I feel because you literally feel what I am feeling."

Monday, May 8

Today was our last class, and I felt frustrated because more than half of it was spent with housekeeping tasks, including filling out two different anonymous teaching evaluations, a qualitative form designed by the English Department and a quantitative form mandated by the university. At the beginning of class students turned in the seventh and last essay, on the following topic:

> Throughout the semester we have focused on the theme of love and loss, equating the latter with death. But there are other types of loss: the loss of one's health (physical or psychological), the breakup of a relationship, the crushing of one's self-esteem or self-respect, the fragmentation of one's family, or the end of one's hopes or ambitions. For your final essay, read *Empathic Teaching* and discuss as specifically as possible three students who have suffered a major loss in their lives. For each student, explore the nature of the loss, his or her response to loss, and the extent to which writing helped each person to deal with loss.

I didn't require students to discuss their own experiences, but I didn't prevent them from doing so if they wished. I suspect that when my present students read about former students' experiences with divorce, drug and alcohol addiction, eating disorders, sexual abuse, depression, and suicide, they will discover that loss comes in many forms, many of which they have written about this semester. My present students are the same age as my past students, studying with the same teacher at the same university, and from the same socioeconomic group. I hoped that my Love and Loss students would be able to identify with my past students and find their stories compelling, as I do. I encouraged everyone to read carefully my former students' essays in *Empathic Teaching* and to witness the breakthroughs that many of them made in their personal writings. Many of these breakthroughs occurred as a result of the self-disclosing classroom. An overwhelming majority of students tell me, in both signed and anonymous evaluations at the end of the semester, that they experienced therapeutic relief when writing about conflicted issues in their lives.

Their experiences confirm the findings of James Pennebaker, who has demonstrated in careful empirical studies that talking or writing about trauma dramatically improves one's physical and mental health. I had the pleasure of serving with Pennebaker on a panel discussion titled "Writing for the Health of It" at the AWP (Association of Writers and Writing Programs) Conference this March in Texas, and during a long lunch following our talks we discussed the healing benefits of writing. A major difference between our research is that he advises students not to reveal their personal writings to anyone lest they regret their self-disclosures. "In many cases, it is wise to keep what you have written to yourself," he cautions in *Opening Up*. "You might even destroy it when you're finished (although many people find this hard to do.)" (41). By contrast, I encourage students in my courses to share their writings with classmates, though some of this sharing is done anonymously, as when I read aloud essays in Love and Loss. Sharing is admittedly risky, especially when students in my Expository Writing courses read aloud their own essays, but the sharing creates a bond of trust between everyone in the classroom, and students discover they are not alone in struggling with personal conflicts.

Since this was the last class of the semester, I was unable to read aloud any of the essays I received today, but I'm looking forward to reading them in the next week. I'm also interested in reading their final exams, which contain essay questions on which I have never asked students to write, such as the importance of gratitude in one's life.

By the time the students completed their anonymous responses to the last writing assignment and the two anonymous evaluations of the course, we had only about thirty minutes left, part of which was then taken up in distributing the take-home final exam questions. I didn't have time to make any overarching statements about the course, but I asked my students to stay in touch with me. I hope they will tell me, via letter or email, whether the course proves helpful to them when they find themselves confronting inevitable losses in the future. I thanked Richard for his participation—it was great having him in the classroom—and then I thanked the students for making the course so meaningful for me. I told them that my two most profound teaching experiences were the spring 2004 section of Expository Writing, the semester when Barbara died, and now the Love and Loss course, which is based on what I have learned from her illness and death. I will always associate both courses with her.

I ended the course by reading from the final pages of *Dying to Teach*. Over the weekend, I had read aloud the conclusion to the book, ensuring that I could maintain my composure. I had no problem with tears today, but I found myself unexpectedly rushing because I did not want to keep the class beyond 4:05, when we are supposed to end. (I could hear students for the 4:15 class waiting impatiently outside the classroom.) I intended to read the following words: "Until Barbara's death, I never experienced loneliness as an adult. Now it is a constant companion. (Once I heard myself blurt to my students that now I am 'married to sadness and loneliness,' but I have been careful not to repeat that melodramatic statement.)." But instead of saying that I am now "married to sadness," I said, "married to madness." It took me a couple of seconds to realize what I said, and then I started laughing, as did everyone else in the room. I admitted that at times it is impossible to avoid feeling after the death of a beloved spouse that one is now married to madness both in the sense of depression and of anger. I then read the last two paragraphs of *Dying to Teach*:

> Barbara's main fear, apart from the fear of the process of dying, was that I would not do well after her death. I had to reassure her repeatedly that, with the love and support of my family and friends, I would be okay. It is still too early for me to

contemplate a future without her. And yet by writing about her, first in the eulogy and now in this book, I have found a way to keep her close to me. Indeed, her presence is most palpable on the days when I write about her. I have spent hours each day reflecting on her and trying to find the words to capture her essence. Just as I often talked about her to my students when she was alive, I continue to talk about her in class, usually with a smile on my face. Both her life and death are noteworthy; she fought to remain alive, and I think she would approve of my efforts to make her death a subject for teaching.

Barbara has left me, but I have not left her. Her face is everywhere in my home and at the university, her timeless beauty preserved for all to see. I continue to wear my wedding ring. Scarcely an hour goes by without my thinking of her. Her name is still on our checks. I continue to use the first person plural pronoun, as in the preceding sentence. When my nine-year-old nephew, Shane, asked me shortly after Barbara's death whether I was going to remarry, I was startled and didn't know how to respond. Hours later, after meditating on the question, I told myself that in the future I would say, "Yes, if I can find another Barbara." I will never find another Barbara, but she now lives within me. Wherever I am, she is, my beloved wife, friend, soul mate, and worrier-warrior. (235–36)

I finished the reading just as our time ended, and to my surprise, the class burst into applause, something that has never happened with the same degree of fervor. Touched by their response, I was at a loss for words, but they could sense my gratitude to them and my sadness that the course was over. I make no effort to conceal my love for teaching. I can't resist saying that I loved teaching this course, aptly named Love and Loss. Throughout the semester I regarded myself not only as the teacher but also as another student, intent on learning how my classmates reacted to death education. We were all in different ways students of sorrow, and we tried to teach each other what we were learning about love and loss. For fourteen weeks we told each other stories of love and loss, joy and sorrow, and each of us was trying to construct healing narratives. "We tell ourselves stories in order to live," Joan Didion states in the opening sentence of her 1979 book *The White Album* (11), and the same belief in writing as rescue may be seen in her 2005 memoir *The Year of Magical Thinking*, the story of her husband's death. I hope my students learned as much from me as I learned from them. I feel sad now that the course is over. We don't often think about the feeling of loss experienced by teachers and students at the end of a good course. I feel this loss at the end of every semester, but it is tempered by the happy realization that I begin summer school in a few weeks. I can't imagine wanting to retire, which is why I hope to be fortunate enough to be teaching until the end of my life.

Now that the course is over, I can begin writing about it, exploring in greater detail the significance of my students' essays on love and loss. The semester flew by so quickly that I did not have time to reflect on everything that was happening. Writing a book about the course will help me to understand how all of us—my students, Richard, and I—were affected by the readings, writings, and discussions. I anticipate that writing this book will produce, as it did when I wrote *Dying to Teach*, what psychologist Mihaly Csikszentmihalyi calls a "flow state," an experience of intense concentration in which one loses a sense of self-consciousness and the passing of time. I was so focused on writing about Barbara's life and death that I forgot I was heartsick and grief-stricken. By losing myself in work, I was paradoxically saving my life. I hope that *Death in the Classroom* will be of interest not only to those of us who participated in the course but also to those who would like to learn more about death education. And I hope that other teachers and students who collaborate in death education will feel the same degree of affection, trust, and sincerity that existed in our classroom—a "warmth" on which Richard comments in his last diary entry:

> One might think that the last class might be anticlimactic; it wasn't. Jeff read about a twenty-minute excerpt from the end of *Dying to Teach*. The description of life after Barbara was wonderfully detailed—tangible to the extent that I'm sure most of the class could almost live it with him. He is intent on recording his Freudian slip of married to "madness" versus sadness. While it is telling, I think what I most observed about the final class was the warmth in the room. I know "warmth" isn't a very good descriptor, but it's most accurate. Elijah—the earlier mentioned student who said in last class, "Well, that's the way she normally acts when I tell her things," suggesting in my mind that he guarded himself against empathic relationships—smiles so genuinely with Jeff in the usual paper exchange that I think I may have misread him most of the term. Today he is more relaxed, less intent on challenging or looking to figure out the classroom game. Now that he knows the class is over, I'm wondering if his previous demeanor was some sort of success act that he learned to play in other classes. Perhaps his sitting in front was a means of being a good student, even if it appeared to me he wanted to challenge the course content. It's strange that I might have misinterpreted challenge for what may have been active learning.
>
> When the students clap at the end of Jeff's reading, it's like the room shifts but only in part because we raise such a thunder. Class ends so suddenly for me—though I'm one of the last ones to leave—that I forget my journal and need to return for it later in a panic that I've lost it. Though this has been a demanding semester for me in my commitments, I'm more shocked that it's over than relieved. I have a lot about which to think.

May 10–18

I've finished reading the *Empathic Teaching* essays and the final exams. As I hoped, my Love and Loss students were intrigued when they read my former students' writings. One person began her essay with an apt quote from Norman Cousins: "Death is not the greatest loss in life. The greatest loss is what dies inside us while we live." I would have read aloud Elijah's essay if I had had more time. In writing about my former students, he reveals much more about himself than he had disclosed in earlier writings. Reading empathically allows him to reach insights that would otherwise be impossible. His essay demonstrates the personal breakthrough he made as a result of the course, a breakthrough that leads not to a sudden epiphany but to the recognition of the subtle ways in which loss has shaped his life. He implies at the end of his essay that this recognition will lead to heightened self-awareness and, perhaps, a more self-fulfilling life.

Elijah: "I Would Much Rather Have Two Dysfunctional Parents Who Fought All the Time or Got Divorced Than Two Dead Parents"

Throughout the semester we have indeed focused on the theme of love and loss, and never have I really felt myself getting emotional with any of the literature we have read. The only time I ever felt anything was when Professor Berman would read from his journal or his books and tell us about his beloved wife. I think the reason I would feel bad is because I have felt loss, and hearing his personal trials puts things into perspective for many of us and made us appreciate life. It was very hard for me to read *Empathic Teaching* because these people were people just like myself; young people, students, and people from broken families.

One of the essays that stood out to me was Matilda's essay about her feelings for her father, his death, and her parents divorce. Throughout our semester people would turn in essays about their parents or about just their mother or father. Many of these essays would be about how they cannot stand their parents or about how their parents mad[e] many [of them] so sick because all they do is argue. I know it is [a] cliche to say but perhaps many of these students do not know what they have until it is gone. I lost both of my parents; my mother passed away from HIV and my father did so many drugs by the time he was in his '30s they took their toll on him and took him away. I would much rather have two dysfunctional parents who fought all the time or got divorced than two dead parents. It seems to bother Matilda a lot that her father was an alcoholic. My father was an alcoholic as well, it often mad[e] me upset and angry and I hated the way he treated my mother but if I could have them back with all their problems I would take them. I think it is a shame it takes a tragedy for people to see reality. I think ever since I lost my parents it has made me a very callous person. I lost my world so I look at it [as] if I have nothing to lose now, there is nothing anyone can take from me that would be worse than what I have lost.

The more I read Matilda's essay the more I thought of my own situation. We have a lot of weird parallels. Both of our fathers were alcoholics, they both are dead now, both of our mothers hated it, her father left for Texas, I am about to leave for Texas. It was very eerie to read somebody else's story who was so similar to mine. Now do not get me wrong, I have a lot of resentment for my father, but I do not wish he was dead. It seems once Matilda went to her father's funeral, she realized that as much as she was mad at him she felt the same way I did. I do not think I ever heard my father say "I love you" and to this day it is not something I long to hear him say. There is a difference between a dad and a father. A father is there for his children, anybody can get a woman pregnant and be a dad. Still, my heart goes out to Matilda because I can relate to her. I was glad to see that she came to terms with herself [and] with her issues through writing.

Charlie's essay about people with eating disorders also stuck with me. It is really hard to read about real people who experienced the same problems as you may have gone through. Reading literature with fictional characters just does not have the same effect. My sister has always fought an uphill battle with a weight problem. She was in and out of clinics for her whole life as a teenager. She tried every fad diet out there and starved herself but nothing seemed to help. Charlie says that "everyone, I believe, worries about their appearance. Especially for teenagers this is a main concern of life." I am not trying to make a sweeping generalization about *all* females, but many females are especially concerned with their weight or looks while they are teenagers. And my sister was no different. She was much older than I so when I was smaller I did not understand that she really had a problem. I just thought she wanted people to feel sorry for her and I hated it. She would hurt herself, she would cut herself, she would fake seizures, whatever it took for somebody to be there for her. When Charlie expresses how he does not understand how "Marcy has a big problem with there being pretty women in the movies and as models," it made me think about how much my sister used to read Cosmo or Seventeen and then just sit and cry. I was only a kid and could not understand how somebody would read a magazine like that and start crying. To me it was just pictures of women. I thought, "Why would that make anyone sad." Now that I am older I better understand what she was feeling and my heart really goes out to her. Charlie was very abrasive in his essay; I do not think he is making a strong attempt to put himself in the other person's shoes. I guess in my case it took me reading about somebody else's problem and another person's abrasiveness for me to really put my own situation into perspective.

Empathic Teaching is a very powerful book. Everybody from all walks of life has family problems and most everyone has experienced loss in their lives. Reading about other people's experiences is very therapeutic especially for somebody like myself. Writing about my problems or listening to other problems never really seemed to fix anything in my opinion. But writing about problems and then reading about other people who are similar to you can really help a person who has a lot of pent up anger or resentment.

I was surprised to hear Elijah say that he became "emotional" not when he read any of the stories or poems on the reading list but only when he heard me speak about Barbara or quote from my diary entries or from *Dying to Teach*. I interpret "emotional" as feeling fully engaged with the course, reacting with his emotions as well as his thoughts. Elijah's word "emotional" reminds us of the "mirror neurons" that enable us to feel another person's emotions. As I suggest in my other books, affective teaching is effective teaching—that's why personal writing is so powerful. Elijah's word recalls the title of Daniel Goleman's influential book *Emotional Intelligence*. "The emotional skills," writes Goleman, "include self-awareness; identifying, expressing, and managing feelings; impulse control and delaying gratification; and handling stress and anxiety." Such competences, explains Goleman, "are interpersonal: reading social and emotional clues, listening, being able to resist negative influences, taking others' perspectives, and understanding what behavior is acceptable in a situation" (259). Hinging "on the link between sentiment, character, and moral instincts," emotional intelligence demonstrates that the "root of altruism lies in empathy, the ability to read emotions in others; lacking a sense of another's need or despair, there is no caring" (xii). [Goleman continues this theme in *Social Intelligence*, which shows that we are neurologically designed for social connection. "Empathy—sensing another's emotions—seems to be as physiological as it is mental, built on sharing the inner state of the other person. This biological dance occurs when *anyone* empathizes with someone else—the empathizer subtly shares the physiological state of the person with whom she attunes" (25).]

Elijah's essay demonstrates the growth of both his emotional and social intelligence. He identified with my loss, as I identified with his, and this identificatory bond made the course more meaningful for both of us. I especially identified with his statement that the loss of his parents was so devastating that he feels he has "nothing to lose"—a feeling I also experience now that Barbara is gone and against which I struggle. I share his belief that it's hard to remain hopeful about the future when one broods over past losses. Nevertheless, his brooding—and mine—are held in check by the realization that there are many reasons for which to live. He acknowledges that the loss of his parents has made him a "very callous person," yet a moment later he reports that his "heart goes out" to Matilda because he can relate to her situation of being fatherless. I don't like to disagree with students' feelings, but I doubt he would be able to feel this way if he were callous. His essay reveals other surprises, as when he admits that until now he has been unable to fathom his sister's conflicts over food. "Now that I am older I better understand what she was feeling and my heart really goes out to her." Once again we see his empathy, which appears to have developed, or at least strengthened, in our Love and Loss course. This is the second time in the essay that he remarks on how hearing another person's experience with loss has put his own situation "into perspective." He thus provides specific examples to support his conclusion that "writing about problems and then reading about other people who are similar to you can really help a person who has a lot of pent up anger or resentment."

Elijah has constructed a new story about his life. He has gone from an uncaring person who believed, as a result of his parents' early deaths, that he had nothing more in life to lose, to one who can empathize with others who have themselves suffered loss. Based on his writings, Love and Loss seems to have been a "psychological turning point" in his life, a term that Elaine Wethington defines as a "period or point in time when a person has undergone a major transformation in views about the self" (39). Elijah can understand for the first time his sister's conflicts: he can not only empathize but also sympathize with her. No longer is he filled with "pent up anger or resentment." One can now see posttraumatic growth, characterized by feelings of rebirth and renewal.

I must admit that whenever I looked at Elijah, a large, imposing man who sat near the front of the classroom, only a few feet away from where I stood, he seemed to have an angry or resentful expression on his face. His scowling expression made me uncomfortable. Richard reacted to Elijah in the same way that I did. I often find myself looking at one or two students in every class, generally because I find their facial expressions friendly and reassuring. But occasionally there are "scowlers" whom I try to win over and make into allies. Only late in the semester did I sense that Elijah found the course meaningful. I discovered this for the first time when I read his final exam question on *Empathic Teaching*, which summarizes his feelings about the course, and then when I read an email he sent me in July, two months after the course ended:

> Since the completion of Love and Loss my whole outlook has changed. It feels very odd to say something like that because through out my college career I usually never leave a class with the feeling that I gained something. The only other times I felt like I gained something out of a class was when I took an upper level English course on William Faulkner [and] when I learned about my history in my Africana studies course. Aside from those two occasions, I always treated school like a job and simply completed the tasks that were asked of me. However, in this class something different happened.

I can remember in the beginning of the term when the books were first introduced to us, I had to admit I was not very excited. I saw a common theme in all of them and I thought to myself "I already have enough sadness in my life, why would I want to study depressing literature?" While reviewing the list of books I noticed toward the end that the professor's name was on one of the books as the author. I was a little skeptical at first but as I began to warm up to the class and understand what the aims were I started to look forward to reading *Empathic Teaching*. As I have stated in other papers, I found *Empathic Teaching* a much more interesting read because of its realness. The idea that there are other people who feel the same way as I do, or have been through very similar experiences is very comforting. Especially considering the book is based on people who took a class very similar to this. It certainly changed the whole class experience for the better.

I would definitely have to agree with the idea that "an empathic approach to teaching enables students to understand themselves and their classmates in ways that are impossible in more traditional argumentative classrooms." College is a very important time in a career-minded person's development. College is also where a person gains a lot of the abilities and experience needed to succeed. At the same time, when a person is a student it is very easy to feel like you are just another student identification number. Empathic teaching changes that type of scenario. Students rarely get close to any of their professors because of large class numbers or simply because the student/professor relationship is more like a business. However, with a class that includes empathic teaching a student is able to open up to his or her professor and I think it makes a world of difference in the student's outlook of the class. Personally, I loved the idea of being able to share my painful moments and confide in somebody who I felt was trustworthy, all the while improving my writing ability. The second advantage of empathic teaching is the support one gets from being around people who share the same pain. Everybody has things in their past or inside that bothers them and it is really therapeutic to be in an academic setting to discuss those types of feelings. Although we were all discussing and writing about painful personal memories I never once got the feeling that we were in some sort of support group. The lectures remained just as professional and always led to positive student feedback.

I do not think I would have ever read a book like *Empathic Teaching* had I not taken Love and Loss. Not to say that I am close minded but a book like that most likely would have not sparked my interest. I find that most English majors do not read enough literature for the sake of reading it. We have to read so much theory that we never have enough time to read other genres of English. This is a shame because it makes me think that perhaps I am missing out on a lot of good literature and books because it is not required in my heavy English curriculum. While reading chapter 6 of *Empathic Teaching* I was a little taken aback to see that there were people out there who did not support the idea. I was even more awestruck to see that the people who did not support empathic teaching were some of Professor Berman's peers and other professors. This made me feel that perhaps these people have not experienced anything painful. Even Professor Berman himself admitted that after the passing of his wife he was much more understanding of his students who had suffered a loss. When I read chapter 6 I kind of got offended because I kept thinking to myself, "How could somebody critique something as powerful as empathic teaching if they have not experienced it for themselves?" Chapter 6 also made me feel that although people doing the critiquing were respected and learned men perhaps they lacked the type of learning that comes with losing a loved one or going through a very trying period.

Empathic teaching is a very powerful tool and I think it is pertinent to the academic field. Students in today's day and age come from broken families and dysfunctional situations where they either had to raise themselves, lost a parent or close friend, or had to go through something difficult. A class like this is important. It gives us a chance to come to terms with our own inner demons through writing. I for one would never consider "writing" about my problems like in a journal or something. However, being in an academic setting made it much more comfortable and healthier.

Hey Prof. Berman,

How is your summer going? I hope it's going good and you are enjoying yourself. Anyway, I wanted to email you because I was really influenced by your love and loss class and I really enjoyed myself. I seem [to] remember you saying that you were going to have either a new book or new material out this summer which would include some of the responses from your last couple of classes. If the book is out what is it called and where can I purchase it? If not, would you mind keeping me posted on when you do come out with it?

Thanks a bunch, hope all is well,

Elijah

Evaluating the Last Assignment

Several students remarked in their anonymous responses to *Empathic Teaching* that with the exception of the essay on *Wuthering Heights*, this was the least personal assignment of the seven. Some people did not like it for this reason. "This was my least favorite writing assignment because it was the least personal," observed one student. "There were only two assignments pertaining to books (this and Wuthering Heights), and I hated them both," stated a second. "I was a little disappointed—I thought there would be a more interesting topic for the last paper," noted a third. Others found it different from the preceding assignments but not necessarily better or worse. "This was a less personal writing assignment and required more attention than usual on the reading." One person found it "intimidating" because it was difficult to write about a professor's book: "Writing a paper to be graded by the author can be quite stressful." Most of the observations, however, were positive:

> I was pleased that we would finally be able to comment on one of your works. It required more thought and you had to write about other people.
> I think that this assignment was a good closure for the course. I don't think it would have worked as well earlier in the course.
> I didn't mind writing it. I felt reading the essays that your former students wrote helped me to appreciate my family and friends more.

My former students' stories in *Empathic Teaching* moved nearly everyone. "I felt connected to the students from the book. I also felt the healing power of writing to be an undeniable force." Those who had themselves experienced therapeutic relief from writing were especially touched by the readings. "I felt emotional because I wrote about how writing has affected my life and inevitably saved it." Many found themselves welling up with tears during their reading. Several identified strongly with the readings. Observed one student, "I felt a kinship with some of the student writers. I felt that reading some of the writings of those that had experienced similar circumstances to what I had brought up some painful emotions, which made objective thinking harder." And another: "I felt for the students who wrote these stories, and I saw myself in some of them." A few remarked that they felt fortunate their families were still intact. Reading the book helped them to understand the "different losses that people go through from divorce and the loss of a parent's relationship." The reading disappointed only a few students. "To be honest, I didn't like the book, sorry. I didn't feel it really went with everything else, and I felt that it could have been left out."

Most students stated that they learned a great deal from the writing assignment. One person learned "just how much kids are forced to deal with, and how many kids have the disadvantage of having to grow up too quickly." Another learned that "life is too short to carry around unwanted guilt." Another learned that "loss comes in all forms." Many learned to be grateful for what they have, including intact families and living parents. They also learned the importance of empathy: "I learned that there are bonds that can be discovered in people who may otherwise be merely strangers." Some learned that they need to improve their relationships with others. "I learned that I'm more emotionally cut off than I ever imagined." Many people commented specifically on the therapeutic value of writing:

> Emotional trauma is lessened through writing.
> I learned how much writing really helps so many people to deal with tough experiences, specifically loss.
> Although this class is not a therapy session, writing can be a therapeutic and helpful tool when dealing with loss.
> I learned how much in fact this assignment made me realize how much writing has helped me.

The next question asked students whether they were glad they read *Empathic Teaching*. I added the following sentence to remind them of the "guarantee" I had offered them. "Remember the promise I made to you on the first day of class. I will refund the money you spent on the book if it disappoints you, provided that you have a sales slip and that you look me in the eye and say, 'Jeff, your book sucks.'" All but three wrote that they liked the book:

> Yes. I couldn't put the book down!!
> I didn't entirely read it, but I fully intend to—my mom wants to read it too.
> I wouldn't give you this book back if you paid me.
> I am very glad and I think I will hold onto it and not even return the book.

The three dissenters remarked: "It wasn't all right"; "Don't know"; and "No, I didn't like it, but I don't have the balls to say it to your face. Plus, I think it would be rude to ask you for a refund. I chalk it up to another book I didn't like and had to read for a class."

The following question—"How did other people respond when you told them you were writing about former students in my book?"—elicited several wry responses:

> I hate when teachers make you buy their book.
> Oh, he's making you read his book?
> My roommate told me I was screwed when I told her my professor was the author.

Forty-three students recommended that I use the writing assignment again. The following comments were typical:

> Yes, I think that learning from past students was insightful and it was similar to hearing my classmates' essays read aloud in class.
>
> Yes. The lesson was very valuable.
>
> Yes. It was a fantastic book and the assignment just made me connect with it more.

Four people did not recommend I use it again and a fifth wrote "possibly."

Finally, I asked everyone to rank the seven assignments. The overwhelming favorite was the essay on "ten things to do before I die," the top choice of twenty-nine students, followed by writing a eulogy, the top choice of eight. The *Empathic Teaching* assignment was the top choice of four students, and the religion-and-death essay and Cathy Linton's letter to her deceased mother in *Wuthering Heights* each received three top choices. The essay on euthanasia and physician-assisted suicide received two top choices. No one chose the obituary assignment as a top choice. In their anonymous evaluations written immediately after the obituary assignment, a large majority of the students recommended I use it again in the future, so the fact that no one selected it as the top choice does not imply that no one liked it. They simply liked the other assignments more.

"A Family inside the Classroom"

I was delighted that my Love and Loss students identified with my former students' writings in *Empathic Teaching,* and for this reason alone I plan to use this assignment the next time I teach the course. "I enjoyed reading about all of these students. It was like listening to the writing assignments read aloud in class; that is always my favorite part. Each student is so unique but very relatable to all teenagers." I agree. Older students can also identify. I'm not surprised that the most common loss with which my present students identify is that of the intactness of their families. "After reading a few of the letters from *Empathic Teaching,* I have realized that many people in this world share similar issues with their parents as I do. I was raised in a single-parent household; my father left home when I was only four years old. I have grown up with a void in my life and a yearning for a normal family. I have spent years wishing that my parents [would] be civil to one another. I have been taut between two opposite worlds for over a decade—two worlds that I desperately wished were one." Students have explored this "tautness" in every self-disclosing literature and writing course that I have taught. The breakup of the family, followed by a parent's absence or premature death, is even more devastating. This was true of Matilda in *Empathic Teaching* and of Breanna as well [see appendix B]: both daughters felt intense anger, grief, guilt, confusion, and, in Breanna's case, shame. Students feel less isolated and stigmatized when reading about classmates' losses. It's not that misery loves company; rather, the knowledge that others have survived painful losses can be empowering.

To an outsider, it may seem that *Empathic Teaching* is unrelentingly bleak, yet I think that nearly everyone would agree that both the book and Love and Loss were more uplifting than depressing. I was the teacher, but my students were also learning from each other and from my past students. To cite one example, Jean observes near the end of her essay that she agrees with Colin's statement in *Empathic Teaching* that "personal writing is a way of developing the process of forgiveness." She then closes her essay with the following affirmation:

> That is why this English course is so profound. I have been seeking a way to describe to my friend just exactly why I am not upset or disturbed by any of the assignments I receive. By putting raw emotions to paper, you are able to step back and truly see what you have endured. You are able to self-sooth[e] through words, a power that I never have appreciated until I took a class with Professor Berman. Every reaction of his students from his book *Empathic Teaching* has run through my body while completing assignments for this class. Yet it is this disclosure that not only helps heal, but it creates a family inside the classroom. It is amazing to know that you are not alone even in the darkest experiences in life.

Gratitude—and Resiliency

We have a choice after the loss of love: to be grateful for what we had or to become bitter over what we have lost. It is seldom a conscious choice—and at times it may feel like we have no volition at all. But unless we are so depressed that we cannot think clearly, each day confronts us with the decision to see the glass as half empty or half full. I chose to write about Barbara immediately after her death and to teach a new course inspired by her. I also chose to dedicate myself to death education, part of her legacy to me and, I hope, my legacy to future students. I am grateful that I was married to Barbara for thirty-five years, grateful that I have a job that enables me to combine my professional and personal lives, grateful that I can remain connected to her memory by writing and talking about her, grateful that my work is my pleasure. And I am grateful that I have been able to construct a meaningful narrative of my experience with love, loss, and *recovery*. I underscore the last word to emphasize the importance of finding a way to live with loss. Recall the Norman Cousins's quotation I cited earlier: "Death is not the greatest loss in life. The greatest loss is what dies inside us while we live." Also recall the epigraph for my book that comes from E. M. Forster's novel *Howards End*: "Death destroys a man: the idea of Death saves him."

I am also grateful to my students, who appreciate my approach to teaching. Their gratitude affirms the value of empathic teaching, affirms the value of trust in the student-teacher relationship, affirms the value of posttraumatic growth from suffering, and affirms the value of mutual compassion, support, and love. It is pedagogical love, teachers loving their students and students loving their teachers: love that is neither transgressive nor exploitive. To borrow Erik Erikson's word, we may describe the teacher's love for students as a form of *generativity*, the "concern in establishing and guiding the next generation" (267). I am only slightly older than my students' parents, and in hearing me speak about the death of my wife, they could imagine the deaths of their mothers and fathers. They could see the sorrow on my face change to joy when I spoke about my children—and my past and present students. In revealing our vulnerability, we also demonstrated our resiliency, our ability to endure suffering and transform weakness into strength.

Those who recover quickly from a relative or friend's death do so because they find a meaning in the loss, explains Timothy Wilson. "People who find meaning, such as believing that the death was God's will, that their loved one had accepted dying, or that death is a natural part of the life cycle, recover more quickly than people who are unable to find any meaning in the loss. Another important factor is the extent to which people find something positive in the experience, such as the belief that they have grown as a person, gained perspective, or . . . that the death has brought other family members closer together" (141). When I was talking about Barbara's illness to my Expository Writing students, I was only dimly conscious that I was teaching them a life lesson, one that I was also learning, but they could see that I was surviving a devastating loss. They could also see that my method of survival, my characteristic response to grief, my "identity theme" as a teacher, to use Norman Holland's term, is to talk and write about sorrow—and to teach it. They could see my resiliency—and as Richard Davidson and William Irwin remark, we can all learn to be resilient by being exposed to a test or stress that challenges but does not exceed our ability to manage. And they could see my undying gratitude for being alive, for bearing witness to loss, for finding a way to appreciate what I still have, and for telling my story and hearing my students' stories. I was struck when reading the final exams by how many students also believe in gratitude. Some of them, like Elijah, have had experiences that make gratitude all the more remarkable:

Gratitude is very important to me; perhaps it is because I have lost so much. However, everything does happen for a reason and I feel because the important things were taken away from me I learned to appreciate all the other aspects of life. I am more than grateful to be alive and it bothers me when people do not appreciate their lives. When I was four years old our house was robbed and the gunmen shot out our windows with a .44 and one of the bullets ricocheted off of a wall and hit me in the stomach. Luckily for me the bullet went in and out cleanly, without hitting any major organs or arteries. Although I was still a small child this put things into perspective for me. I realized that anything could happen to anybody at anytime. If a four-year-old could be shot and almost killed over some drugs then anybody could be taken away.

When people get in a comfort zone they tend to no longer have gratitude. They do not remember what it is like to be one of the "have nots" and with that comes the lack of appreciation and gratitude. We analyzed and discussed a plethora of characters and they all lost something. Constantly reflecting on other people's loss made me think about my losses. I became disturbed at first because all I could think about every time I walked into this class was my mother. However, as time went by and I came to terms with the loss of her I began to appreciate my life even more. I began to look at my situation through the lens that I am alive and I need to make the best of it in order to live for her.

I think as time goes by and I get older I will gain more gratitude for life. I am only 22 and I feel like I have the rest of my life ahead of me. However, I am sure when I am middle aged I will reflect on my younger days and wish I could relive them. Hopefully, with those sentiments will come gratitude and appreciation for life.

11

~

A Teacher's Self-Eulogy

Jeff Berman's fantasy came true yesterday when his body was found in his office minutes after teaching the final class of the semester. For decades the popular English professor had disclosed to his students that he wanted to expire teaching, dying in harness. The bizarre wish came true. He was eighty-two years old and had been teaching at the University at Albany for fifty-four years, longer than any other faculty member in that institution's history. The news stunned his devoted students, though one expressed the hope that his teacher had submitted final grades in the course before passing on. Administrators also expressed sorrow, but one admitted privately that he thought Berman should have retired years earlier. Upon turning seventy, Jeff boasted that he planned to continue teaching for as long as he received the top teaching evaluations in his department—a statement that a dean, who wished to remain anonymous, believes manipulated students into giving him higher evaluations than he deserved. Few of his colleagues could be reached for comment, since those who were still alive had retired long ago and moved to Florida.

Jeff could never adequately explain to others or to himself his passion for teaching. Throughout his career he believed that his university underappreciated and undercompensated him, yet he also knew that he was getting paid for something he loved to do, and secretly he thought he should have paid his students for the privilege of teaching and being taught by them. Until the death in 2004 of his beloved wife, Barbara, whom he met in his college freshman English class in 1963, he believed he was the luckiest person in the world, in love with both his wife and work, twin passions that complemented each other.

Barbara's death profoundly affected Jeff's teaching, and in his memoir *Dying to Teach* he affirmed the power of writing to memorialize loss and work through grief. He did not idealize her, as Clym Yeobright in Thomas Hardy's novel *The Return of the Native* idealizes his mother, in whose death he is implicated. A harsh, vindictive mother who never accepts Clym's marriage to an equally wilful woman, Mrs. Yeobright is rendered into a "sublime saint" by her guilt-ridden son, who has attempted to lock her out of his heart and house and who, in the process, loses his eyesight. Jeff also had problems with his vision and, later in life, with his hearing, but he did not spend the rest of his life preaching his wife's death. He maintained, however, that it was pedagogically appropriate to speak about her when discussing death scenes in literature. An overwhelming majority of his students agreed with him, believing that death education was valuable both academically and psychologically. Hearing him speak about his wife's death, they made comments like,

> For the first time in my college career, I was able to relate to my professor on a personal, human level.
> You never spoke like you were above us but as though you were one of us.
> I believe when a professor is able to share not only his personal life, but also his emotions, it helps the students relate to him/her.
> I found that I can learn the basics in any English class but I learn "life lessons," so to speak, when professors choose to speak about personal experience.

Several students stated that hearing their professor talk about his wife helped them to get to know him better as a person, which in turn motivated them to work harder. They felt a close connection to him as a result of his self-disclosures, and they believed that his candor and openness encouraged these qualities in their own writings.

Jeff's students described his pedagogy as "teaching from the heart." "It is fine to teach by the book, but the chance of students relating to literature and finding interest in it is so much less. To teach from the heart requires a lot of courage both by the professor and the students." The same person believed that Jeff's self-disclosures "allowed students to be completely free and open within class discussion and in their papers. It was very calming to be able to be open in such a way. It allowed our class to be a support group for one another." Jeff believed in teaching from the heart and the mind, and, perhaps, the soul, in which he had only a vague belief. He never lost faith in the power of teaching to transform lives, and his students appreciated his confidence in them.

Jeff became identified with the pedagogy of personal writing, and many of his books explored the extent to which teaching based on understanding the other can transform the classroom experience. Unlike most of his colleagues in English studies, who theorized the other without attempting to find out specifically how their students felt about teachers, Jeff was constantly soliciting his students' reactions to his teaching. His students wrote weekly reader-response diaries in literature courses, and they often filled out anonymous questionnaires at the end of the semester. In addition, he interviewed many of his students months and sometimes years after they completed courses with him.

Few of Jeff's colleagues shared his enthusiasm for self-disclosing writing. Empathy, which was the cornerstone of his teaching, attracted more interest from psychology professors and psychotherapists than from those in his own discipline. His colleagues' lack of interest in empathic teaching disappointed him at first, but he welcomed the challenge to develop a pedagogical approach that enabled students to write about vexing life issues. As he wrote at the end of his book *Empathic Teaching*, "I have not discovered anything new; Heinz Kohut and Carl Rogers were tireless advocates of the use of empathy in psychotherapy, and they both recognized its application to education. Other teachers and researchers have investigated the dynamics of self-disclosure in a variety of settings. My contribution is to show how empathy and self-disclosure can be combined safely and productively in the classroom" (374).

Jeff did not believe that personal writing was superior to traditional argumentative writing, based on critique, but he sought to redress the imbalance that favored the latter over the former in academia. Most of the English majors whom he taught told him that he was the first college teacher to allow them to use the first person pronoun when they wrote. As a student remarked, "I have encountered professors who, after I disclosed that I was taking Love and Loss, emphatically stated that it was not a professional approach to teaching. More importantly, I was told, it was not appropriate to encourage students to write personally about their lives, as it allowed a professor a more personal interaction with his or her students. It's not condoned, I was told once, and it creates the risk of overfamiliarity with students. Previous to this course, I would have agreed, but after learning what I have learned, it's impossible to imagine learning a more valuable lesson. In order to become a better human, I believe now, it's integral to be able to connect and empathize with people." Jeff himself did not use "I" until the epilogue of his third book, *Narcissism and the Novel*. He agreed with Gerald Graff that the "opposition between persuasive and creative/personal modes of writing is needlessly overdrawn" (248) and that college teachers should encourage both types of prose.

Radical and Conservative

Jeff's teaching was both radical and conservative. His commitment to the self-disclosing classroom and emphasis on "risky writing" were considered not only radical but also dangerous. Few rhetoric and composition scholars endorsed such "risky teaching." His decision to emphasize the "basics of writing"—

grammar, diction, style, compression, voice, point of view—was perceived as conservative if not reactionary, particularly during an age in which rhetoric and composition were influenced heavily by cultural studies, with its implicitly Marxist bias. As he remarked in *Empathic Teaching,* his emphasis on grammar in writing courses differed from the "bonehead English" courses satirized by Bernard Malamud in his novel *A New Life,* and it also differed from the "back to basics" approach championed by conservative educators such as Allan Bloom, E. D. Hirsch, and Dinesh D'Souza. Instead of writing about their summer vacation, Jeff's students wrote about being depressed during their summer vacation, or about grieving the loss of a loved one. The knowledge that only their writing skills would be critiqued, not their emotions, enabled students to write openly and truthfully about the most important issues in their lives.

Jeff was radical and conservative in other ways. In the mid 1970s he taught the first psychoanalytic literary course at his university, and he demonstrated in his 1994 book *Diaries to an English Professor* that introspective diary writing was a powerful educational and psychological experience. Many students told him that they learned more about themselves by writing weekly psychoanalytic diaries than by spending months in psychotherapy. Psychoanalytic diary writing was radical not because it demonstrated that writing promotes self-mastery and self-healing—writers have long known this—but because he showed that the teacher did not need to play the role of therapist for students to experience therapeutic relief. Yet at the same time Jeff was conservative, preferring literature to theory, and agreeing with James Hynes's definition of literature in his satirical academic novel *The Lecturer's Tale:* "A literary work is any work of imaginative writing—prose, poetry, or drama—that is inherently more *interesting*—rich, complex, mysterious—than anything that can be said *about* it" (24; emphasis in original).

To determine how teachers make a difference in their students' lives, Jeff kept a folder of unsolicited letters and emails he received over the years. Some former students wrote to him asking for a letter of reference, but most wrote simply to express gratitude for his teaching. The folder grew thick over time, and when he began reading them closely, he discovered that most students saw him in the same way. Students did not praise his originality or brilliance, qualities that he did not see in himself. Nor did they generally refer to his publications, which occupied so much of his time and attention. A few praised the writing and reading skills he taught them, but most appreciated his passion for teaching, which made his courses challenging, and they especially valued his ability to relate literature to life. "Thank you for everything you taught me about Hemingway and Fitzgerald," wrote one student. "Most of all thank you for teaching me about the quality of being human and humane. I'm a better person because of your teaching." What they valued most was his interest in their education and his belief in their potential. He was particularly struck when a former student, who had written about his father's suicide, sent him a letter from graduate school and quoted from a passage that Jeff used in *Empathic Teaching*: "I came across the Henry Adams quote the other day, the one that says, 'A teacher never knows where their influence really stops,' but yours definitely has not. I still feel that your class truly helped me to continue to face my situation. Unfortunately, I had a friend take his life this past year. Though it was his third time trying, and we all knew that eventually he would succeed, it is still very hard. But your influence continues with me."

Jeff's students saw him as approachable, warm, down-to-earth, and honest. They were not intimidated by his knowledge, fearful of his judgments, or confused by his language. He enjoyed bright students but he also welcomed average students, who sometimes learned the most from his courses. He believed that education was reciprocal. "Many of the ideas that I hold important about teaching were expressed by you during our classes," wrote one man who desired to be a college professor. "One, at the top of this list, is a teacher must know he or she will learn from their students every day. You knew that." Another student, who took Jeff's Age of Freud course, wrote that "I remember a different feel in the classroom that I never felt anywhere else. When the course was done, right after the final [exam], I remember everyone taking a moment, one after the other, to come up and shake your hand and say 'Thank you' and that was how I knew it was different from any other previous course."

Jeff's critics, of whom there were many, did not see him in the same way. The reviews of his books were often mixed; those who praised his approach to teaching asserted that not many professors could encourage personal writing without traumatizing their students, and those who criticized his books claimed that he was voyeuristic, narcissistic, and predatory. Jeff was stung by the negative criticisms, but he believed that his students were the most accurate judges of his work.

Jeff often made jokes at his own expense, believing that they helped to make the student/teacher relationship closer to friend/friend. Many of his students later became lifelong friends. He knew how to maintain professional boundaries. He did not have affairs with students; did not go drinking with them, as many of his colleagues did; and did not dress like them. Indeed, as he grew older, he was one of the few male teachers who always wore a tie and jacket to class. But he tried to understand his students' lives and published several books containing their life writings. Jeff grew up in the 1960s, when the word "relevance" became the slogan for educational reform, and he urged his students to make connections between their lives and those of the fictional characters discussed in class. He believed in motivating them to do their best work and fulfilling their potential, but he also sympathized with their difficulties and encouraged them to write essays and diaries in which they engaged in problem-solving.

Jeff believed in what Kay Redfield Jamison calls exuberant teaching, in which teachers' joy and passion infect their students, motivating them to do their best work. Throughout his life he loved teaching, but it became increasingly important to him after his wife's death and helped to fill a huge void in his life. As he turned sixty, he read George Steiner's book *Lessons of the Masters*, and he was struck by the three types of pedagogical relationships discussed by the eminent literary critic:

> Simplifying, one makes out three principal scenarios or structures of relation. Masters have destroyed their disciples both psychologically and, in rarer cases, physically. They have broken their spirits, consumed their hopes, exploited their dependence and individuality. The domain of the soul has its vampires. In counterpoint, disciples, pupils, apprentices have subverted, betrayed, and ruined their Masters. Again, this drama has both mental and physical attributes. . . . The third category is that of exchange, of an eros of reciprocal trust and, indeed, love. . . . By a process of interaction, of osmosis, the Master learns from his disciple as he teaches him. (2)

Jeff identified with the third pedagogical relationship, based on reciprocal trust and, within professional boundaries, love. He did not regard himself as a master—he was keenly aware of the deficiency of his education, which was strikingly clear from his unfamiliarity with many of Steiner's wide-ranging literary, philosophical, and religious allusions. (He would have done almost anything to have Steiner's encyclopedic memory, command of languages, and magisterial prose style.) Nor did he regard his students as disciples—on the contrary, he required his students to disagree, in their essays, with his interpretations of literature. He believed that he learned as much from his students as he hoped they learned from him. He agreed wholeheartedly with Steiner that "there is no craft more privileged" than teaching: "To awaken in another human being powers, dreams beyond one's own; to induce in others a love for that which one loves; to make of one's inward present their future: this is a threefold adventure like no other." For Steiner, and for Jeff, one need not be a master teacher to reap the rewards of teaching: "Even at a humble level—that of the schoolmaster—to teach, to teach well, is to be accomplice to transcendent possibility" (183–84).

Like most academics, Jeff valued knowledge and wisdom, but he placed the highest worth on goodness. He loved reading about real and fictional characters who sought, with varying degrees of success, to be good. He was fortunate to have been married for thirty-five years to a good woman to whom he was devoted, and who inspired him to do his best. He sought to keep Barbara's memory alive after her death, first by speaking about her to his students, then by writing a book about her, and finally by teaching new courses on death education that allowed him to teach to others what he was himself learning. He taught many thousands of students over a career that spanned more than half a century, and although he forgot most of their names, he never stopped feeling affection for them, even love. He never taught James Hilton's story *Good-Bye, Mr. Chips*, but as he grew older, he identified with the venerable pedagogue, who also lost a beautiful wife to premature death. If Jeff could have bid farewell to his students, it might have sounded like Mr. Chips's valedictory speech to the pupils of Brookfield Academy: "I have thousands of faces in my mind—the faces of boys. If you come and see me again in years to come—as I hope you all will—I shall try to remember those older faces of yours, but it's just possible I shan't be able to—and then some day you'll see me somewhere and I shan't recognize you and you'll say to yourself, 'The old boy doesn't remember me.' [Laughter] But I *do* remember you—as you are *now*. That's the point. In my mind you never grow up at all. Never" (89). Jeff's students could tell from his voice, even when he grew old and frail, that his passion for teaching remained, and that Barbara was never far from him.

Appendix A

"Helping or Harming Students?": Reflecting on Love and Loss

Richard Bower

A tenured community college professor who is now pursuing a doctoral degree, Richard Bower took my Age of Freud graduate course in the summer of 2005, and partly as a result of that experience, he became interested in the pedagogy of self-disclosure. I was delighted when he offered to attend Love and Loss in the spring of 2006 as a coparticipant/observer. I asked him to examine as rigorously as possible whether he thought the course helped or harmed the students. Richard was attentive to every aspect of Love and Loss, including the teacher-student relationship and the visible (and often invisible) intellectual and emotional responses of everyone in the classroom. He attended nearly all the classes; taught two classes; read all the students' writings, which came to a staggering twelve hundred double-spaced pages, not to mention another twelve hundred pages of midterm and final exams; and graded one set of papers for grammar and style, providing students with constructive comments. In addition, he wrote journal entries for every class, which amounted to more than eleven thousand words. He also interviewed twenty-two students and wrote a detailed report of his findings, which he presented to me after final grades were submitted. And he wrote the following reflective essay in which he offers his impressions of the course.

> I felt emotional because I wrote about how writing has affected my life and inevitably saved it.

> I felt connected to the students from the book. I also felt the healing power of writing to be an undeniable force.
>
> —Two anonymous responses to the *Empathic Teaching* writing assignment

In fall 2003 one of my students died early in the semester in an automobile accident. Rachael (pseudonym) was a twenty-one-year-old single mother taking my first-year composition class in preparation for our nursing program. I was visibly shaken for a number of days. As a commuter campus, my college had lost a few students in the four years I'd taught there. I'd been well aware of the risk community college students face in their commutes as they ap-

227

proached me annually to say how their cars had been totaled in an accident. But in the past they had always been physically unhurt. I'd never lost a student in the middle of a semester, and for me this death in my classroom felt extremely personal. Typically, I take it personally when any student of mine cannot finish a course because of the craziness of life obligations in providing for their children, job exhaustion, or illness. I know this is not my fault, just as students unwilling or currently unable to master the course materials and performances are not my fault, yet I feel the "unfinishedness" like sour bombs bursting in my belly every time a student fails.

This particular student was struggling but far from failing. She enthusiastically participated in class discussion and peer reviews. She was unafraid of asking questions and asked them with a strength built up from years as a single working mother. She always showed up to class tired, nervous about her work, and with circles under her eyes from pulling night shifts as an LPN in Syracuse. She was taking only my class, so she could concentrate on it and succeed enough to enter the RN (registered nurse) program, but with work and the childrearing of her four-year-old son, she lived at least three lives in any given day.

In the previous semester I had a student with a heart condition take my creative writing class online. She was socially and cognitively underdeveloped because of poor blood flow to the brain since birth. Her greatest love was to write about teddy bears. Because fragments best captured her world, she wrote some aesthetically pleasant and poetic lines. Even if the poetry bordered on the sentimental, she was a master of line breaks. When it came to short fiction and workshops, the online students responded poorly to her work. She had written many pages daily before this course. Writing gave her great joy and no doubt provided instrumental development for a young woman who lived with a severe lisp, where people sometimes reacted by shying away or not knowing how to respond to her bubbly cheerfulness in being alive and having the chance to meet or talk with someone new. When the students turned on her in workshop, it was the worst and best thing to happen; it demonstrated the limitation of a text-centered discussion and presented her with an important moment for herself as a writer and me as a teacher. She and I talked privately, and of course, she was disappointed by her classmates' reactions yet was determined to get people to see the greatness in teddy bears, bears that had comforted her throughout all the years she spent in hospitals: sick, anesthetized, and lonely. I was honest when I told her that many audiences would not be able to see the purpose in what she was writing and that they would question her inability to spell or compose beyond simple three- to seven-word statements. I also said I thought the students were wrong in their criticisms because who were they to say how she might spend her time?

While talking with her, I also was thinking, "Who was I to tell this young woman that she couldn't enjoy the writing she produced or that no one was going to read her writing in the coming years?" In general, most of us are not going to be read by wide audiences; this is a petty romantic belief writers often hold in ourselves. It was fine to be realistic about one's writing, but no one had the right to suggest she couldn't find productive purposes for her work. She had found the means to bypass earlier course prerequisites, get around the institutional gate-keeping system, because she wanted to take creative writing, a course that symbolized her struggle with language and a life where her heart underwent several bypasses. The brutal honesty of her classmates' criticism paralyzed her from writing for nearly a week; then through some encouragement she produced nearly forty more pages of her struggling story, completing eighty pages by semester's end, nearly three times what the rest of the class did. While still not what readers would call literary, her writing did improve. As in the past while depressed, she wrote her way out. She discovered that literary models weren't the right goal for her work, and she claimed she would write every day she was well enough to do so. She died the following spring in her sleep, but I'm certain she kept her promise. She would not fail herself after refocusing her purposes in that workshop.

The memorial book filled out in the library spoke to how students, faculty, and staff were glad to have known her. She had one of the worst lives possible for a child and young adult growing up in Central New York, but she developed a fervently positive attitude through her dedication to writing and teddy bears. And ultimately, she had at least one receptive audience for her writing. After she died, the young woman's mother appreciated having every word that her daughter had struggled to produce. It was the truest remembrance she had of her daughter.

The weekend after my student died in the car accident, a counselor from Student Development met me outside the classroom beforehand. She was a tremendously kind person, sensitive and soft-spoken, who had called me the day before to tell me about Rachael's accident. She would offer counseling sessions for any of Rachael's classmates who needed it. I entered the classroom first, giving the students the news, explaining how calling hours would be two days away. I had already planned on attending, and in telling the students this I nearly broke into tears. Several of Rachael's classmates also had redness forming in their eyes, lips drawn tight together. Students wanted to know what happened. "Her car skidded off 481 on her way to work." The students nodded their heads, knowing the speed involved in this main commuter corridor leading from Oswego to Syracuse. I didn't say how Rachael had been trying to pass a truck, hit a patch of road grit, and slid into the median that dipped to collect rainwater between the south and northbound lanes, propelling her car into the air then rolling upon landing. She had been speeding to get to work and had not been wearing a seatbelt. One young woman who commuted the I-81 corridor north to see her fiancé stationed at Fort Drum whispered worriedly about Rachael's son, "Who would take care of him?" The counselor had more answers than I did; however, she focused on inviting students to come see her either during or after class if they needed. Her eyes caught mine as she left as if to say, "Let me know who might need me."

The room was silent, and I don't know what I said to fill the empty air. Something caring, I know, but I wasn't really present in the room anymore. I was disconnected from everything and everyone. I think I said we'd get to our course materials after we took a moment to talk about this incident. The room seemed dark in the fluorescently lit classroom without windows, and I couldn't focus on anyone very well. Then a fairly outgoing and social student asked, "Who's Rachael? Which student was she? Where did she sit?"

Admittedly, it was only the third week of classes and not all students bond in their rapid circulation through our front doors, but the question stopped me. I'd expected that this student being one of the more socially networked would have known Rachael—personally. It's a small community, and people know one another at our college. Students whispered him the details in embarrassed tones. If possible, I felt worse than I had. It's not as though this student didn't care; he didn't know her, just as all of us didn't know much about her.

I also don't know if anyone went to see the counselor. I watched for students to observe if they were at risk, and while sad, I didn't see any signs. They were merely somber the rest of the week. I was seemingly the most troubled by having lost Rachael from our class, but I don't know this for sure. After going to the wake and seeing her family, her son wandering the crowd with his father continually picking him up to hug him, and her parents and brother, I cried much of that night. In order to deal with the uncontrolled emotions of the situation, I wrote a short story in which a middle-aged professor was sympathizing with the death of his student such that he was contemplating suicide. I wasn't feeling suicidal, but her aggressive driving without a seatbelt felt like an act of suicide that needed balancing—even sharing in the grief at the calling hours among her friends and family did not reconcile my feelings. However, writing the story let me take a few good steps toward dealing with what I thought an unnecessary death. In the story I fictionalized much of the ambivalent anger and love her friends and family expressed at the wake, even if I could not provide meaning or completely isolate and "theorize" the stages of grief we faced over losing Rachael. In the following excerpt from my story, the wake scene was one of mixed blame and praise:

A shiny-headed, bald man squinted his eyes as if he needed glasses. A man with a mullet and wearing a leather NASCAR jacket dabbed his nose with a white hankie. A girl with a baby face and blond hair hanging down her back all brittle and starchy whimpered how SHE had been such a "good girl." Others were talking about Rachael too, but none used her name. There was no need. She was a good girl. Pearl Jam music played from speakers in the ceiling. A thin young man said, "She loved this band." Another said, "She would have wanted it this way." The voices were a polyphonic eulogy. Rows of compressed faces, people peered through one another, even I with my bulk. One uncle type said, "I warned her about her driving. She drove like a demon." No one said much after that until a middle-aged couple a few people ahead said they had to leave. They had to go and would quickly pay their respects. This couple stepped from the line and cut through a side room to enter the mourning room at the front. The line progressed back toward the entrance—a prolonged slowdown. One young man who entered turned left to cut into the line. He was round and plump in his middle, his head a smaller pudgy double for his belly. Like most, he looked about twenty.

I was struck by my moment of anger at this young man. Why would I be so trivial as to want him to go to the end of the line and wait? Did I think that the ritual of politely waiting in line mattered for Rachael or that this one person cutting the line really hurt me? No. I took offense at the uncle-figure implying Rachael gave cause for her own death through her "driving like a demon", but I knew I felt the same. Deep inside me, I thought that if Rachael had abided by the rules of the road, we would not be at this wake feeling her loss.

After paying my respects and while driving home, I saw the young line cutter "outside a fast food restaurant laughing with his friends and kicking at a pile of dirt by the roadside." For me this image was rich with possible interpretation, but what was important at that moment was that I shared in some small amount what that young man must have felt, just as I had earlier felt the way I did about the derisive comment on Rachael's driving. At some point, we all blame the victim as part of grief; we all want to fix and rectify the loss that happens around us, even when it can't—and perhaps *especially* when it can't—be rectified.

Still, better than the wake and similar to my student with the heart ailment, putting the emotional events onto the page, communing and navigating my experience through words, let me take control of the loss; at the same time, I was writing fictionalized versions to know the loss better. Often I've seen writing can have emotional purposes and possess emotional catharsis for the writer. The idea that catharsis should be reached solely through reading or through watching a play never sat well with me.

Later that week when I read my usual stack of notebooks and papers, I had forgotten that Rachael's writing sat at the bottom of the pile. Did I have the strength to read it? I had intentionally forgotten about it because I didn't know what to do with it. When I gave my respects to Rachael's mother, I told her that I was Rachael's writing teacher and that I'd especially enjoyed her in class. I said I liked her writing, and she responded by telling me how much Rachael cared for writing and how she always looked to find more time to write in her journal. Rachael's body was propped in the casket behind this 4'10" woman who began crying again as if she hadn't cried enough in the last few hours. Rachael wore a makeup smile on her lips and a large fishing hat to hide the damage done to her forehead upon impact with the windshield, her face gray and plastic. This was no longer the smiling student I'd had in class, and I chose to skip kneeling before her in prayer because I didn't want to see or remember her in that way. I'd never wanted to think of her as a "dead fisherwoman." But I knew I could not avoid these remains in her writings. She had written them for herself and for me. I also hoped the writing might provide more meaning in light of the meaninglessness of her death, and it did provide a powerful comment on the circumstances facing my students who are caught between work, family, and aspirations of the American dream. In my short fiction, I translated her feelings in a way my unfortunate hero could make sense of his disconnection from his students and begin to make choices that might mend the academic work a professor does in the classroom with the humanity of loss. The following sample adapts and submits us to the metawriting protocols Rachael experienced as best as I made sense of them:

> This damn computer with its carpal tunnel starting keys; it's making my wrists tighten up. Now my topic is lost and I need five pages. One more lousy page. I know it's important for me to pass!!!!!!!!!!!!!!!! I need to pass I want to enjoy class it sucks I can't enjoy it due to my absolute hell of a schedule right now workallnight tillclass inthemorning tendmyson betray him to-my-ex aftersupper anap study whenIcan atwork. I wish there was an infinite time for me to learn.

Then, the word "fuck" was crossed out with the word SORRY written in red letters over the top. "This sucks," she continued. "I know I know I can do better be better work harder motivation is key to spelling. How can I be more? I hate it so much frustration nothoughts of hope in me. Shit." Then she ends her vent as if thinking that no one would care to listen to a night shift LPN or a single mother's complaints. The switch to an academic voice is striking but not artificial when considered what she worked through in her notebook:

> Learning has suffered greatly in this time of technology; there is the notion that "there's got to be a better way" in the mind of every schoolboy and girl. Who am

> I to question technological advances that spawned a culture of such great writers
> and thinkers in our generation and the many generations before us? We now
> have a better life, don't we? People say "if it's not broken, don't fix it," but I think
> we should question and be encouraged to challenge developments. Maybe ques-
> tioning could even help us in our racing pursuit for improvement. But again,
> what do I know? I'm not broken.

The irony is obvious. Her feelings of hopelessness may be fleeting and tempo-
rary, but they are also self-destructive. The push to work, to be intelligent
critically, and to sublimate or eject emotion from her life: these are my interpretations of what Rachael faced in the week before her death. I sense she was
mostly alone in these problems, except for her writer's notebook, except for me
in being willing to listen instead of tossing her last written words out, and
except for readers of this essay who take Rachael with them.

In my sharing this story, I don't want to dwell on the unfairness of the
accident or the sociopolitical inequities that young, single mothers like
Rachael face daily. The economic consequences of people pushed into these
living conditions are quite obvious. The dreams and desires of America over-
ride our psychological well-being and healthy attitudes toward risk and real-
ism. Instead I want to concentrate on how death is not part of the typical
classroom. Classrooms are primarily arenas of youth and life. Our colleges are
training grounds for people beginning or midcareer. The knowledge of hospice
is not generally invited into classrooms, and if it is, the material is treated
clinically. Increased life span in the United States of more than 35 percent in
the last hundred years alongside the removal of the elderly from the home has
given Americans a deluded sense of immortality and likely an inability to deal
with death. Americans wish to be active (and happy) until they die in their
sleep, and with an aging population and overextended—soon to be failing—
healthcare system, the current generations of Americans are unprepared to
encounter the new faces of death.

In the spring semester of 2006, Jeff asked me to assist with what he called
the "greatest educational challenge of his career." He wished me to be a
coparticipant/observer in his Love and Loss class in order to investigate the
feasibility of a humanities course in death education. The course would read
relevant literature, but more importantly, it would allow students their own
empathic discourse opportunities to navigate their experiences and those of
others including Jeff's own loss of his wife to pancreatic cancer in the spring of
2004. As with all his previous classroom research, Jeff was particularly concerned with the students' well-being and that I be present to witness if students were helped or harmed by this course. Thus I undertook reading the
literature and students' essays produced throughout the course in addition to
talking with students voluntarily about the value and risk of the course for

them. I was able to attend all but two classes and kept a journal on important weekly events.

Before pointing out any evidence for a conclusion about this unique course, I want to explain the classroom composition. The course consisted of mostly female students, making up about 80 percent of the enrollment. This section of English 226 was one of the department's large sixty-student electives for English and non-English majors. Most students were English majors, and a strong cohort selected the course knowing its content would include affective as well as cognitive learning. The room was overly wide, loud with echoes, and ill suited for student-to-student interaction. After several weeks of asking students to arrange their desks in a semicircle, Jeff allowed the students to sit in a less crowded row formation. Some teacher-to-student conversation would be possible, but predominately, Jeff would need to carry the class from the front at its lectern. Neither the class size nor the room conditions promoted what empathic teaching typically embodies. To compensate, Jeff prepared his lectures carefully with a mix of personal disclosure and quality literary passages. He would also emphasize empathic teaching. The standard class time consisted of 45 percent readings—mostly from student essays and responses—and 40 percent lecture with some participation in the form of surveying the class or question/discussion. The remaining 15 percent was required for paper passing, syllabi reminders, and assignment logistics.

The initial week replicates the emotional challenges this course presented for its participants. The first day Jeff invites students to name anything worse than death. Two students have answers to this. One is "rape," which Jeff acknowledges as a horrible trauma in lives. As recorded in my journal, Jeff asks apologetically what he says is a terrible question, "Would you rather have your mother experience rape or death?" The student admits she'd prefer to have her mother alive. Jeff then receives an answer that shows there are worse things than death when a second student gives an account of how he works with the brain dead. The resulting pedagogy is thus one of inviting engagement with the subject of death but acknowledging when Jeff or our current research doesn't know all the answers. This folds well with the fact that we cannot know death, and as I mentioned earlier, we know it less and less with views of cure-all medicine and the removal of the dying from the home. The deaths we encounter are presented through media or entertainment drama; thus they are not actual experiences but encountered figuratively and consumed pleasurably as theatrical acts.

The disclosures Jeff makes about his wife in the second class by reading his eulogy for her attempt to mend this disconnect between our fantasy of loving and dying and the reality few of us are prepared to face. In hearing Barbara's eulogy, students are startled by its honesty and the implied difference this course will take from other standard classes. In hearing Barbara's eulogy, students must acknowledge their professor as real and experienced with the subject. Through this reading, many students share in Jeff's sadness and love for his wife; a few tense up like a muscle around a wound. And I'd say this pedagogy of addressing wounds, not merely dressing injuries in an attempt to hide them, is what Jeff looks to undertake as the healing mechanism for this course. As a mission statement, it might look like the following: "Stake out our individual and collective dreams compared to the hard reality of life; then allow students the space to engage in these presently incommensurate forces that make our losses so incredibly difficult. Support differences throughout."

When Jeff asks students to think for next class about what they would like their last words to be, he's charged them with a task that introduces the possibility for life-changing actions. The assignment's a common literary trope in which a hero or heroine gets the chance to say his or her last words before expiring. And yet, to ask students to compose this figurative text is to begin engaging them beyond the usual boundaries for what they might expect and dream. The following class, even with this challenge as will be explored continually over the course of the semester, the pedagogy is playfully engaging and safe as Jeff reads the responses anonymously. Some of the responses are even funny such as when students' last words say,

I'll be back.
Meet me at the stoplight after the gate.
When you have to go, you gotta go!
Put something funny on my tombstone.
This sucks, give me a beer.

In fact, the compositions are supportive in that all engage in the challenge and are respected in their opinions. Interestingly enough, one last word was "Teddy," reminiscent, I think, of the comfort my bubbly student wished to (re-)create in her writing. Some students take the opportunity of last words to offer advice such as,

I wish I could live forever. Since I can't, I hope to be remembered forever. I love the people who have impacted my life, positively or negatively, because I would not be the person I am without them. I am grateful for the life I've led.
Remember me with smiles, not tears.
Move on, for if you don't, you're as useful to this world as I am right now. (Dead.)
Keep your head up. I'm only dying physically.
Love and be free.
Please don't be afraid. I won't be alone. I'm not scared.

Just because I'm gone, doesn't mean I'm not going to be here. What's lost
   shouldn't be forgotten.

Listeners to these responses hear that others apart from themselves have
similar outlooks and similar misgivings. Through these words students document the importance of closure in the form of thanks and love:

Thank you to everybody who has touched my life. I will miss being here with
   you. I love you.
I'm going to miss the people I love, and the people that love me.
Life is the most beautiful gift I ever got. Thank you, to whoever the giver
   may be.
I appreciate everything—the good and the bad.
I'm going to be with my dad again.
Thank you, God, for a wonderful life.
I love you.
To my husband or family: "I owe whatever I was in life to your hope that
   would not give me up, to your love that saw me still as good." Edgar Lee
   Masters

Regardless how we categorize these responses, what is certain is that the
students in Love and Loss are not spectators. The class bonds through the
common enterprise of attempting to know more about what is fearfully
avoided and a subject that while common to life is impossible to know fully. In
connection to this, the students and I find Jeff's disclosures about his wife
absolutely necessary to the course, but the reasons for this are slightly different.
As a teacher, I find the disclosures essential as a pedagogical centering around
one subjective reality, one true experience of death. Because Jeff shares Barbara's dying words in the form of photocopied reproductions for the class, his
relationship with death becomes less abstract compared with our media and
entertainment bombardment of it.

   Seeing Barbara's last words in her own shaky handwriting—obviously in
pain and with misspellings and cross-outs—links unromantically loss to reality. Students admire Jeff's personal expertise in love and loss, but the disclosures for them are more about how a professor may be a person, how the
personal does matter, and how sufferers are not really alone if we were to open
ourselves to the people who experience similar pain around us.

   With the safety precautions of anonymity and the understanding that
essay grades are based on one's ability to write SAE (Standard American
English) and not one's willingness to self-disclose, students commented to me
privately that they felt safe and supported in their explorations of this risky
subject. In each writing assignment, students could choose not to have Jeff

read what they had written before the class by printing "No" on the front page. Further, while some students commented that they found the course emotionally challenging because of past encounters with loss, none felt the course placed him or her in psychologically harmful situations or seriously "at risk." I talked to a few students who wondered how anyone could feel at risk in such a supportive and welcoming classroom. But again, this speaks to the skill with which Jeff molds his classroom environment.

Reading the essays as I did, I witnessed how students navigated safely important yet "risky" issues for them. Their writing space could be used for their own individualized purposes. For example, in commenting on divorce and depression, one student wrote: "When I was 13 years old, I bought a box of razors from CVS. They were not attached to plastic handles; they were exposed as if they were made for my purpose. I did not expect the clerk to sell them to me. I swore that my intentions were written across my forehead, visible through my parted bangs. I had never mutilated my body before, but I acted as though I was a professional. I cleaned my skin with rubbing alcohol before I carved in the outside of my right arm: E M P A T H Y. My teachers spotted it before my parents did. When I was forced to show my mother, she asked me what it meant."

While it's notable that written language does not cure this writer's concerns or the trauma that caused them, the student does frame the problem based in people trying to figure her out. As intoned by the student's mother and in the essay's conclusion where she says, "I keep seeking a definition, but all I am finding are more words," she articulates how language itself cannot solve all misery. Whereas writing as a poststructuralist play like what this student observes in her never-ending litany of words is not enough to help her completely write her way to reality through language or have her mother appreciate her otherness, empathy is surely part of what's needed. According to medieval definition, discourse centers on reasoning. But reasoning is not what my two former students who died needed; reasoning is not what this student needed and may still need. This student understands that empathy itself can be a problem when others have too little or one has too much empathy in one's own life. She understands its limitations, including its absence on the part of her mother and "problem-solving" therapist; nevertheless, she can identify with Gabriella's essay on depression in *Empathic Teaching*. She empathizes with this real life "character" and is less alone in her worries when her pressures and emotions are not uniquely hers, even if they are still scary. This was missing in me when I thought I suffered so greatly from my student's accident; this was missing when my writers' workshop attacked my student who wanted to write about teddy bears but did not know her purpose for writing about them.

In writing some of the assignments like the eulogy, students worried that they would "jinx" themselves by writing about loved ones as if they are dead. This superstition links the same unwillingness our culture has, in general, to not talking about death. Likewise, when death happens outside or inside the classroom, we tend to isolate each other when collective significance might be possible. Educationally, Jeff's discourse pedagogy may be traced to James Britton and the London group that posited the need to think of language for its usage, not simply its modality. Britton, like Freud, imagined language as formed through parental interactions and relationships. Routinely, expressivist writing is considered narcissistic and romantic, but what critics forget about expressivist pedagogy is that a parental audience is still a social construction of language, albeit ideally an encouraging and not an isolating one. Parents are the first to show us we are not alone. No doubt parents are also not to blame for everything traumatic in one's life, and blaming them for genes they could not control is another attempt at guilt-produced reasoning where logical reasoning cannot exist. I don't claim that empathy can solve all these "disconnecting deaths" between people, but developing increased classroom empathy might support the kind of expressive place for language that Britton's 1971 article "What's the Use?" originally intended: "We would hope, for instance, that expressive language may be increasingly seen to play a key role in all learning (even the most subject oriented) as well as in learning to use language. . . . We see such activities indeed as reflecting a concern for 'the compleat man': for it is the corpus of an individual's experience that makes him the person he is; that generates the pluses and minuses of his fluctuating verdict on the world, his fluctuating acceptance of the human condition, his fluctuating faith in himself" (218–19).

Throughout the reader and writer responses that Jeff shared with everyone, he spent much class time presenting the other side of student critiques of his assignments and lectures. After interviewing students who spoke so enthusiastically in favor of his class and what he allowed them to achieve, I find that Jeff gave undeserved weight to criticisms of his teaching. But this willingness to show fluctuating evidence, to let the students be the best judge of his work and its impact on them, is noteworthy. Jeff's Love and Loss course builds trust by paradoxically allowing students to express their doubts. This pedagogical strategy creates a discourse community that enables students to articulate and develop their views on religion, euthanasia, dreams, forgiveness, and love and loss.

As some students confided in me, "This class is not for everyone. The course description should be very clear in what people are getting into." But I'm not sure I agree in its lessons not being for everyone. Without doubt, forcing students to enroll in a death education course, as part of a sensitivity training or general education requirement, is a mistake and like many unilateral requirements undercuts effectiveness. One caution I do have is that few teachers have the direct experience to teach a course like this. After ten years of college teaching, I don't have enough experience to teach a course like this, and while I think death education is instrumental for our forthcoming generation of college students, teachers need to attend to empathic teaching concertedly. Bureaucrats and parents may not take empathy as seriously as grammar and mathematical accounting. The business of academia does not train us as well in "empathic discourse" as the university does in its disciplinary subjects and associated logics. This is not to say that I find universities unsupportive learning environments, merely not focused around empathic teaching, and this is a loss in our potential to learn in new forms.

But to return to my initial question, are students helped or harmed by taking a course in death education? According to the students, who may be the best judge in this, and through what I observed, students are helped immensely and found the course firmly useful.

Coda

In fall 2003, three weeks after Rachael's death, midterm grades came due. Looking at my grading sheets, I noticed that her name was not on my class roster. I checked the computer records, and she was nowhere to be found, as if she had never existed according to the database. Approaching a dean, I discovered her family had been given a refund, and she'd been "unenrolled" to prevent failing grade reports being accidentally generated. I'd recycled her papers earlier in the semester, as holding on to them depressed me. Her classmates had formed new peer groups and discussed writing strategies without her. Again, I felt as sick as when I found out she had died or when I met her parents and son, with her body, which no longer resembled her, resting in a coffin in the same the room. Once buried in the ground and nearly forgotten, it was like she'd been erased. In Love and Loss many students talked of moving on in one's life after death, but I think it's essential to note that on this point Jeff needed to share how he didn't want to forget the dead in moving forward with his life—and neither do I. I can't go back in time and put Rachael's seatbelt on her nor can I quite forget her, and I shouldn't. What I have is a story based on where she entered and exited my life, and though the story is a fictionalized account based on her writings, I find this vision of her struggles important in understanding what most of my students face in their monthly bills, heavy workloads, loves, and many deaths. I think it's important that all these categories—all the messiness of students' complexities—be kept if I am to continue to teach them in their lives as well as throughout my own circumstances. If I lose their history, I lose a necessary part of my ability to empathize and to understand.

Appendix B
"Writing Has Saved My Life": Breanna's Story

In nearly all her writings, Breanna kept returning to her father, who died on Thanksgiving day, 2001. Her writings reveal an ever-deepening examination of the dark emotions produced by this event, which remains the most traumatic experience in her life. She wrote about this experience first in a diary immediately after her father's death and then in my course. Writing enabled her to acknowledge that she needed help in coming to terms with his death—help in the form of a psychotherapist, whom she began seeing while enrolled in my course. By talking about her feelings to a therapist, and by writing about her feelings in Love and Loss, she demonstrated that the "talking cure" and the "writing cure" are parallel journeys toward self-knowledge and self-healing. In what follows, I reproduce her writings on her father and the complex emotions it awakened within her, including toxic shame. She wrote insightfully about the literary texts in the course, but I have not included these writings.

Breanna's obituary begins with a religious image. "The golden gates of heaven swung free on October 15, 1986, to let a single angel free from heaven to bless the earth." Childhood for her and her brothers "was more war than love, but the siblings reflect fondly on their younger years." Her early years passed quietly, but high school was a "true learning experience" for her. "Thirteen brought not only the gravity of finally entering the teenage years, but the unexpected shock of her parents' separation," followed by the death of her father two years later:

> In the insecurity of her young age, not having the same accessibility to her father was devastating, but with great strength and maturity she was able to see the logic of the situation: if her parents were happier this way then she would find a median to be happy as well. Two short years later, shock struck again when her father was stricken with lung cancer. For six long months, she struggled to watch her father fight the battle before he finally let himself succumb to the illness on Thanksgiving morning of 2001. Disbelief was her initial reaction to her father's death, but in her maturity she was able to look back with fond memories of what her father brought to her life. The insight and guidance her father left her with helped to steer her through the days when he wasn't physically near.

That is all we learn about the father's death. There is no indication that Breanna had difficulty coping with the loss, and the rest of her obituary is upbeat. She graduated from college, earned a master's degree in education, moved to Manhattan to become a high school English teacher, married the "man of her dreams," retired at the "ripe old age of 65," and then returned with her husband to upstate New York. "She passed in her sleep at the age of 91. She lays to rest now in her hometown near her beloved mother who passed away thirty years before her. Behind her, she leaves a legacy of three children and twelve grandchildren to carry on her name, her memory, and her love."

Breanna eulogizes her father in the second writing assignment. "He was Superman, a hero, and my father," she observes in the opening paragraph. The eulogy contains only loving memories of this larger-than-life patriarch who seemed to center his life on "Daddy's little girl." She cites many concrete examples of his devotion to her. He would dilute her cough syrup with water so that it wouldn't taste so bitter to her; he would be there every day after school when she came home from elementary school and help her with her homework; he would make popcorn for her with his special recipe; he would tell his daughter "yes" after her mother had said "no" to her; and he would protect her from her brothers. In the most striking detail of the eulogy, Breanna describes one of her favorite night rituals:

> Before going to bed, he would tuck me in and I would smell Listerine on his breath. Of course, he would use the worst smelling mouthwash. But he also did something very strange before bed. I would always smell freshly sprayed cologne on him as he would kiss me goodnight. When I had asked him why, he said he sprayed cologne on him[self] before he went to sleep, so that if he died in his sleep, he would go to heaven smelling good. It was the strangest thing I have ever heard of, but I will never forget that Aramis cologne he wore every day and every night. He never seemed afraid of death and he thought, when he faces death and meets our Father, he will at least face Him smelling great.

The eulogy contains no mention of divorce, though she states without further comment that her father moved out of the house to another part of the state as she grew older. "We must have tried every restaurant in town and then talked about which one was the best. We would first sit at the bar and play the quick draw lotto. He always let me pick the numbers and gave me whatever we won. He just liked to see me happy." The image of a child sitting at a bar with her father may seem unusual, especially following an earlier reference to her father who would "come home from work, get a beer, and turn on Oprah," but she does not seem to find these details disturbing. She presents us with an idealized portrait of a father who promised to include her in all his plans. "We would talk about all the things we were going to do and all of the places we were going to travel to. He went to Ireland once and told me all about it and said we would go there someday together." She ends the eulogy with a strong religious affirmation. "Dad passed away, but his presence has not at all left us. I can still smell his cologne, still feel his touch, and I can still pretend that I will see him tomorrow. He returns to our Father now, and leaves us with his endless love and unveiling faith."

Breanna opens her third essay by disclosing the importance of her faith as a Roman Catholic. "I believe there is heaven and hell and, depending on how you live your life, you will go to one of these places." She affirms her close relationship with God, believing that one day she will "return to Him." She then discusses how her faith sustained her when her father was dying:

> When my father passed, I did not know how to react. You could say that I had no reaction but pure shock. He suffered for six months from lung cancer and I watched him struggle every day as he went to chemotherapy. When he passed away, I was shocked because I never believed that my father was actually no longer living and that he would not be there to hug me every day. It was hard to cope with at the time, of course, but as time passed, I realized that he was not holding my hand anymore, but he is looking over my shoulder every day and watching everything I do. He suffered terribly for so long, and I began to believe that he is much happier now with God and that he is not suffering so much. Of course, I wish he was still here for me to call every day on the phone and go to the movies together like we used to do, but I believe he is with me always every day in my heart and helping me through everything I encounter. Because of these religious beliefs, I have been able to go through everything I have encountered due to the simple fact that I knew I was not alone. I believe my father is with me every day and in my heart I know what he would say in whatever choice I make.

Later in the essay Breanna declares that she was upset when her father died but nevertheless believed that he was "safe and healthy with God now and, more importantly, no longer suffering." Religion played a large part in comforting her. "Personally, my religion has helped me cope with my father passing away and accepting the fact that I, too, will die someday and be with God and my father once again."

The first hint of Breanna's difficulty in coping with her father's death appears on her midterm exam discussions of C. S. Lewis's *A Grief Observed* and Emily Brontë's *Wuthering Heights*. Lewis's crisis of faith following his wife's death from cancer encouraged Breanna to acknowledge her own crisis after her father's death:

I will say that my religious beliefs were tested when my father passed away, and they were even questioned, as they were with Lewis. When I heard the footsteps of a family friend come to our door on that black morning, and upon hearing him say, "Jimmy died this morning" to my mom, I felt as if time had stopped. I closed my eyes to try and fathom what had just been said. I could not breathe, and I could not even cry. I could not do anything at that frightful moment but to look for God for help. I remember asking, "why?" and not being able to understand anything that I have believed in up to that moment. I had gone to church every Sunday before that, worshiped this God that I have accepted into my life, and did not know why my God would take away the only person I had looked up to in the world. I found that I had not gone to church much after that, for it was too unbearable to worship this God that had taken him from me. You could say that I questioned my faith entirely, and I wondered if my father was still with me in spirit. I was in the car one day soon afterward, and I had seen a license plate on the car in front of us that said, "Jimmy," with an arrow pointing up. My affirmation that my dad was safe and no longer suffering became more and more evident. It took about two years before I actually started going to church again on a regular basis. I cannot sit here and tell you that [I] have reached a complete affirmation of my faith, for it would be a lie. Just as I could not sit here and tell you that I have completely accepted the death of my father. What I do believe is that he is out there somewhere, looking over my shoulder, and guiding me in the right direction as he always had when he was alive. He is alive in me, in my heart, and that is what is important to me.

Breanna's crisis of faith is not surprising; indeed, it would be unusual if a father's premature death did not cause a daughter to lose faith, if only temporarily. But what is surprising, even startling, is Breanna's self-disclosure following her discussion of healthy and pathological forms of grieving in *Wuthering Heights:*

When my father passed away, I was just fifteen years old. Afterward, I did not know how to cope with the loss of this love. As a result, I had a very unhealthy response to his death. I kept going from church to church, I stayed out late, snuck out of my house when I was punished, turned to alcohol and drugs, and ended up getting arrested at the age of 17. Looking back now, I see that I should have talked to someone about his death, but I thought at the time that my wrongdoings were justifiable in rebelling through coping with my fathers death. I hurt myself in the end, and I hurt others around me. I could have gone about his death much healthier, but, being a fifteen-year-old girl is confusing enough, and losing my father at this age left me lost. I fear for others that go through this at a young age, and I fear they will have the same response as I did. Today, I am going through therapy, and I am learning to cope with my mistakes and most of all, the loss of my father. I am lucky to be where I am today because of the help and support of my friends and family, but, unfortunately, others in my position may not be so lucky.

Breanna doesn't mention the word "shame" here, but we can infer that it lurks throughout her description of her "unhealthy" response to her father's death. Léon Wurmser, perhaps the leading psychoanalytic theorist of shame, offers a vivid definition that captures its complexity:

> The word shame really covers three concepts. Shame is first the *fear* of disgrace, it is the *anxiety* about the danger that we might be looked at with contempt for having dishonored ourselves. Second, it is the feeling when one is looked at with such scorn. It is, in other words, the *affect of contempt* directed against the self— by others or by one's own conscience. Contempt says: "You should disappear as such a being as you have shown yourself to be—failing, weak, flawed, and dirty. Get out of my sight: Disappear!" One feels ashamed for *being exposed*. . . . Third, shame is also almost the antithesis of the second one, as in: "Don't you know any shame?" It is an overall *character trait* preventing any such disgraceful exposure, an attitude of respect toward others and toward oneself, a stance of reverence." (67–68; emphasis in original)

The three concepts of narcissism discussed by Wurmser may be seen in Breanna's writings. Shame anxiety, the fear of disgrace, prevented her from disclosing her unhealthy behavior until she felt trust in her teacher and classmates. Shame affect made her feel weak, flawed, dirty, leading to self-destructive behavior. And shame as a preventive attitude compelled her silence in her early essays, since self-expression would threaten self-respect.

Breanna's self-disclosure is an example of what I call "risky writing," which arises from an "unsettling or destabilizing subject" and which "threatens nothing less than the writer's identity and self-respect. Shame is the key emotion in risky writing, and the writer [may experience] shame even when he or she has done nothing wrong" (*Risky Writing* 9). Breanna makes no attempt here to conceal behavior that she now regrets. To acknowledge feeling devastated after a parent's death is difficult enough, but to acknowledge acting out, drug and alcohol addiction, and criminal behavior is disclosure of a different magnitude. As I suggest in *Risky Writing*, self-disclosure and shame exist in a reciprocal relationship: "The more one self-discloses, the greater the threat of shame" (22). To expose one's darkest secrets is to risk rejection, misunderstanding, and ridicule. Students like Breanna are willing to make these painful or shameful self-disclosures only when they believe that their teacher and classmates will respond empathically, not judgmentally.

Breanna's next important reference to her father occurs in the "Ten Things to Do before I Die" assignment, in which she lists her desire to write a book. "I am an English major, and I love to write. When my father passed away, I did not know how to cope with many things in my life. In trying to cope with his passing, I began to write, and I felt as if it had helped a great deal to write down my feelings on paper and analyze them. I would love to write a book one day, perhaps discussing my difficult childhood. I feel as if I have found comfort in reading stories and watching movies that I can relate to, and I would love to reach out to others and have this same effect on those going through similar situations. I do not care how much profit the book makes in selling; if my book comforts one person, and touches one soul, I will feel as if writing my book was worth every minute." She returns to her father in the seventh writing assignment, on *Empathic Teaching*:

"I Felt Shame, Guilt, Sadness, Fear, and Every Other Emotion When He Died"

"Jimmy passed away this morning." These are the words that have echoed in my head for years when I was told my father lost the fight against cancer. Every day, we encounter loss whether it is the loss of a friend, one's health, or the breakup of one's relationship. We all handle it in our own way like by writing about it, for example. We never truly "get over" a great loss in our lives, but we do learn ways to handle the loss and cope with it. Jeff Berman discusses the theme of love and loss in his book *Empathic Teaching*. Jeff introduces many students to us through their writing, and we see many themes of loss in their lives. What the reader notices is that their losses are all different, and their responses to [loss] vary greatly. As seen in this book, there is no way of "getting over" a loss in one's life, but people handle loss in a way that works for them.

One student we are introduced to is Cory. Cory struggles with the difficulty of his father's absence in his life. Physically, his father was there, but emotionally, he never let his father in his life. He recognizes his father's thinking in a long phone call he had with him one night. He also begins to notice that he never really let either of his parents into his life. Cory's mother felt as if she did not even know who her own son was. "She wanted desperately to meet her twenty-year-old son" (Berman, 156). His mother wanted to *meet* her son, Cory, as if he were a stranger she passed on the street. Because Cory never thoroughly opened up to her, their relationship was almost strictly biological, not emotional. Through writing, he attempts to end his silence, and he begins to "open up." As he writes, Cory reaches insight into his family life. Instead of going through life in his silence, Cory begins to write down his thoughts, and he realizes he is not angry with his father, but with his father's silence.

Another student, Danielle, experiences the breakup of her parents. One image that stuck out to me as it did to Jeff was "the shattered remains of the antique mirror were scattered around the stairway like ashes of the dead" (164). Danielle thought it was normal to have divorced parents when she did not realize the issues that surrounded it. When her parents separated, this "dream" became a horrifying reality as her brother ran to her room to escape from the words that "flew like artillery." This image is so powerful, and it creates a vivid image in the reader's mind. She loses her father to alcoholism, and she is then forced to care for the family on her own when her mother falls into a depressed state. In writing this essay, Danielle conjures up memories of who she was when she [was] younger, and who she is now. In doing so, she realizes many things about her family that she now understands. Her parents may have forgiven each other, but they are not healed. As the bruises fade, the scars remain as Danielle focuses on her life now as a grown, mature adult.

Although the assignment was to write on three students in *Empathic Teaching*, I felt I needed to illustrate the role writing has had in my own life. In reading about Cory and Danielle, memories of my own life came into thought as I found similarities among us. I was born into a "classic" family consisting of a mother, a father, and two brothers. I thought my mother and father, like most people, fell in love, got married, and were living happily ever after. As I grew into an adult, I realized this was not true, for I began to find out the truth behind their relationship. When my parents were just married at twenty-one years old, my father had an affair with a woman named Lynn. My mother then became pregnant with my brother, and my father ended his relationship with Lynn. Growing up, I thought it was normal for my father to drink a six-pack of Budweiser after work, and then have more during dinner. My father was an alcoholic. Whether he knew this himself, I will never know. In his drinking, he and my mom would argue over different things. I found myself, like Danielle's brother, running into my room to escape the "words that flew like artillery." I remember glass breaking, and my mother telling me to have my brothers gather up a change of clothes so that we can spend the night in a hotel. I also remember being afraid of my father when he argued with my mom because my mother and I were close to each other. When he hit her, I did not know this man my mom had married. I became afraid and distant from him, physically and emotionally, as my mom drove us to the local hotel. I had mixed feelings about everything as I was afraid of my father, and I was forced to take sides with my mom. I was angry at my dad for how he acted, although I did not understand it. I was angry at my mom for dragging me to a hotel as I felt embarrassed that someone at school might find out.

This was something normal to me and my brothers as we sat in the car and cried with my mom because daddy was drinking again. I began to write in a diary when he passed away when I was fifteen. I realized I felt shame, guilt, sadness, fear, and every other emotion when he died. In those six months he fought in chemotherapy against the cancer, I spent time with Lynn, as he was now engaged to her when he and my mother divorced two years earlier. We watched him suffer through it as he got sick very often, and I began to really see my father for the first time, not just the man my mom had married twenty-five years ago. Maybe it was because he was forced to quit drinking, but it did not matter to me when we looked into the future together as we watched the sun set. We looked toward my wedding, a possible trip to Ireland, and taking a trip across country. He promised me he would see me do these things when he got better.

On Thanksgiving morning of 2001, I found out that was not possible. I looked at his death as if he had broken his promise to me, and I felt furious toward him as I looked at his closed casket. It took me four years to talk about his death as I took your class, Jeff, and realized in writing seven essays throughout the semester that I needed to talk to someone before it was too late. As I looked toward sexual relations with random guys to feel that male connection I had lost with my dad, as my brothers and I stopped talking to each other, I saw my life crumbling before my eyes. The next day I made the phone call to make an appointment to talk with my psychologist. I truly believe writing has saved my life, for it made me realize many things about my family. In my talks with her, I am now working through many things I ran away from as a child. Clearly, writing has saved my life as I saw it dwindling down toward suicidal thoughts. The role of writing is crucial in one's coping with loss as seen in the lives of Cory, Danielle, and my own. Bruises do fade, but the pain remains the same as the scars are still evident. We are forced to confront these scars, and stop running away from them in coping with these losses. Unfortunately, some never confront those scars, and they let them hang over them into adulthood. Thank you, Jeff.

Strictly speaking, Breanna did not do what I asked of her, since she did not write on *three* students in *Empathic Teaching*, but I did not penalize her because her decision to write about herself struck me as fulfilling the spirit of the assignment. She writes empathically about Cory and Danielle, and I suspect the reason she wrote about herself as the "third" student is because she identified so closely with being the daughter of an alcoholic father—an identi-fication that is all too common among my students. I gave her a "plus" on the essay because it was so well written—there are only a few grammatical mis-takes, including a dangling modifier ("In reading about Cory and Danielle, memories of my own life came into thought") and an incorrectly positioned pronoun (her sentence should read, "This was something normal to my brothers and me"). Apart from praising the quality of her writing, I raised one substantive question at the end: "Did taking this course enable you to begin grieving your father's death and to acknowledge your anger toward him? If so, this course had a meaningful effect on you!"

Only in her seventh essay does Breanna mention feeling shame follow-ing her father's death. Nothing in the earlier writings hints at his physical abuse of his wife, the severity of his drinking problem (though there are clues about this in her eulogy, when she mentions sitting at a bar with her father and when she describes him drinking beer while watching Oprah), or, most ominous of all, her shame and guilt leading to suicidal thoughts. But these are precisely the details she explores in her seventh essay. The diary in which she began writing immediately after her father's death allowed her to discover, presumably for the first time, the "shame, guilt, sadness, fear and every other emotion" she was feeling. As important as diary writing is, it is a solitary and introspective experience, and it apparently did not help her to realize that others were struggling with similar emotions arising from their own losses. Nor did diary writing alone motivate her to enter therapy. That motivation came from our Love and Loss course, as she explains on two different final exam questions, in which she first offers additional information about her struggles after her father's death and then explains her decision to speak to a therapist at the university counseling center:

When my father passed away, I blamed myself for not getting to know him better, and I blamed him for breaking his promise to me that he would be there to walk me down the aisle at my wedding. My only dream in life was to have him walk me down the aisle and give me away to my husband. When he passed away, I began to feel as if he had broken that promise, and any hope for this dream to come true was nonexistent. I turned to sexual relations with random guys to feel that male connection I had with him. I was hurting myself in the end when each month I had to worry about being pregnant. I truly believe that had my father still been alive, I would not be the person I am today. I would not have been as promiscuous as I was after his death, and I would have had higher self-esteem, for I felt as if I was not good enough because he was not alive. I constantly wonder what kind of person I would have been, had he still been alive

Although my life did crumble before my eyes after he passed away, I had learned many things about myself and my family. My father was an alcoholic, and this was the basis for many arguments between my parents that drove them toward divorce. When I was younger, I thought it was normal for my father to have six beers after work and more during dinner. It was difficult growing up, but I believe I became a stronger person because I learned from his actions, the way he treated my mom, and the type of person that I want to be. Had my father still been alive, I know he would continue his drinking habits, and I am afraid that he may have hurt more people around him including his new fiancée. His death taught me to value the people I still have in my life, and to not take anything for granted. All he wanted in his life was to see me succeed, and this led to my consistent success in college as I am working toward an English degree. His death has taught me to cherish what I have and to take advantage of every opportunity I get. I have lost many friends to death, drugs, jail, and other influences, and each friend that crumbles shows me that is who I do not want to be.

～

It was fall semester, and I was registering for classes to take in the spring of 2006 semester. I came across an English class called Love and Loss in Literature and Life. As I read the description for this class, I imagined we would be discussing love in Shakespearean literature, for example, like in *Romeo and Juliet*. Instead, I experienced something that I never had in any class before. Jeffrey Berman, my professor, assigned us his book that he wrote called *Empathic Teaching*. We read this book at the end of the semester so that we would get a full understanding of it. Professor Berman, or as his students call him, Jeff, taught in a way that no teacher has ever taught in my other classes. He taught us how to be better writers not by having us summarize a reading we did (like other classes), but by having us write about personal experiences with love and loss, and to connect them with readings from the book. His empathic approach to teaching was brilliant and successful in his students' eyes.

Being in this class was not like being in any ordinary class because this was not just an ordinary class. My father died four years ago, and I never really talked about it with anyone. Sure, I cried with my family, and I was comforted by my friends, but I never actually talked about how I felt about his death. I felt as if my whole life crumbled one event after another when he died. I lost my father, my hero whom I looked up to my entire life. He was Superman, the man that could not be stopped by any creature on earth. I was wrong though. He was stopped by an ugly creature called lung cancer. It made him suffer for six months before it killed him on Thanksgiving morning of 2001. I never got the chance to talk about how I felt except in my diary. However, even in my diary, I tried to write about other things in my life so that my father's death did not affect me too much. The truth is, I ran from his death and hid it away somewhere so I did not have to visit it again. My brother and I were always so close, especially after my father died, and he became my father figure that I looked up to. Two months ago, my brother and I got into a fight, and we are not talking anymore. This is yet another hurdle I encountered.

In Jeff's class, we were told to write about personal experiences, and in doing so, grammar was corrected so that we became better writers. I found myself beginning to write about my father and my relationship with my family. For the first time, I wrote down on paper how I felt about these issues. Falling into depression after the fight with my brother, I felt as if I could not find a way to rise again. I fell toward suicidal thoughts, and did not have any idea how I would get back up. In writing about personal experiences, and in hearing other classmates' stories, I began to feel that I was not alone after all. Still, I realized I needed to talk to someone.

I began talking to Julie, a psychologist at the counseling center. She helped me realize that since my father's death, I have been searching for that male connection with others around me, whether it was my brother or random guys that I let disrespect me. I began to rise as she [held] out her hand to help me up. I may not have my father in my life anymore, and I may not have a relationship with my brother, but since I have talked to Julie, I have grown to see that I can make it on my own without that male connection. I began to talk about my father's death for the first time with someone who would not judge. As I see a couple of my friends pregnant and with children right now, and another friend living with AIDS, I realized I was headed in the same direction. Through my talks with Julie every week, she helped me realize that I love myself more than that, and I am a stronger person than I look at myself as. Now, I look back, and I realize that I probably would not be alive today if I had not taken Jeff's class. Through his empathic approach to teaching, I wrote about my personal experiences for the first time, and I talked to Julie about my life for the first time. In my other classes, I was forced to remember equations and the biology of the human brain. However, in Jeff's class I was taught how to become a better writer by writing about personal experiences. It was as if the class was therapy for me. Perhaps it served the same purpose for my classmates as well, but I am glad it did.

As I began reading *Empathic Teaching*, I understood exactly what Jeff was talking about on each page. He discussed the way his students learned the basics of writing, and how in doing so, that is the first step in becoming a great writer. Jeff taught us this idea, and it was proven in my advancement of the grades I had received on my papers. The first paper was filled with red marks and comments on each page, and I got a B on it. By the sixth paper, I found very few corrections and more positive comments. I got an A on that paper. Although I was taught to become a better writer, I was also taught indirectly (through Julie) that I was a better person than I thought I was. Jeff's approach to empathic teaching, in a way, saved my life.

In reading *Empathic Teaching*, I had a clear understanding of his way of teaching. If I had read this book without taking his class, I would not have gotten as much out of it because I would not have had a firsthand account of his teaching. I may have gotten bored in reading the book because I would not have been interested in why Jeff taught me the way he did. I thoroughly enjoyed this book, for his teaching may have saved my life. Maybe we just need that extra voice forcing us to talk about our lives once in awhile. I do not feel like enough people talk about their lives because they do not believe it will do anything. The reality is that we all have issues. What we do with them, and how we handle the unfortunate events that take place in our lives is what makes each of us the people we are.

It is gratifying to hear that one's teaching has "saved" a student's life, but how does one respond to such high praise? How does a teacher know when such testimony is true or exaggerated? Many teachers want to make a difference in their students' lives, and some may acknowledge that students have made a difference in their own lives, but it is not "pedagogically correct" to admit the desire to "save" students—though teachers will probably feel comfortable in expressing the desire to improve the world or, if they are ecologically oriented, to save the planet. Yet why shouldn't teachers strive to help students conquer their fears and, in the process, save their lives? Donald Murray's observation is relevant here: "Donald Barthelme told us to 'write about what you're most afraid of.' When I do, I survive the terrors that silence me. While writing, the dark clouds rise, the monster shadows retreat. Graham Greene explains, 'Writing is a form of therapy; sometimes I wonder how all those who do not write, compose or paint can manage to escape the madness, the melancholia, the panic fear which is inherent in the human condition.' Writing is my therapy" (56).

Was Breanna projecting onto me the fantasy of being "Superman," the word she used to describe how she had once viewed her father? If so, she may have rendered me into an idealized father figure, and idealization is, by definition, a distortion of the truth. Her perception of me may have been influenced by transference, a phenomenon that exists not only in psychotherapy but in education as well. An element of unreality inheres in transference relationships, when patients (or students) project onto analysts (or teachers) feelings that arise from significant others in their lives, such as parents. I should point out, moreover, that her comments appear on the final exam; she may thus be telling her teacher what he wants to hear—or at least what she thinks he wants to hear. Is she offering praise—or flattery? "Flattery is strategic praise, praise with a purpose," Richard Stengel declares. "It may be inflated or exaggerated or it may be accurate and truthful, but it is praise that seeks some result, whether it be increased liking or an office with a window" (14–15). Or, we might add, flattery is praise that seeks an A on a final exam. In short, one would like additional proof that Love and Loss saved Breanna's life—proof in the form of a follow-up interview five or ten years in the future, to see if she still feels the same way.

Notwithstanding these caveats, notice that Breanna does not claim *I* saved her life: she singles out an *empathic approach* to teaching, not the *teacher*. Love and Loss allowed her to write about her feelings toward her father's death and to hear her classmates' experiences. She then decided to consult a therapist. She implies the course was therapeutic, largely because she was able to express her feelings without the fear of judgment. Neither Breanna nor I transgressed our roles as student and teacher: there were no boundary violations. To the best of my memory, she never spoke to me outside of class. At no time did she ask me for advice about her personal problems, nor did I offer any. Most of my comments on her essays focused on grammatical and stylistic suggestions for revision, which helped her to become, as she correctly notes, a better writer. That her last essays are so well written demonstrates her academic success in Love and Loss and validates her claims about the course's impact on her life.

Breanna states unambiguously on her final exam that writing has saved her life, words that I have chosen for the title of the present chapter. Surely some readers will believe that these words are an exaggeration. Can writing actually save a person's life? Yes, if we believe the writers who have affirmed the therapeutic benefits of art. In three of my earlier books, *Joseph Conrad: Writing as Rescue, The Talking Cure,* and *Surviving Literary Suicide,* I document how novelists and poets like Conrad, Virginia Woolf, Ernest Hemingway, Sylvia Plath, and Anne Sexton asserted the life-saving nature of writing. As Plath records in her *Journals,* "Fury jams the gullet and spreads poison, but, as soon as I start to write, dissipates, flows out into the figure of the letters: writing as therapy?" (255). I realize, of course, that all of these writers eventually committed suicide except for Conrad, who attempted suicide early in his life and who projected his suicidal feelings onto his major characters. Art is a necessary but not always sufficient part of an artist's support system. As I remark in *Surviving Literary Suicide,* "Writing allowed Woolf to express and work through feelings that might otherwise have overwhelmed her. Writing was not a perfect therapy, but there is little doubt that it extended her life and gave her a reason to live. If, as a result of chemotherapy or radiation therapy, a patient's cancer goes into remission for several years but then returns, we do not question the value of the treatment that has prolonged life. The same is true for Woolf" (99)—and for many other artists.

Writing may have saved Breanna's life in another sense. As a student observed after reading this manuscript, "perhaps 'saved' means not rescuing but preserving, recording, collecting. It occurs to me that in *Dying to Teach* you saved Barbara's life, and through your books about teaching you have saved the lives of your students. I think it's the most beautiful act a person can carry out. Writing does save lives, in so many ways."

Writing was indeed a part of Breanna's support system. She confirmed this eight months after the course ended, when I emailed her for permission to use her writings for this chapter. She agreed enthusiastically, and she also provided me with detailed answers to several questions about her classroom self-disclosures. As Sidney Jourard and Lynn Miller and David Kenny have shown, self-disclosure begets self-disclosure, and my willingness to talk about my wife's death emboldened Breanna to write about her father's death. "When you spoke about Barbara in class, I think we all felt that you put us on a personal level with you because not many teachers are willing to bring their personal lives into the classroom. You also made it very easy for us to open up our personal lives with you and not be afraid to write about things that are on our mind. Doing this put us on a more comfortable level with you in the classroom." Significantly, she did not expect to be so self-disclosing when she signed up for the course. "In the beginning of the semester, I was unenthusiastic about taking your class because I had seen the *seven* writing assignments on the syllabus, and I was not looking forward to the assignments. My feelings changed as I began writing about personal experiences in my writings, and it was even helpful for me to do so."

Breanna confirmed my suspicion that she decided to reveal her father's alcoholism after reading the chapter in *Empathic Teaching* about my former student Danielle, who had written about *her* father's similar problem. "I had read about Danielle's father, and I sympathized with her, and it made me feel as if I wasn't alone. Writing about this perhaps may make someone else feel as if they are not alone—it was almost strangely comforting to me to know there was someone else feeling the same pain." Hearing me read several essays aloud, anonymously, also confirmed that she was not alone in feeling the pain of loss. "I was almost very happy that you read my essays in class because I had written personal stories, and hearing other student's stories provided me with some comfort in knowing that we are all fellow mourners over someone or something. Reading our writings in class makes us all connected in some ways by listening to others' pain." She felt this connection not only to her classmates but also to her teacher. "I feel you and I had some kind of connection as we were fellow mourners helping each other cry. Sometimes we need to cry—it is the only way to let your emotions out."

Only by writing about her father's death did Breanna realize that her life was spinning out of control. This is perhaps the major insight to be drawn from her story: introspective writing is a powerful way to discover painful or shameful feelings about oneself and find solutions to vexing problems. [As the native American novelist Leslie Marmon Silko observed in a talk sponsored by the New York State Writer's Institute on 30 January 2007, "I write to find out what I know."] Breanna wrote to find out more about herself, especially the tangled feelings arising from her father's death. "What made me reveal these events where I responded in unhealthy ways was because at that point, I had just realized that they were unhealthy! In writing about my father's death, I came to the realization that there was a definite correlation between the unhealthy things I did and my father's death. In writing, we reveal things about ourselves that we sometimes never realized until that moment. I think this is what happened to me in your class, Jeff, as well as help from Julie." The discovery of these dark emotions arising from her father's death was so wrenching, Breanna added, that she "began to have suicidal thoughts because I was ashamed of who I had become. I felt this way more and more as I had written those assignments. In not appreciating life and hurting those around me, I realized that I needed help from a professional. You cannot force someone to go to a psychologist because they need to decide to do so when they realize they need it themselves and they want to go." Quite apart from the educational and literary benefits she derived from Love and Loss, the course was for Breanna a psychological odyssey in which she moved from acting out to working through her feelings of grief, anger, guilt, and shame resulting from her father's death five years earlier.

Sandra Lee Bartky maintains in "The Pedagogy of Shame" that women are typically more shame-prone than men, a phenomenon that she attributes to a patriarchal society (226). Females tend to write more frequently about low self-esteem than do males, but over the years I have had hundreds of men and women disclose in literature and writing courses shameful experiences. Some of these self-disclosures occurred in essays the students read aloud to their classmates; other self-disclosures, like Breanna's, I read aloud anonymously, with the authors' permission. Only in an empathic classroom will students feel emboldened to share such risky self-disclosures with their classmates and teacher. I never analyze—or psychoanalyze—these self-disclosures. Rather, I limit my comments, as I did in Breanna's Love and Loss class, to grammatical and stylistic suggestions for revision. I help my students find the best words to express themselves. Paradoxically, my refusal to analyze my students' personal writings encourages their own self-analysis. Writing about shame becomes a counter-shame strategy, and students discover through the pedagogy of identification that their classmates can understand and empathize with them.

In *Risky Writing* I discuss the protocols I put into place in my expository writing courses to minimize the possibility that students who write about traumatic experiences are retraumatized in the process. These protocols include empathizing, avoiding critique, observing professional boundaries, allowing students not to write on topics that are too personal, grading pass/fail whenever possible, permitting anonymity, prescreening essays, protecting self-disclosures, balancing risky and nonrisky assignments, having conferences, and knowing how to make appropriate referrals. I used many of these protocols in Breanna's Love and Loss course. She never regretted a self-disclosure, never felt unsafe in the classroom. Writing about shame and other dark emotions creates the opportunity for posttraumatic growth, the positive changes that may arise from a crisis. As I observe in *Empathic Teaching*, posttraumatic growth implies that "people have the ability to re-create their lives following a devastating loss and grow in new and unexpected ways. Growth includes changes in perception of self, interpersonal relationships, and meaning of life" (124). Such posttraumatic growth may be seen in Breanna's writings.

Breanna revealed in her email to me that she began seeing a therapist during the middle of the semester as a result of her personal writings in the course. Did she see me as a therapist? "Because you allowed us to open up with you as you had shared your experiences, in that way you became like a therapist to us, or to me at least. Until then, I had not been able to really open up with anyone directly. In your class, you gave us a chance to indirectly open up to someone whether it was you, your TA, or other students. Someone was listening either way, and in that way you became a therapist for us. Too many professors are black-and-white, up-and-down, right-and-wrong. There were no binaries with you, it was just a listening ear, and our writing improved as you had helped with our grammar at the same time."

As Breanna indicates, teachers can have a therapeutic impact simply by listening attentively to their students and by allowing them to express themselves without the fear of being criticized or judged. The word "simply" may be misleading, however, because we live in what Deborah Tannen calls an "argument culture" in which verbal assault masquerades as the pursuit of truth. There is nothing simple about the effort to understand the other. Empathy has received little attention from literature and composition professors, and many teachers fear that they will be emotionally burdened if they attempt to empathize with their students. Yet empathy need not result in a teacher's depression or burnout. To empathize with students is to realize their resiliency in confronting their problems. Education can be transformative, as we can see from Breanna's response to reading this chapter:

> It is now my junior year at SUNY Albany, and it is extremely stressful. Jeff Berman got in touch with me a few weeks ago to discuss using my writings in a book of his and in a scholar's book as well. More than happy to, I was honored to have him use my writings because although my writings were assignments, to me they were my "public diary" in a way. I did not stress over these assignments, and I rather enjoyed writing them because it gave me a chance to focus on my thoughts and feelings about certain issues in my life. In reading this chapter written by Jeff, I began to focus upon my feelings about my life once again. Interestingly enough, this past Thanksgiving was the anniversary of my father's death as he had passed away five years ago now. It feels like yesterday when I found out he was gone. A lot happens in five years, and you don't even realize it.
>
> Since I have taken Jeff's course, many things have occurred that have changed my life. I had mentioned that my brother and I were not talking for a little while. Over the summer, I had come home from work one day, and my mother told me my brother was in a street-bike accident, and he was in the hospital. My heart sank, and I could barely breathe. It felt like the morning of Thanksgiving 2001 when I learned of my father's death. Thankfully, he survived the accident, with a mandatory knee surgery, stitches, 2 broken wrists, and a broken arm.
>
> Up to this point, he and I had not been talking (over what I don't think either of us can really say), and my feelings of guilt and sadness once again had taken over my mind. If he had died in that accident, I would have lost another "male connection" in my life, and I realized that this fight could not continue. I

thought I had learned to not take for granted the people I do have in my life, yet I realized I did not when my brother got into the accident. He and I are talking, yet I do not think our relationship will ever go back to the way it once was, but it is okay because I will cherish anything with him right now. This accident made us both realize that we were taking each other for granted when you never know if the other person will be there tomorrow. We never spoke of the fight, and we never talked about why we were mad; the only thing that mattered was that I picked him up from the hospital when my mother could not, and we were family—nothing could change that.

Over the summer, I began to clean myself up a bit. I stopped doing drugs, slowed down the sexual relations with friends, and met a guy, Vinnie, who is my current boyfriend. Finding the trust to put into this relationship is still difficult today, for I am haunted by my father's death and the emotions I continue to feel about it. This year has been extremely stressful for me, and I tended to let my anger out on Vinnie. He still remained by my side and put up with my "crap," yet the words, "Jimmy died this morning" continue to echo through my head. In reading this chapter, I reflected on my writings Jeff used, and remembered how I felt at the time.

I am no longer seeing Julie, for my dependence on her diminished somehow. Yet, I still find myself writing poems, writing them at home before bed, in class, and at lunchtime. I do not care if anyone reads them, for they are simply my thoughts down on paper. Being so close with Vinnie scares me, for I constantly fear that I will become too close, and I will lose him as I lost my father. Yet, today, he has been my backbone in helping me cope with family drama, medical problems of mine, and academic stress. I felt myself dwindling down toward suicidal thoughts once again. Julie made me see that my sexual relations with men in the past were a function of finding the male connection I have with Vinnie, to catch me when I do dwindle to these thoughts once again.

Jeff Berman's class, as he says in the chapter, assisted students in reflecting on their lives as they read of other student's lives. Jeff and I were teacher and student, yet we were each other's support in class as we mourned for our losses. Having Jeff read us his own diaries in class put us on an equal level with him, as he was not demanding we hand in an assignment; rather, he was asking to share with each other our lives as he had shared his with us.

This past month, I lost a friend to epilepsy. She died on Halloween 2006. She sings with the angels now, and my faith once again helped me cope with her death. I wrote many poems about it, and after I write my poems, I put them away, perhaps to read them some other time in the future. I do not care who reads these poems, for their main function was to put down my thoughts on paper. I had done this exact thing in Jeff's class. I put my thoughts down on paper and handed it to him. That was it. He improved our writing through writing about death.

Death consumes our minds sometimes, and writing about it cleanses one's soul. I compare my writings in this chapter to the way I feel now, and they are completely different. They are different because every day babies are born, loved ones pass away, the wind blows, and time continues. Death does not stop time, and this is the realization that I have come to through these writings of mine and through Jeff's empathic approach to teaching. Time continues, the leaves fall, the seasons change, and life continues to throw you curveballs to make you stronger in the end. Death does not stop time unless you let it.

Breanna's response to her own story, as she narrated it in Love and Loss, reveals the central importance of reading and writing in death education. Writing continues to "save" her life, not as a one-time therapy that results in a lifelong cure nor as a method to seek "closure," but rather as a daily practice that is necessary for her ongoing recovery from grief. Recall Donald Hall's observation in *The Best Day the Worst Day:* "Poetry gives the griever not release from grief but companionship in grief" (118). So too did the texts on our reading list give all of us, students and teacher alike, not release from grief but companionship in grief. Teachers who are sympathetic to courses like Love and Loss will be reassured by Breanna's statement that she enjoyed the seven writing assignments, which she found stress reducing. She acknowledges candidly that she is still "haunted" by her father's death, but she has been able to regain control of her life. Fear of abandonment continues to be a problem, but it has not prevented her from maintaining a close relationship with her boyfriend, who has been her "backbone."

Breanna felt no hesitation in granting me permission to use her writings, and the only disguise she required was changing the name of her father's fiancée. (To be cautious, however, I changed most of the other names as well.) I showed her every draft of this chapter, which she approved. I wish her name could be listed as the coauthor of this work, but we both concluded that it would be better for her to remain anonymous. Our collaboration on this project was mutually enjoyable—our "pedagogical alliance" was not unlike the patient-analyst "therapeutic alliance." There are many parallels between therapists writing about patients and teachers writing about students. Judy Leopold Kantrowitz concludes that most patients feel validated when they read what their therapists have written about them; my experience suggests that students feel validated when they read what their teachers have written about them. This validation requires, however, that therapists and teachers receive written permission from their patients and students, respectively, to use their words—and, I would add, for patients and students to be shown *in advance* how their words are being used. The validation also depends on patient and therapist, student and teacher reaching similar conclusions about their collaborative work.

Based on my students' signed and anonymous evaluations of the course at the end of the semester, as well as interviews conducted by Richard Bower, Love and Loss was a successful experiment in death education. The course helped not only Breanna but also many of her classmates to work through the death of loved ones. Part of the reason for this was the interactive nature of the course. Before handing back the seven writing assignments, I read three or four aloud, always anonymously, with the authors' permission, and with no class discussion afterward, so that students could reach their own conclusions about what they had heard. They closely identified with their classmates' stories about love and loss, and such identification enabled them to feel less isolated. "We all have issues," Breanna states at the end of her final exam. Her issue was her father's death; my issue was my wife's death. We were student and teacher, but we were also fellow mourners, each moved by the other's story. Multiply this by the sixty students who were in the course, and one can begin to see the extent of our death education. By talking about my wife's death, and by encouraging students to write about their own losses, I affirmed an intersubjective model of education in which each of us played the role of teacher and student. My self-disclosures narrowed the distance between students and teacher, leading to a more equal relationship based on reciprocity and on what Jessica Benjamin calls mutual recognition: "the necessity of recognizing as well as being recognized by the other" (23).

I identify with Breanna's statement about the need to write books that help others cope with the problems of living—and dying. That is why she wants to be an author. "I do not care how much profit the book makes in selling; if my book comforts one person, and touches one soul, I will feel as if writing my book was worth every minute." My feelings precisely. Samuel Johnson, the great eighteenth-century lexicographer and man of letters, famously opined that only a blockhead writes for no money. By his standards, I am a blockhead, for I have given up all royalties from *Empathic Teaching* to keep the price as low as possible so that students will be able to buy the book. The gratification of writing a book like *Empathic Teaching* or *Death in the Classroom* is that they demonstrate how students can make educational and psychological breakthroughs in their lives. Just as my present student Breanna identified with past students like Cory and Danielle, so will, I hope, future students identify with Breanna, discovering in the process that they too can learn to cope with loss. As she aptly observes, "We never truly 'get over' a great loss in our lives, but we do learn ways to handle the loss and cope with it."

Appendix C

"Literature, If Anything, Will Save Me": Confronting Multiple Sclerosis in Love and Loss

Sara E. Murphy

Sara was a member of my Hemingway course in the summer of 2005. During this time she was diagnosed with multiple sclerosis, a cruel irony in that she was working as a neurological researcher and suspected before her physician did that she had developed the disease. She enrolled in Love and Loss hoping it would help her understand the psychological dimension of her frightening new situation. I invited her to write an essay, after the semester ended, to discuss whether the course was helpful to her in coping with loss. Sara's essay reveals how a literature course may serve as a form of mourning, allowing one to acknowledge grief and begin the healing process.

When I registered for English 226, I did so with a recognized and intentional purpose: to come to terms with personal loss. When the course began in January, however, I was uncertain as to the path it would take or how it would affect me. My only certainty was that I needed to be there.

I returned to academic study part-time in fall 2004; I felt old and out of practice, actively missing my life in politics and inactively battling profound boredom in Albany. After one English course with a brilliant and inspiring professor, I realized that I wanted to pursue the study of literature. I was despondent about the amount of time it would take to earn a degree; I had switched careers and continued to work all day, dashing from my clinical research patients to SUNY-Albany at night. I remember that I frequently bemoaned the idea of graduating at thirty; it was the worst scenario I could imagine.

In May of last year, between appointments with an Alzheimer's patient and a multiple sclerosis patient, I was struck with vertigo. It was the first day of summer classes, and I was irritated at having to drive to class so dizzy. I assumed that I was getting the flu. When my physician prescribed an antivertigo drug, I complained to her because I was spending the upcoming weekend in Boston for my best friend's bachelorette party and I thought that the medication would interfere with my ability to drive there and participate in the festivities once I arrived. At some point over the next ten days, I became convinced that

261

my symptom of vertigo—soon joined by overwhelming fatigue, imbalance, pain, and double vision—indicated that I had multiple sclerosis. Patted down by my employer, a research-oriented neurologist who had seen sympathetic symptoms among his staff in the past, I nonetheless underwent MRI scans and a spinal tap.

The spinal tap was scheduled to take place during the second meeting of a literature course that Jeff was teaching over the summer and in which I had enrolled. I was worried about beginning the course on the wrong foot and attempted to drive to campus for the following class, only to turn back home once I was overcome by a painful spinal headache. When I returned to classes, I met with Jeff about my absences and he suggested that I withdraw from the course. We were in his office and I remember that I could not focus on his face as he said this to me. My vision had not yet corrected itself; I was so angered by that—by the idea that my body was pulling all sorts of tricks on me—that all I could think to say was "I would prefer not to," Bartleby the Scrivener's line of protest in Herman Melville's famous short story of that name. The spirit of Melville was commuted, apparently, because I was allowed to remain in the course.

I had just left class the day I received my diagnosis. We had been discussing *The Sun Also Rises*; it was sunny out, and I felt less wretched than I had in the preceding few weeks, and the class discussion had been a good one. As soon as I reached my car, I switched on my cell phone and it rang right away. I was asked to stop by the office of my employer, now my doctor, immediately. I was in such an upbeat mood from the class that it did not occur to me that I would be given bad news. When the news arrived, my previous suspicions were confirmed, and I was diagnosed with multiple sclerosis.

It is difficult to find the words to describe the first year with MS. The plunge from good days to awful ones can occur without warning, or it can come with a sinking, instinctive sensation. There have been days when I have felt nearly normal; there have been days when I can barely walk. The majority occupy the space between. Since my initial attack, I have had one relapse, which occurred this spring. Although many people who are not familiar with the disease believe that in periods of remission everything is fine for the patient, the truth is that the symptoms of MS never really leave me; rather, they continually fluctuate in severity. It seems so much longer than a year since May 2005, when this entirely new way of living began.

Following my diagnosis, I left my job and threw myself headlong into the life of a full-time, impoverished college student. For the most part I have enjoyed it, and I have generally avoided sharing information about my disease with the faculty and students. I am a good student, and I feel naturally suited to English studies. The problem in returning to college full time, however, was that I began to feel useless. I had worked since I was seventeen, and invariably my work has been both exciting and rewarding. I felt that I was not contributing to society; in addition, I secretly harbored a fear that I would not be able to contribute in the future.

The myelin sheath that covers the brain acts as protection to the unfathomable and intricate message system encased therein. Shortly before I returned to classes following the winter break, I learned that the two original lesions detected in the summer had been joined by three more. My doctor was so concerned that I not invest the lesion load with import that I immediately began to invest it with import. I actually anthropomorphized the lesions, imagining invisible, insatiable mice nibbling away at my brain, much the way rodents chew insulation off electrical cords, and certainly with the same result. At the beginning of the semester, I was still feeling bitter, and the bitterness lasted a long time. To be honest, it still recurs, although I have stopped trying to make a list of all of the people who should have been blighted with MS instead of me (actually, I never progressed much further than the entire Bush administration).

Over the last year, I have chosen not to seek therapy, although there were days and nights when undoubtedly it would have proven helpful to speak to someone about what I later recognized were symptoms of grief. I am adamant about refraining from the use of any antidepressants to cope with fluctuating emotions; although I realize that many people suffer from mental illnesses that make such drugs necessary, in order to come to terms with my life with MS I need to do so while clearheaded and honest with myself. Instead of therapy, I enrolled in Love and Loss. When the course began, I was aware that in rearranging my schedule to participate in it I had, in effect, made a conscious effort to force myself to face this disease and attack my fears about it, even as it continued to attack me. This awareness tinged my view of the course with a lens of need and expectation. I was not disappointed. The literature chosen for the class was moving, the essays thought provoking, and the writing process cathartic. I had sought a coping mechanism, but I found personal strength.

As the class progressed, I began to sense a secondary interest emerging. Although my primary interest in the study of love and loss was one of personal need, I found myself increasingly interested in the concept and method of empathic teaching. Once I had committed to a major in English, the possibility of teaching literature at the college level had immediately intrigued me; throughout this course, I began to observe the style in which Jeff teaches as well as the parameters that he sets for the emotional safety of students. I have become quite a fan of empathic teaching, and I hope that I will be able to use the methods from this course should I ever reach the other side of the academic world.

The literature and accompanying writing assignments allowed me to improve as a reader and writer; I have read extensively since infancy and continue to read literature across all genres, but until this class, I had not read the literature of loss with a gaze of personal loss. Likewise, the writing assignments honed my stylistic and grammatical skills while forcing me to reflect on issues that affect me now or will undoubtedly do so in the future. The format of the course forced me out of my self-absorption; although I wrote several essays pertaining to my battle with MS, I also wrote on literature, on the issue of loss through death, and on euthanasia. I have never lost a close friend or relative to death, and when I do, I believe that I will turn to my memories of this class for some solace as well as methods of coping.

There have been many difficult aspects to the first year with MS; many seem balanced on contradictions. I abhor needles, yet I learned to inject myself thrice weekly with interferon in an effort to slow the progression, and thus disability, of the disease. I was dependent on my career and defined myself by my position; now, I am a mere student without income or prestige. I lived a life, in Washington and Albany, of seemingly limitless energy, characterized by an overbooked social life and spontaneous travel, yet I am now forced to nap almost daily just to avoid falling apart. I loved to go dancing, and I can no longer trust my balance. Balance, in a sense, is what I have found in this class—an emotional balance that allows me to accept several metaphorical monsters from which I previously ran. I have lost a great deal of myself over the year, more than mere myelin. The course has allowed me to accept the losses as well as to accept that no permanent adjustment will occur with a disease this insidious. I do not try to guess when or where the next symptom will occur, nor do I attempt to speculate about the future; rather, I am learning to accept each day as an individual challenge.

Perhaps the most difficult aspect of the last year has been communicating about what I am going through. Unlike many of the men and women living with MS, I immediately informed my family and friends of the diagnosis. My mother, in fact, accompanied me through the diagnostic process and has been an unshakable rock of support. Within several months, however, I soon learned that MS planted a minefield within my familial and social circles. My relatives run the gamut from concerned listeners to single-minded optimists to those who simply ignore the disease. As deeply as I appreciate the former group, I am irritated by the latter two. In a related pattern, several of my friends have been so "there" for me that they deserve medals; other formerly close friends have quite literally disappeared from my life, as if I carried the risk of some contagion. When I am among the friends and family who still surround me, I choose my words carefully; I have become tired of depressing my mother and closest friends and adding to their emotional toll, although they accept the burden with love. To others, I downplay the day-to-day strain of the disease, because they so desperately wish me to be well that they have closed their minds to the fact that I am not. The need to step so tentatively in speaking to my loved ones created a heightened need to communicate honestly about the physical and emotional challenges I am experiencing.

The course itself was emotionally challenging, a fact that Jeff predicted from the onset. It also contained an undeniably therapeutic element. In the class responses to the writing assignments, many students expressed the catharsis they experienced in writing about a loved one who had died or the empathy they had felt in hearing the essays read aloud. For my part, hearing my essays read aloud predictably made my words seem more real to me. Hearing the essays of my classmates about the losses they had experienced made my problems seem less horrific. I sank into the literature, reading all the required texts before the course began and again throughout the semester. Because of the literature, I recognized my emotional tumult as grief, and in realizing it, I began the process of mourning. As morbid as that may sound, I feel that such an experience was necessary in accepting the permanent place disease now has in my life.

I recognize that I have studied for the last four months under the guidance of a professor who has been frequently criticized for the way in which his classes operate. In previous books, he has written that outraged academics have accused him of playing therapist to his students' patients, and in doing so, putting his students at risk. I would cheerfully and emphatically refute any such accusations and, with these people, share my story. For me, the therapy provided by this class prompted a cycle of acceptance and healing, for which I am immeasurably grateful, but it was not dealt out by some charlatan. There was no pretense within the course that the sixty students would supplicate themselves in front of the professor and thus be cured of whatever pain ailed them. Instead, tools were provided—the act of reading literature, the act of writing, the act of listening—that seemed so simplistic at first but so necessary by the end. These tools were made available, and if students like me chose to use them, the healing could begin.

In a personal diary entry from February, I reflected on my anger at struggling through a bad day with MS, then wrote, "literature, if anything, will save me." Rereading the entry, I recognize the melodramatic sense born from physical pain, but I continue to agree with the statement. This course has given me the tools to craft a new life for myself, one in which obstacles have their place but not the starring role. Although this may constitute an emotional breakthrough, at no point did I feel like a psychological test subject. The respect with which the class was conducted enforced the tenants of empathy; only in an environment fostering self-inquiry, expression, and deference to the feelings of others can these breakthroughs occur. This course achieved all three to a remarkable degree while focusing on the varied forms of love and loss experienced by students and expressed throughout literature.

In my memory, my first year with multiple sclerosis will always be insepa-rable from this course. I am a woman who hopes to teach English one day, and the class provided me with a method of teaching that I only hope I can replicate successfully. I am also a woman who is living with disease, and the focus of the class allowed me to confront and accept that fact while expressing my feelings about it more freely than I had ever felt able to before.

In conclusion, I add a further testimony to the effects of this course in both method and focus. Two months ago, I initiated meetings with the direc-tors of the local chapter of the National Multiple Sclerosis Society to talk about the lack of discussion among younger people living with MS. Before this course began, I felt unable to fully express the effects and implications of this disease to my family and friends, let alone talk candidly with others who are coping with it as I am. Now, thanks in part to this course, I have assumed the position of a self-help group leader for the MS Society. I am working with a wonderful man from the area in organizing this new group, which will serve as a forum for local adults in their 20s through their 40s to respectfully and openly discuss all the ways in which MS has affected us. I believe that I never would have taken this step if it were not for my participation in Love and Loss. I feel optimistic about taking a positive and proactive step in tackling the disease, and I look forward to employing the methods of empathic teaching for the group.

This class has been a haven and a refuge, and it has facilitated both learning and introspection. I am grateful to have been part of the course, and I am gratified to be passing on the benefits to others.

Appendix D

English 226: Love and Loss in Literature and Life

Spring 2006, Monday, Wednesday 2:45–4:05
Social Science 134, Course No. 7563
Jeffrey Berman

Love inevitably ends in loss: this is one of the oldest themes in literature. In this course we will focus on the ways in which writers portray love and loss and seek to find consolation through religion, nature, art, deeds, or memory. The reading list includes a course pack containing selected eulogies, elegies, poems, and the Book of Job. (I will distribute the course packs on Wednesday; each will cost $3, which is below the price charged to me at Shipmates.) In addition, we will read Emily Brontë's *Wuthering Heights*, C. S. Lewis's *A Grief Observed*, John Bayley's *Elegy for Iris*, Ernest Hemingway's *A Farewell to Arms*, Anna Quindlen's *One True Thing*, and Jeffrey Berman's *Empathic Teaching*. (These books are available at the campus bookstore.) I will also be reading in class passages from my forthcoming book *Dying to Teach: A Memoir of Love, Loss, and Learning*, about the death of my beloved wife, Barbara, on April 5, 2004.

Please note that this will be an emotionally challenging course. There may be times when some of us cry. How can one not cry when confronting the loss of a loved one? Tears indicate that we are responding emotionally as well as intellectually to loss; tears are usually a more accurate reflection of how we feel than are our words. I'll try not to make the course morbid or depressing—indeed, I promise that there will be many more smiles than tears in the course. I'll ask each of you to indicate your own tear-to-smile ratio.

Required Books

	The Book of Job
C. S. Lewis	*A Grief Observed*
John Bayley	*Elegy for Iris*
Emily Brontë	*Wuthering Heights*

Ernest Hemingway   *A Farewell to Arms*
Anna Quindlen   *One True Thing*
Jeffrey Berman   *Empathic Teaching*

Requirements

There will be seven short essays, each about three pages long (typed, double-spaced). They will constitute 50 percent of your final grade. There will also be a midterm exam (worth 25 percent of the final grade) and a final exam (worth the remaining 25 percent).

I will not grade the essays on content—the topics on which you will be writing do not have right or wrong answers. Rather, I will grade your essays mainly on the quality of writing. Each essay will be graded with a plus (a grade in the A range), a check (a grade in the B range), or a minus (a grade C or below). Please make two copies of each essay so that Richard Bower, a doctoral student who will be helping me teach the course, will have a copy. Well-written essays will have few grammatical errors, especially comma splices, punctuation errors, colloquialisms, and wordiness. (I will go over in class how to avoid these problems.)

Please note that I will not accept late papers unless you can provide a doctor's note or a convincing explanation why you couldn't turn in the essay on time. I have indicated on the syllabus when the essays are due. I will return the essays to you the following class or, at the latest, the following week. Save your essays, and on the last day of the semester, May 8, I will ask you to submit all of them to me in a folder, all of which I will have read except for the last one. I will return them to you, with a letter grade, during the final exam, on May 17.

I would like to read about three or four essays aloud before I return them to you the next class. If you do *not* want me to read your essay aloud, please indicate with the word *no* on the top of the essay; otherwise, I will assume that you are giving me permission to read your essay aloud. I will always read the essays anonymously—no one will know the writer's identity. Nor will there be a discussion of the essays afterward. Your grade will not be influenced by the number of your essays I've read aloud.

Jan 23   Introduction
Jan 25   Selected eulogies in course pack: Emerson on Thoreau, *NY Times* on Buber, Robert F. Kennedy on Martin Luther King, Lincoln's Gettysburg Address, Elie Wiesel, Henry James
Jan 30   Emily Dickinson—selected poems in course pack

Feb 1	Emily Dickinson
Feb 6	Poems in course pack: John Donne, Dylan Thomas, W. H. Auden
Feb 8	Poems by Sylvia Plath, Anne Sexton, and Donald Hall
Feb 13	The Book of Job
Feb 15	The Book of Job
Feb 27	*A Grief Observed*
Mar 1	*A Grief Observed*
Mar 6	*Elegy for Iris*
Mar 8	*Elegy for Iris*
Mar 13	*Wuthering Heights*
Mar 15	*Wuthering Heights*
Mar 20	*Wuthering Heights*
Mar 22	*Wuthering Heights*
Mar 27	Midterm Exam
Mar 29	*A Farewell to Arms*
Apr 3	*A Farewell to Arms*
Apr 5	*A Farewell to Arms*
Apr 17	*A Farewell to Arms*
Apr 19	*One True Thing*
Apr 24	*One True Thing*
Apr 26	*One True Thing*
May 1	*Empathic Teaching*
May 3	*Empathic Teaching*
May 8	*Empathic Teaching*
May 17	(Wednesday) 10:30–12:30 Final Exam

First essay: Writing Your Classmate's Obituary	Due February 1
Second essay: Writing a Eulogy	Due February 13
Third essay: How Your Religious Beliefs or Disbeliefs Influence Your Attitude toward Death	Due March 1
Fourth essay: Cathy Linton's Letter to Her Mother in *Wuthering Heights*	Due March 22
Fifth essay: Ten Things to Do before I Die	Due April 17
Sixth essay: Your Attitude toward Euthanasia or Physician-Assisted Suicide	Due April 26
Seventh essay: What I Learned about Love and Loss from Reading *Empathic Teaching*	Due May 8

～

Attendance is very important. You are allowed three excused absences. If you miss more than three classes without a good reason (such as a documented medical problem or a death in the family), then you will not pass the course. Please try to come to every class. If you can't make a class, please email me.

> Office: HU 348
> Office Phone: 442-4084
> Home Phone: 355-4760 (please call before 9 p.m.)
> Email address: Jberman@Albany.edu
> Office Hours: Monday and Wednesday, 1:45–2:45, and by appointment

～

English 226: Take-Home Midterm Exam
March 27

Write on Question 1, either 2 or 3, and 4, for a total of three questions. Write 2–3 pages (typed, double-spaced) for each of the three questions. Be sure each answer is well written: I will be grading you mainly on the quality of your writing, as I have been grading the writing assignments. The exam is due in my mailbox or office no later than 4:05 on Monday, March 27.

This is not a research-oriented exam, but if you do use research (such as library work or the Internet), be sure to footnote ideas that are not your own. If you are quoting another person, use quotation marks and a bibliography. (There's no need to use footnotes if you are quoting one of my class statements.) You can discuss your answers with classmates, but I won't look kindly upon two exams that are identical. It's probably a good idea to let a friend proofread your exam before you submit it.

1.   Discuss three different moments in the Book of Job that challenge your own religious belief (or disbelief). Quote one or two lines (but no more) from each of these three moments in the story and explain how they challenge your own thinking on the subject. To what extent did you find yourself thinking about other biblical chapters that agreed or disagreed with these moments? (It's not a problem if you don't answer this question.) Do you believe that our discussion of Job will permanently influence your religious belief? If so, in what way?

2. With which do you identity more closely, C. S. Lewis's questioning of his faith at the beginning of *A Grief Observed* or his affirmation of faith at the end? Do you believe your own religious faith will be tested by the suffering and death of a loved one, as Lewis's was? What value if any is there in "observing" one's grief? How does Lewis convince you that he has closely observed his own grief?

3. Describe three different ways in which Alzheimer's disease has affected Iris Murdoch. What kind of caregiver is John Bailey? How does he convince us that her illness has strengthened rather than weakened his love for her? What kind of caregiver do you think you will be?

4. *Wuthering Heights* presents us with many different responses to the loss of love. Discuss one response that you see as "healthy" and another response that you see as "unhealthy." Then describe a third response to the loss of love in the novel that defies such black-and-white characterizations. Speculate on your own response to the loss of a loved one.

~

English 226: Take-Home Final Exam
May 17

Please write on all four questions; each question should be about three pages long, typed, double-spaced. I will be grading both on content and writing (except for question 3, in which I will be grading entirely on writing). The exam is due in my mailbox or office no later than 12:30 on Wednesday, May 17. I don't return final exams, but if you want your final grade early, enclose a self-stamped postcard with your exam or send me an email.

This is not a research-oriented exam, but if you do use research (such as library work or the Internet), be sure to footnote ideas that are not your own. If you are quoting another person, use quotation marks and a bibliography. (There's no need to use footnotes if you are quoting one of my statements in class or from *Empathic Teaching*.) As with the midterm, you can discuss your answers with classmates, but I won't look kindly upon two exams that are identical. It's probably a good idea to let a friend proofread your exam before you submit it.

1. The fifth writing assignment, "Ten Things to Do before I Die," was due during the week in which we finished our discussion of *A Farewell to Arms*. I chose this writing assignment because Frederic

seems to have little to do after he deserts the war. Apart from making love with Catherine and drinking alcohol, he doesn't know what to do with his life.

Agree or disagree with the preceding sentence. Include in your discussion Frederic's attitude toward his child (both before and after the baby is born), his relationship with Catherine, his reactions to her death, and his attitude toward the future. Agree or disagree with Leslie Fiedler's famous observation that Catherine would have turned into a "bitch" if Hemingway had not killed her off at the end of the novel.

2. Caring for a dying person is the most agonizing experience imaginable short of, perhaps, death itself. Caring for a dying person is physically and emotionally exhausting, depressing, and overwhelming. The caregiver must not only attend to the dying person, often around the clock and without a break, but must also cope with dark emotions: fear, anger, sadness, and guilt. Indeed, caregivers may often wish that they can trade places with the dying person to end their own suffering. Such a wish is not only useless but it may also be selfish, as the historian Arnold Toynbee observes in his book *Man's Concern with Death*:

> My answer to Saint Paul's question, "O death, where is thy sting?" is Saint Paul's own answer: "The sting of death is sin." The sin that I mean is the sin of selfishly failing to wish to survive the death of someone with whose life my own life is bound up. This is selfish because the sting of death is less sharp for the person who dies than it is for the bereaved survivor. This is, as I see it, the capital fact about the relation between living and dying. There are two parties to the suffering that death inflicts; and, in the apportionment of this suffering, the survivor takes the brunt.

Nevertheless, without invalidating the preceding observations, I believe that the dying person gives to the caregiver a precious gift: that of entrusting his or her final days, weeks, or months alive to a trusted and dedicated relative or friend. This is a gift that the caregiver may experience as a curse during the period of illness; it is usually perceived as a blessing only after the loved one's death.

Discuss how Ellen's life has been changed for the better as a result of taking care of her mother in *One True Thing*. What *specific* changes in Ellen's life have been made possible by the gift of taking care of her mother? Speculate on how her life might have been different had she not taken care of her dying mother. What will you remember the most about this novel if you find yourself in the position of a caregiver?

3. Chapter 5 of *Empathic Teaching*, "The Age of Melancholy," focuses on the course Literature and the Healing Arts that I taught in the spring of 2002. There were many parallels between that course and the one you are currently taking. Both were taught under the rubric of English 226; both contained sixty students; both involved writing self-disclosing diaries or essays that I read aloud anonymously and without comment; both involved bearing witness to loss; and both encouraged students to write about experiences and feelings that are generally deemed too "personal" for most college courses. Many of the diaries and essays that I read aloud in these courses were emotionally charged, painful to write and difficult to hear.

Now that you have completed Love and Loss in Literature and Life, discuss how your experience of the course confirms or disconfirms the conclusions I reach in chapter 5. Based on your experience in Love and Loss, do you agree or disagree with my statement in *Empathic Teaching* that "an empathic approach to teaching enables students to understand themselves and their classmates in ways that are impossible in more traditional argumentative classrooms" (354)? Speculate on how your reaction to *Empathic Teaching* would have been different if you had not taken Love and Loss. Include in your discussion your response to chapter 6, "Risky Teaching," in which I discuss educators who have called into question the value of encouraging students to write about their lives.

4. Throughout the semester we have discussed real or fictional characters who responded to the loss of loved ones. Many though not all of these characters express gratitude for being alive despite suffering a grievous loss. Select three different characters—one from *A Farewell to Arms*, a second from *One True Thing*, and a third from *Empathic Teaching*—and explore their attitude toward gratitude. Your discussion of these three characters should be about two pages.

For the final page of this question, discuss your own attitude toward gratitude. Do you often feel grateful for being alive? Please explain. What emotions or thoughts make it difficult to feel gratitude? Has the course heightened your awareness of gratitude? Speculate on how your attitude toward gratitude will change as you grow older.

Works Cited

Adams, Henry. *The Education of Henry Adams*. Boston: Houghton Mifflin, 1961.

Adamson, Joseph, and Hilary Clark, eds. *Scenes of Shame: Psychoanalysis, Shame, and Writing*. Albany: State University of New York Press, 1999.

Alcorn, Marshall. *Changing the Subject in English Class*. Carbondale: Southern Illinois University Press, 2002.

Aries, Philippe. *The Hour of Our Death*. Translated by Helen Weaver. New York: Knopf, 1981.

Armstrong, Karen. *A History of God: The 4000-Year Quest of Judaism, Christianity, and Islam*. New York: Ballantine Books, 1993.

Banville, John. *The Sea*. New York: Knopf, 2005.

Bartky, Sandra Lee. "The Pedagogy of Shame." In *Feminisms and Pedagogies of Everyday Life*, edited by Carmen Luke, 225–41. Albany: State University of New York Press, 1996.

Bates, Ernest Sutherland, ed. *The Bible: Designed to Be Read as Living Literature*. New York: Simon and Schuster, 1936.

Battin, Margaret Pabst. *The Least Worst Death*. New York: Oxford University Press, 1994.

Bayley, John. *The Character of Love*. New York: Collier, 1963.

———. *Elegy for Iris*. New York: Picador, 1999.

———. *Iris and Her Friends: A Memoir of Memory and Desire*. New York: Norton, 2000.

Benjamin, Jessica. *The Bonds of Love*. London: Virago, 1990.

Berman, Jeffrey. *Dying to Teach: A Memoir of Love, Loss, and Learning*. Albany: State University of New York Press, 2007.

———. *Empathic Teaching: Education for Life*. Amherst: University of Massachusetts Press, 2004.

———. *Joseph Conrad: Writing as Rescue*. New York: Astra Books, 1977.

———. *Narcissism and the Novel*. New York: New York University Press, 1994.

———. *Risky Writing: Self-Disclosure and Self-Transformation in the Classroom*. Amherst: University of Massachusetts Press, 2001.

———. *Surviving Literary Suicide*. Amherst: University of Massachusetts Press, 1999.

Berman, Jeffrey, and Patricia Hatch Wallace. *Cutting and the Pedagogy of Self-Disclosure*. Amherst: University of Massachusetts Press, 2007.

Bernard-Donals, Michael, and Richard Glejzer. *Between Witness and Testimony: The Holocaust and the Limits of Representation*. Albany: State University of New York Press, 2001.

Blacker, David. *Dying to Teach: The Educator's Search for Immortality*. New York: Teachers College Press, 1997.

Blanchot, Maurice. *The Writing of the Disaster*. Translated by Ann Smock. Lincoln: Bison/University of Nebraska Press, 1995.

Bloom, Harold. *Jesus and Yahweh: The Names Divine*. New York: Riverhead Books, 2005.

Borrie, Cathie. "A Harbinger of Birds." Typescript.

Britton, James. "What's the Use? A Schematic Account of Language Functions." *Educational Review* 23, no. 3 (1971): 205–19.

Brontë, Emily. *Wuthering Heights*. Harmondsworth, Middlesex, Eng.: Penguin, 1965; rpt. 1985.

Byock, Ira. *Dying Well: Peace and Possibilities at the End of Life*. New York: Riverhead, 1997.

Caine, Lynn. *Being a Widow*. New York: Penguin, 1988.

Cassell, Eric. *The Nature of Suffering*. 2nd ed. New York: Oxford University Press, 2004.

Chodorow, Nancy. *The Reproduction of Mothering: Psychoanalysis and the Sociology of Gender*. Berkeley: University of California Press, 1978.

Choron, Jacques. *Death and Western Thought*. New York: Collier Books, 1963.

Csikszentmihalyi, Mihaly. *Flow: The Psychology of Optimal Experience*. New York: HarperCollins, 1990.

Dalai Lama, and Howard C. Cutler. *The Art of Happiness: A Handbook for Living*. New York: Riverhead, 1998.

Davidson, Richard, and William Irwin. "The Functional Neuroanatomy of Emotion and Affective Style." *Trends in Cognitive Neuroscience* 3 (1999): 11–21.

Dickinson, Emily. *Collected Poems of Emily Dickinson*. New York: Gramercy Books, 1982.

Didion, Joan. *The White Album*. New York: Simon and Schuster, 1979.

———. *The Year of Magical Thinking*. New York: Knopf, 2005.

Du Maurier, Daphne. *The Rebecca Notebook and Other Memories*. Garden City, N.Y.: Doubleday, 1980.

Eckstein, Jerome. "An Old Man Contemplates Genesis." Typescript.

Edelman, Hope. *Motherless Daughters: The Legacy of Loss*. New York: Delta, 1995.

Elbow, Peter. Foreword to *A Way to Move: Rhetorics of Emotion and Composition Studies*, edited by Dale Jacobs and Laura R. Micciche. Portsmouth, N.H.: Boynton/Cook, 2003.

Erikson, Erik. *Childhood and Society*. 2nd ed. New York: Norton, 1963.

Famous Last Words, Fond Farewells, Deathbed Diatribes, and Exclamations upon Expiration. Compiled by Ray Robinson. New York: Workman, 2003.

Felman, Shoshana. "Education and Crisis, or the Vicissitudes of Teaching." In *Trauma: Explorations in Memory*, edited by Cathy Caruth, 85–99. Baltimore: Johns Hopkins University Press, 1995.

Forster, E. M. *Howards End*. New York: Buccaneer Books, n.d.

Gilbert, Sandra M. *Death's Door: Modern Dying and the Ways We Grieve*. New York: Norton, 2006.

———. *Wrongful Death: A Memoir*. New York: Norton, 1997.

———, ed. *Inventions of Farewell: A Book of Elegies*. New York: Norton, 2001.

Gilligan, Carol. *In a Different Voice*. Cambridge: Harvard University Press, 1982.

Goggin, Peter, and Maureen Daly Goggin. "Presence in Absence: Discourses and Teaching (In, On, and About) Trauma." In *Trauma and the Teaching of Writing*, edited by Shane Borrowman, 29–52. Albany: State University of New York Press, 2005.

Goleman, Daniel. *Emotional Intelligence*. New York: Bantam Books, 1995.

———. *Social Intelligence: The New Science of Human Relationships*. New York: Bantam, 2006.

Gorer, Geoffrey. *Death, Grief, and Mourning in Contemporary Britain*. Salem, N.H.: Ayer, 1965, rpt. 1987.

Graff, Gerald. *Clueless in Academe: How Schooling Obscures the Life of the Mind*. New Haven: Yale University Press, 2003.

Greenberg, Moshe. "Job." In *The Literary Guide to the Bible*, edited by Robert Alter and Frank Kermode, 283–304. Cambridge: Belknap Press of Harvard University Press, 1987.

Greenberg, Sidney, ed. *A Treasury of Comfort*. New York: Crown, 1954.

Greenspan, Miriam. *Healing through the Dark Emotions: The Wisdom of Grief, Fear, and Despair*. Boston: Shambhala, 2003.

Hall, Donald. *The Best Day the Worst Day: Life with Jane Kenyon*. Boston: Houghton Mifflin, 2005.

———. *Without: Poems*. Boston: Houghton Mifflin, 1998.

Harris, Sam. *The End of Faith: Religion, Terror, and the Future of Reason*. New York: Norton, 2004.

Hartman, Geoffrey. *Scars of the Spirit: The Struggle against Inauthenticity*. New York: Palgrave Macmillan, 2004.

Heilbrun, Carolyn. *Writing a Woman's Life*. New York: Ballantine, 1988.

Hemingway, Ernest. *A Farewell to Arms*. New York: Scribner's, 1929.

Hennezel, Marie de. *Intimate Death: How the Dying Teach Us How to Live*. Translated by Carol Brown Janeway. New York: Vintage, 1998.

Hilton, James. *Good-Bye, Mr. Chips*. New York: Little, Brown, 1962.

Holland, Norman. *Meeting Movies*. Madison, N.J.: Fairleigh Dickinson University Press, 2006.

Hynes, James. *The Lecturer's Tale*. New York: Picador USA, 2001.

Jamison, Kay Redfield. *Exuberance: The Passion for Life*. New York: Knopf, 2004.

Jourard, Sidney. *The Transparent Self: Self-Disclosure and Well-Being*. Princeton, N.J.: Van Nostrand, 1941.

Kahn, Jack. *Job's Illness: Loss, Grief, and Integration*. Oxford: Pergamon Press, 1975.

Kantrowitz, Judy Leopold. *Writing about Patients: Responsibilities, Risks, and Ramifications*. New York: Other Press, 2006.

Keats, John. *Selected Poems and Letters*. Cambridge: Riverside Press, 1959.

Kübler-Ross, Elisabeth. *On Death and Dying*. New York: Macmillan, 1970.

LaCapra, Dominick. "Trauma, Absence, Loss." *Critical Inquiry* 25 (Summer 1999): 696–727.

———. *Writing History, Writing Trauma*. Baltimore: Johns Hopkins University Press, 2001.

Laub, Dori. "An Event without a Witness: Truth, Testimony, and Survival." In *Testimony: Crises of Witnessing in Literature, Psychoanalysis, and History*, by Shoshana Felman and Dori Laub, 75–92. New York: Routledge, 1992.

Lawrence, D. H. *The Letters of D. H. Lawrence*. Vol. 2, edited by George J. Zytaruk and James T. Boulton. Cambridge: Cambridge University Press, 1981.

Lewis, C. S. *A Grief Observed*. San Francisco: HarperSanFrancisco, 2001.

Martin, Robert. *Tennyson, the Unquiet Heart*. Oxford: Clarendon Press, 1980.

Martin, Terry, and Kenneth Doka. *Men Don't Cry . . . Women Do: Transcending Gender Stereotypes of Grief*. Philadelphia: Brunner/Mazel, 2000.

Miller, Lynn, and David Kenny. "Reciprocity of Self-Disclosure at the Individual and Dyadic Levels: A Social Relations Analysis." *Journal of Personality and Social Psychology* 50, no. 4 (1986): 713–19.

Miller, Nancy K. "Memory Stains: Annie Ernaux's *Shame*." In *Extremities: Trauma, Testimony, and Community*, edited by Nancy K. Miller and Jason Tougaw, 197–212. Urbana: University of Illinois Press, 2002.

Miller, Nancy K., and Jason Tougaw, eds. *Extremities: Trauma, Testimony, and Community*. Urbana: University of Illinois Press, 2002.

Mitchell, Stephen, trans. *The Book of Job*. San Francisco: North Point Press, 1987.

Moffat, Mary Jane, ed. *In the Midst of Winter: Selections from the Literature of Mourning*. New York: Vintage 1992.

Moller, David Wendell. *Confronting Death: Values, Institutions, and Human Mortality*. New York: Oxford University Press, 1996.

Morris, Virginia. *Talking about Death Won't Kill You*. New York: Workman, 2001.

Murray, Donald. *Crafting a Life in Essay, Story, Poem*. Portsmouth, N.H.: Boynton/Cook, 1996.

Neruda, Pablo. *The Book of Questions*. Translated by William O'Daly. Port Townsend, Wash.: Copper Canyon Press, 2001.

New Oxford Annotated Bible. Edited by Michael Coogan. 3rd ed. New York: Oxford, 2001.

Nuland, Sherwin. *How We Die: Reflections on Life's Final Chapter*. New York: Vintage, 1995.

Nussbaum, Martha. *Upheavals of Thought: The Intelligence of Emotions*. Cambridge: Cambridge University Press, 2001.

Payne, Michelle. *Bodily Discourses: When Students Write about Abuse and Eating Disorders*. Portsmouth, N.H.: Boynton/Cook, 2000.

Pennebaker, James. *Opening Up: The Healing Power of Expressing Emotions*. New York: Guilford Press, 1997.

Plath, Sylvia. *The Bell Jar*. New York: Harper and Row, 1971.

———. *The Journals of Sylvia Plath*. Edited by Frances McCullough and Ted Hughes. New York: Dial Press, 1982; Ballantine, 1991.

Quindlen, Anna. *One True Thing*. New York: Dell, 1995.

Rogers, Carl. *A Way of Being*. Boston: Houghton Mifflin, 1980.

Sacks, Oliver. *The Man Who Mistook His Wife for a Hat*. London: Duckworth, 1985.

Schultz, Patricia. *1,000 Places to See Before You Die*. New York: Workman, 2003.

Silin, Jonathan. *Sex, Death, and the Education of Children*. New York: Teachers College Press, 1995.

Solomon, Maynard. *Beethoven*. New York: Schirmer, 1977.

———. *Late Beethoven: Music, Thought, Imagination*. Berkeley: University of California Press, 2003.

Sontag, Susan. *On Photography*. New York: Farrar, Straus and Giroux, 1977.

———. *Regarding the Pain of Others*. New York: Farrar, Straus and Giroux, 2003.

Stearns, Ann Kaiser. *Living through Personal Crisis*. New York: Ballantine, 1985.

Steiner, George. *Lessons of the Masters*. Cambridge: Harvard University Press, 2003.

Stengel, Richard. *You're Too Kind: A Brief History of Flattery*. New York: Simon and Schuster, 2000.

Stewart, Garrett. *Death Sentences: Styles of Dying in British Fiction*. Cambridge: Harvard University Press, 1984.

Tannen, Deborah. *The Argument Culture: Moving from Debate to Dialogue*. New York: Random House, 1998.

Tedeschi, Richard, Crystal Park, and Lawrence Calhoun, eds. *Posttraumatic Growth: Positive Changes in the Aftermath of Crisis*. Mahwah, N.J.: Lawrence Erlbaum, 1998.

Terkel, Studs. *Will the Circle Be Unbroken? Reflections on Death, Rebirth, and Hunger for a Faith*. New York: New Press, 2001.

Theroux, Phyllis, ed. *The Book of Eulogies: A Collection of Memorial Tributes, Poetry, Essays, and Letters of Condolence*. New York: Scribner, 1997.

Toynbee, Arnold. *Man's Concern with Death*. St. Louis: McGraw-Hill, 1969.

Trillin, Calvin. *About Alice*. New York: Random House, 2006.

Twain, Mark. *Letters from the Earth*, edited by Bernard Devoto. New York: Harper-Perennial, 1991.

Wallace, David Foster. *Brief Interviews with Hideous Men*. New York: Little Brown, 2000.

Warren, Robert Penn. *All the King's Men*. New York: Bantam, 1973.

Wethington, Elaine. "Turning Points as Opportunities for Psychological Growth." In *Flourishing: Positive Psychology and the Life Well-Lived*, edited by Corey L. M. Keyes and Jonathan Haidt, 37–53. Washington, D.C.: American Psychological Association, 2003.

Wilson, Timothy. *Strangers to Ourselves: Discovering the Adaptive Unconscious*. Cambridge: Harvard University Press, 2002.

Wurmser, Léon. "Shame: The Veiled Companion of Narcissism." In *The Many Faces of Shame*, edited by Donald L. Nathanson, 64–92. New York: Guilford Press, 1987.

Yalom, Irvin. *Love's Executioner*. New York: HarperCollins, 2000.

———. *The Schopenhauer Cure*. New York: HarperCollins, 2005.

———. *When Nietzsche Wept*. New York: Basic, 1992.

Student Writers

Alen
Anna [from *Cutting and the Pedagogy of Self-Disclosure*]
Ava
Baxter [from *Cutting and the Pedagogy of Self-Disclosure*]
Belle
Breanna
Brooke
Carly
Cassie
Chad
Charlie [from *Empathic Teaching*]
Chuck
Clarissa
Connie
Cory [from *Empathic Teaching*]
Cyana
Danielle [from *Empathic Teaching*]
Dean
Elijah
Elle
Esther
Gabriella [from *Empathic Teaching*]
Gladys
Hannah
Jackie
Jean
Jo
Joy
Kelly
Kitty
Krystal
Lily
Madison
Malechi

Mandy
Mariela
Matilda [from *Empathic Teaching*]
Raymond
Sara E. Murphy
Scarlett
Scotty
Zoe

Index